Schwarz on Residence and UK Taxation

Schwarz on Residence and UK Taxation

22nd Edition

Jonathan Schwarz
BA, LLB (Witwatersrand),
LLM (University of California, Berkeley), FTII
Barrister (Middle Temple)
Barrister, Ireland
Advocate of the High Court of South Africa
Barrister and Solicitor: Alberta, Canada

Bloomsbury Professional
LONDON • DUBLIN • EDINBURGH • NEW YORK • NEW DELHI • SYDNEY

BLOOMSBURY PROFESSIONAL

Bloomsbury Publishing Plc
50 Bedford Square, London, WC1B 3DP, UK
1385 Broadway, New York, 10018, USA

Bloomsbury Publishing Ireland Ltd
29 Earlsfort Terrace, Dublin 2, D02 AY28, Ireland

First published in Great Britain 2025
1

British Library Cataloguing-in-Publication Data

A catalogue record for this book is available from the British Library.

ISBN:	PB:	978-1-52653-459-0
	Epdf:	978-1-52653-458-3
	Epub:	978-1-52653-460-6

Typeset by Evolution Design & Digital Ltd (Kent)

For product safety related questions contact productsafety@bloomsbury.com

PREFACE TO THE 22ND EDITION

'we'll soon shake your windows and rattle your walls, for the times they are a-changing.'

Bob Dylan 1964

The law governing personal attachment to the UK for both individuals and legal persons remained remarkably stable throughout the twentieth century and before then. That stability provided the context for Neil Booth's original work in 1986: Residence, Domicile and UK taxation. These concepts were largely built up by the courts. The United Kingdom, long an open economy and an open society, thrived on the mobility of individuals, capital and business. Worldwide liability to tax of individuals was determined on the basis of a graduated system by reference to residence, ordinary residence and domicile. The greater the UK connection, the greater the liability to tax.

Pressures on the system were already apparent when I first took over authorship of the 12th edition in 2008, driven by unprecedented mobility of individuals, capital and business that has resulted from technological change in transport and communication as well as a reduction in legal impediments to free movement. Since that time, the last 10 editions have reflected rapid and dramatic change across all areas. Key milestones are:

- HMRC have actively and systematically contested non-domiciled status, as well as the residence of individuals, companies and trusts, giving rise to a substantial volume of decisions by the tax tribunals and higher courts, including landmark cases for both domestic law and tax treaty purposes.
- The residence of trusts and estates addressed by statute in Finance Act 2006.
- The remittance basis for non-domiciled resident individuals expanded the meaning of remittance to the UK with byzantine complexity by Finance Act 2008 along with the introduction of a charge for claiming the relief.
- 2013 saw the introduction of the Statutory Residence Test for individuals along with the abolition of ordinary residence for income and capital gains taxes.
- Finance Act 2015 increased the remittance basis charge.
- OECD BEPS Action 6 and the MLI abolished the place of effective management for resolving dual residence of companies and trusts in favour of pure administrative agreement.

- Finance Act 2017 deemed resident non-domiciled individuals to be UK domiciled if they were born in the UK or have been resident for 15 out of 20 years.
- On 31 December 2020, the UK departed from the EU, depriving UK citizens of the right of British citizens to reside in EU Member States and both individuals and companies of non-discriminatory treatment.
- Finance Act 2021 introduced higher rates of Stamp Duty Land Tax on non-resident purchasers of residential property than those applicable to UK resident purchasers, which would have been prohibited by EU law. It included a new, self-contained, statutory definition of residence applied to this tax only.
- Finance Act 2025 largely abolished domicile as a connecting factor for tax purposes, plus the remittance basis. New concepts – long-term UK residence and qualifying new residents – have been introduced.

This 22nd edition has been restructured and substantially rewritten to reflect the fundamental changes in this area of law. It aims to provide a comprehensive treatment of the law of residence for taxation of individuals, companies, trusts and partnerships in light of the latest legislation, case law and HMRC practice. All forms of taxpayer are now subject to statutory residence rules in varying degrees. Only companies and partnerships continue to be governed by common law principles. Ordinary residence continues to play a key role for National Insurance Contributions and tax credits. Domicile remains relevant for the future for individuals who were resident but not-domiciled before 6 April 2025. The Statutory Residence Test has been in place for over 12 years. For this reason, the chapters that deal with the earlier case law and HMRC practice on individual residence and moving to and from the UK have been deleted. However, as the Statutory Residence Test and the long-term UK residence test may in some cases require a look back to periods prior to 6 April 2013 for individuals, readers are directed to the previous edition of this work for an explanation of the earlier law.

Changes in this area have been advanced on the basis of fairness. I leave others to judge whether that is achieved or whether old anomalies are replaced by new ones and how that fairness should be determined. A principled exercise of taxing jurisdiction based on sound connecting factors is likely to be internationally attractive and domestically legitimate in a democratic society, as well as provide a stable revenue base for governments. A grab-what-you-can tax policy encourages escape-what-you-can tax subjects.

My thanks go to Hannah Collins, Dave Wright, Chris Harrison and all the Bloomsbury Professional editorial and production team for all their hard work in bringing this edition to fruition, which is generally up to date to the beginning of November 2025.

Jonathan Schwarz
Middle Temple,
London
November 2025

CONTENTS

TABLE OF STATUTES

[*References are to paragraph number*]

TABLE OF STATUTORY INSTRUMENTS

[*References are to paragraph number*]

TABLE OF HMRC MATERIAL

[*References are to paragraph number*]

HMRC GUIDANCE MATERIALS

OTHER HMRC MATERIALS

HM TREASURY MATERIALS

STATEMENTS OF PRACTICE

TABLE OF EC MATERIALS AND INTERNATIONAL CONVENTIONS

[*References are to paragraph number*]

TABLE OF CASES

[*References are to paragraph number*]

C

F

G

H

I

J

K

Decisions of the European Court of Justice are listed below numerically. These decisions are also included in the preceding alphabetical list.

CHAPTER 1

United Kingdom taxation

I am a stranger and a sojourner with you

Genesis ch 23 v 4

1.01 State practice in exercising taxing jurisdiction

In the field of direct taxation, state practice in exercising taxing jurisdiction universally recognises that either the person subject to taxation, or the item of income (or gain), that is the object of taxation, must be within the territory of the taxing state. Taxation by the country of the source of the income is often described as 'limited taxation', in that the liability is limited to income (and gains) from sources within that state's territory. 'Unlimited liability', on the other hand, applies to persons whose personal connection, typically residence, is within the state's territory, because the liability is in respect of income (or gains) regardless of where they arise.[1]

Most states adopt a single factor connecting persons with their territory, namely residence. The UK has long adopted a more nuanced approach in relation to individuals, applying instead several connecting factors: residence, ordinary residence, domicile and nationality. In general, the more connected the person has been to the UK, the greater the exposure to UK taxation. This approach has contributed to, and is a product of, an open economy, a diverse and tolerant society and a central position as a leading centre of international commerce, finance and creativity.

Recent reforms have largely eliminated ordinary residence as a factor,[2] confined the relevance of domicile in most cases[3] and introduced temporary

1 For an examination of these issues worldwide, see 'Source and residence: new configuration of their principles' *Cahiers de droit international*, Vol 90a (International Fiscal Association, 2005).

2 See Chapter 2, **2.1**, Chapter 4, **4.01**.

3 See **1.8.**

non-residence,[4] qualifying new residence,[5] long-term UK residence,[6] as well as residence with split-year treatment,[7] as new factors. These changes have increased complexity of the tax system exponentially. It is too soon to say what their effect will be on UK society and its economy.

Questions of sovereignty

1.02 The right to levy tax

It was 1199 when King John began to convert the elaborate and well-ordered fiscal system he had inherited from Henry I and Henry II into an instrument of arbitrary and merciless extortion, but it was not until 15 June 1215 that 'in a Thames-side meadow called Runnymede, … the taxpayers … combined to control the tax-imposer'[8] by forcing the monarch to set his seal to Magna Carta. Clause 12 of the charter provided that 'no scutage or aid shall be imposed in our Kingdom unless by the Common Council of our Realm' but, even then, the control was incomplete. In the fourteenth century, Edward III imposed massive taxation to finance his long war with France and the price of the people's consent to such taxation was that future taxation would be conditional on the 'common consent of prelates, earls, barons and other lords and commons of the realm'.[9]

Although this was 'a major step on the road to parliamentary control of taxation',[10] it was not until 1689 that the prerogative rights of the British monarchy were finally and completely abrogated in that regard. In 1681, Charles II had dissolved the Parliament and begun to rule absolutely. In 1685, he was succeeded by his brother James II and, in 1689, upon the accession to the throne of William and Mary, Parliament secured the passing of the Bill of Rights which vouchsafed for it ultimate supremacy. Ever since then, the British monarch has reigned but not ruled, so that today, just as in 1689, 'levying moneys for or to the use of the Crowne by pretence of prerogative without grant of Parlyament … is illegal'.[11]

In recent years, as the sophistication, complexity and volume of tax legislation has grown, concerns have been expressed about the reality of parliamentary control. A 2005 International Monetary Fund working paper found that the UK had some of the weakest powers in the world for budget

---

4 See Chapter 3, **3.13**.
5 See Chapter 3, **3.14**
6 See Chapter 3, **3.15**.
7 See Chapter 3, **3.02**.
8 Arthur Bryant, *Set in a Silver Sea* (Collins) pp 130–132.
9 Bryant, p 226.
10 Bryant, p 226.
11 Bill of Rights 1688.

scrutiny. The Tax Law Review Committee of the Institute for Fiscal Studies said in 2003, 'The truth of the matter is that the House of Commons has neither the time nor the expertise nor, apparently the inclination, to undertake any systematic or effective examination of whatever tax rules the government of the day places before it for approval.' A Confederation of British Industry task force report in 2008 concluded, 'it would not be unreasonable to say … there is no genuine scrutiny of the finance bill under the present system.' To illustrate, Sch 7 to the Finance Act 2008 (the Remittance Basis) is some 50 pages in length and had 135 government amendments introduced at the committee stage but received the attention of the Public Bills Committee for less than a full day. In response to these criticisms, a Working Party chaired by Lord Howe of Aberavon published a report in July 2008 taking forward the Forsyth Tax Reform Commission's recommendations on the making of tax law.[12] A discussion document setting out the government's proposals shaping a new approach to tax policy-making was published as part of the 2011 Budget documents.[13] It proposed a more considered approach, including consultation on policy design and improved scrutiny of draft legislative proposals.

Schedule 45 to the Finance Act 2013, which introduced the Statutory Residence Test, is 67 pages in length. Together with Schedule 46 (abolition of ordinary residence), which is 20 pages, it commanded under 30 minutes of the Public Bills Committee's time. This legislation was however the subject of public consultation over a period of nearly two years.[14]

1.03 Jurisdictional limitations

It is a matter of constitutional law that, because the sovereign power of Parliament is absolute, unless Parliament chooses voluntarily to abrogate its powers,[15] it may legislate contrary to the requirements of international law, for 'international law … yields to statute'[16] and, 'if the language of the statute is clear, it must be followed notwithstanding the conflict between municipal and international law which results'.[17]

The primary characteristic of law is that it is enforceable by sanction (ie fine, suspension of rights, imprisonment, etc). Before a court may order enforcement, however, it must be competent to hear and determine the alleged non-compliance, and, in the English courts, such competence rests solely on

12 *Making Taxes Simpler. The final report of a Working Party chaired by Lord Howe of Aberavon* (July 2008).

13 HM Treasury and HM Revenue & Customs, *Tax policy making: a new approach* (June 2011).

14 See **1.17**.

15 As, for example, when, on 1 January 1973, Britain acceded to the Treaty of Rome and became bound, as a European Community Member State, by Community legislation. This is now largely irrelevant after 31 January 2020 as a result of Brexit.

16 *Cheney v Conn* (1967) 44 TC 217 at 221, per Ungoed-Thomas J.

17 *Maxwell on the Interpretation of Statutes* (12th edn) p 183.

whether a claim has been served on the defendant in person. This – following from the fact that a writ is essentially an assertion of sovereignty and that sovereignty itself is territorial – gives rise to the

> '… broad general universal proposition that English legislation … is applicable only to English subjects or to foreigners who by coming into this country, whether for a long or a short time, have made themselves during that time subject to English jurisdiction.'[18]

Personal taxing jurisdiction has developed by reference to these same common law principles in relation to the matters with which this book is concerned.

1.04 Enforcement overseas

Although the requirement of service of process on a defendant personally may prevent an action for the recovery of taxes from a person abroad being brought before an English court, what is to prevent such an action being brought before the court of the foreign state in which that person is present and being heard there in accordance with the principles of international law? The short answer is simply that 'it is the practice of nations not to enforce the fiscal legislation of other nations'.[19]

The principle on which this practice is based emerged over two centuries ago when, in upholding a French individual's claim for the purchase moneys due in respect of goods which were to be smuggled into England by their purchaser in violation of English revenue laws, Lord Mansfield enunciated the proposition that 'no country ever takes notice of the revenue laws of another'.[20] Stated thus, the proposition may be too wide – and may, indeed, no longer even be of application in the circumstances with which Lord Mansfield was concerned.[21] What may be said, however, is that:

> '… a foreign government cannot come here – nor will the Courts of other countries allow our government to go there – and sue a person found in that jurisdiction for taxes levied and which he is declared to be liable to by the country to which he belongs.'[22]

The rationale behind the principle thus stated is that:

---

18 *Re Sawyers, ex p Blain* [1874–80] All ER Rep 708 at 710, per James LJ.

19 *Clark v Oceanic Contractors Inc* [1983] STC 35 at 41, per Lord Scarman.

20 *Holman v Johnson* (1775) 1 Cowp 341.

21 In *Regazzoni v K C Sethia (1944) Ltd* [1957] 3 All ER 286 at 292, Viscount Simonds said: 'It does not follow from the fact that today the court will not enforce a revenue law at the suit of a foreign state that today it will enforce a contract which requires the doing of an act in a foreign country which violates the Revenue laws of that country.'

22 *King of the Hellenes v Brostrom* (1923) 16 Ll L Rep 167, per Rowlatt J.

> '... a claim for taxes is but an extension of the sovereign power which imposed the taxes, and ... an assertion of sovereign authority by one State within the territory of another ... is (treaty or convention apart) contrary to all concepts of independent sovereignties.'[23]

Were the payment of tax a contractual obligation, the situation would, of course, be different and the contract would be not only recognised but enforced if necessary, by the courts of a foreign state in accordance with the principles of private international law. Tax collection is, however, 'not a matter of contract, but of authority and administration as between the State and those within its jurisdiction'.[24] Accordingly, foreign courts will not entertain a suit for the direct or indirect[25] enforcement of UK revenue laws and, this being so, the limitation implicitly imposed on the legislature's legislative power by the principle of action *in personam* cannot be circumvented (at least so far as revenue laws are concerned) by recourse to a foreign forum.

This principle is now increasingly limited by international treaties. In 2007 the UK signed the Multilateral OECD/Council of Europe Convention on Mutual Assistance in Tax Matters, which, likewise, facilitates collection of taxes by one signatory state for the others.[26] The UK has also started to include such provisions in its bilateral tax treaties.[27] The EU Mutual Assistance in Recovery of Taxes Directive[28] also requires Member States to collect unpaid taxes of all kinds on behalf of each other. Authority to extend this assistance beyond the European Union by treaty has existed since 2006.[29] Following

23 *Government of India v Taylor* [1955] 1 All ER 292, per Lord Keith of Avonholm.

24 *Government of India v Taylor* [1955] 1 All ER 292, per Lord Somervell of Harrow.

25 In *Peter Buchanan Ltd and Macharg v McVey* [1954] IR 89, the director of a Scottish company made a deal with the Inland Revenue on which the Revenue authorities subsequently reneged. The director promptly stripped the company of its assets and removed them – along with his private assets and himself – to the Republic of Ireland where he proceeded to 'snap his hands in the face of the disgruntled Scottish Revenue'. The Inland Revenue, realising that a direct attempt to recover taxes through the courts of Eire would fail, attempted to do so indirectly by suing the director on the grounds that he had acted in breach of his duties as a director. The court looked beyond the action, however, and, seeing that it was no more than an indirect attempt to enforce UK revenue laws in the Republic of Ireland, dismissed it. See also *Skatteforvaltningen v Solo Capital Partners LLP* [2022] EWCA Civ 234 and [2023] UKSC 40 for a full exposition of the rule.

26 OECD/Council of Europe Convention on Mutual Assistance in Tax Matters signed by the UK on 24 May 2007.

27 See, for example, Protocol of 7 November 2007 to United Kingdom-New Zealand Double Taxation Convention of 4 August 1983 (SI 1984/365 as amended).

28 Current legislation is Council Directive 2010/24/EU on mutual assistance for the recovery of claims relating to certain levies, duties, taxes and other measures; implemented in the UK by FA 2006 s 173 and the MARD Regulations SI 2011/2931.

29 FA 2006 ss 173–176.

Brexit, this directive continues to apply to the UK for a period of five years after the end of the transition period.[30]

1.05 Territorial limits

In interpreting a parliamentary enactment, however, the courts have been committed to carrying the principle of territorial sovereignty no further than they need. Almost a century ago, Lord Esher MR expressed his conviction that:

> 'Parliament ought not to deal in any way, either by regulation or otherwise, directly or indirectly, with any foreign matter or person which is outside the jurisdiction of our Parliament, and … the Courts ought always to construe … general words to apply only to the person or thing which will answer the description in them, but which person or thing is also within the jurisdiction of our Parliament.'[31]

Those same sentiments have been echoed by Lord Asquith, who was adamant that:

> '… an Act of the Imperial Parliament today, unless it provides otherwise, applies … to nothing outside the United Kingdom: not even to the Channel Islands or the Isle of Man, let alone a remote overseas colony or possession.'[32]

In the context of taxation, in *Clark v Oceanic Contractors Inc*,[33] the House of Lords held that, because Oceanic, a non-resident company, had an address for service in the UK and carried out operations in the designated areas of the North Sea (the profits of which were to be treated under FA 1973 s 38(4) as profits from a trade carried on by it in the UK and, as such, to be liable to corporation tax, it had a trading presence in the UK and that such a trading presence was sufficient to impose an obligation on the company to operate a PAYE scheme for the collection of tax in respect of emoluments chargeable to tax under Schedule E.

Lord Scarman also noted in that case that 'the principle is a rule of construction only' and that 'British tax liability has never been exclusively limited to British subjects and foreigners resident within the jurisdiction'. Lord Wilberforce[34] referred to the 'territorial principle' as being 'really a rule of construction of statutes expressed in general terms'.

---

30 Agreement on the withdrawal of the United Kingdom of Great Britain and Northern Ireland from the European Union and the European Atomic Energy Community, (2019/C 384 I/01), art. 100. The Withdrawal Agreement had effect in UK law by the European Union (Withdrawal) Act 2018 as amended by the European Union (Withdrawal Agreement) Act 2020.

31 *Colquhoun v Heddon* (1890) 2 TC 621 at 626.

32 *A-G for the Province of Alberta v Huggard Assets Ltd* [1953] 2 All ER 951.

33 [1983] STC 35.

34 At p 427; 152.

On the other hand in *Agassi v Robinson (HM Inspector of Taxes)*,[35] a non-resident company, set up by a famous tennis star, entered into endorsement contracts with two manufacturers of sports clothing and equipment, neither of which was resident or had a tax presence in the UK. The company received payments abroad from the manufacturers pursuant to the contracts. The House of Lords by a majority concluded that the foreign entertainers' tax applied to the payments as a matter of legislative intendment.

Questions of territory

1.06 Territory of the UK

The UK has three constituent units, each subject to the ultimate sovereignty of the common Parliament at Westminster. The three units are England and Wales, Scotland, and Northern Ireland. Legislation has now been passed which establishes a Parliament for Scotland with powers of primary legislation in some areas, including a limited power to vary income tax; a National Assembly for Wales which has, jointly with Westminster, some powers of primary legislation; and an Assembly for Northern Ireland with powers of legislation in certain areas.[36] England, Wales and Scotland are described collectively as Great Britain,[37] and the UK consists of Great Britain and Northern Ireland.[38] Scotland and Wales both have an element of autonomy in relation to income tax. A 'Scottish taxpayer' may be liable to the Scottish rate of income tax under Part 4A, Chapter 2 of the Scotland Act 1998. Similarly, a 'Welsh taxpayer' may be subject to the Welsh rate of income tax under the Government of Wales Act 2006 Part 4A.[39] The Isle of Man and the islands of Jersey, Guernsey, Alderney, Sark, Herm and Jethou (ie the Channel Islands) are British Isles outside the UK[40] and have their own systems of private law and taxation.

1.07 The territorial waters

In addition to the land mass described at **1.06** above, the UK includes territorial waters. These include internal waters such as rivers, lakes and the area of sea which lies upon the landward side of the low-water line along the coast

35 [2006] UKHL 23.
36 Scotland Act 1998 and 2012, Government of Wales Acts 1998 and 2006, and Northern Ireland Act 1998.
37 Royal and Parliamentary Titles Act 1927.
38 Interpretation Act 1978 s 5 and Sch 1.
39 See **2.44** on the meaning of 'Scottish taxpayer' and 'Welsh taxpayer'.
40 As to the Channel Islands not being part of the UK, see *Navigators and General Insurance Co Ltd v Ringrose* [1962] 1 All ER 97.

(including the coast of all islands and low-tide elevations comprised in the territory) or, in the case of a bay, the area of sea which lies on the landward side of a straight line (not more than 24 miles in length) joining the low-water lines of the natural entrance points of the bay.[41] They include also the territorial sea which consists of those parts of the sea over which the UK's sovereignty is subject to the right of innocent passage by foreign ships[42] being any part of the open sea which lies within one marine league[43] on the seaward side of the base-line from which the areas of internal waters are determined.[44]

The relevance of territorial waters in the context of revenue law may not be immediately obvious. As we shall see, however, the precise place where a person is present or the time at which a person leaves the UK may be critical in the context of the establishment of non-resident tax status,[45] and that time is the time at which a person moves out of the UK's territorial waters (or out of the air space above them).

The scope of territorial waters is suggested by two cases brought by the Post Office under the Wireless Telegraphy Act 1949 s 14(7) against a so-called 'pirate' radio station in the Thames estuary. The defendants, who operated from Red Sands Tower, a structure which rests on the seabed more than three nautical miles from the nearest low-water lines of the Kent and Essex coasts, contended that their operations were performed on the high seas outside the UK's territorial waters and that they did not, therefore, come within the UK's jurisdiction. It was held, however, that the Red Sands Tower lies within the bay contained by a straight line drawn between the Naze and Foreness Point (the natural entrance points of that coastal indentation which forms part of the Thames estuary) and is accordingly within the internal waters of the UK.[46] Had Estuary Radio Ltd sought to escape UK taxation on the grounds advanced in its defence, it would, it seems, have been bound to fail for identical reasons.

One of the questions raised in the cases described was whether or not the jurisdiction of a magistrates' court could extend over an area of territorial water. As the territorial waters in question adjoined the county of Kent, it was held that the Kent justices did indeed have jurisdiction. On the same premise, therefore, it seems clear that, where matters of revenue law are concerned in relation to persons or sources of income or gains within territorial waters, the General Commissioners (whose function is similar in connection with revenue law to that of the justices in connection with criminal law) appointed for the adjoining tax division will have jurisdiction to the same extent as they

41 Territorial Waters Order in Council 1964, Arts 2–5.
42 Convention on the Territorial Sea and Contiguous Zone, Cmnd 2511, Art 11.
43 That is three nautical miles.
44 Territorial Waters Jurisdiction Act 1878 s 7.
45 See **2.01** in relation to the Statutory Residence Test and **5.08** for years to 5 April 2013 below. See also **9.16** below in relation to domicile.
46 *Post Office v Estuary Radio Ltd* [1967] 1 WLR 1396 and *R v Kent Justices, ex p Lye* [1967] 2 WLR 765.

would have jurisdiction were the person or source located on the area of land contained within that division.

1.08 Territorial extension

Although Parliament is not, for all the reasons stated thus far, presumed to generally legislate beyond the limits of the territory over which it has sovereignty, there is nothing to prevent it so doing if the inhibiting constraints of international law are removed by international treaty. This will, of course, happen only rarely, but one instance of its occurrence may be cited.

In 1958, the Geneva Convention on the Continental Shelf[47] secured agreement at international level concerning exploration or exploitation rights in relation to all resources in the seabed and subsoil of the North Sea continental shelf. Certain of that Convention's provisions were brought within the municipal law of the UK[48] by the Continental Shelf Act 1964 and that Act provided that areas of the continental shelf outside the UK's territorial waters might be designated by Order in Council[49] as areas within which the UK might exercise rights of exploration and exploitation.[50] The Act recognised that any areas so designated would not thereby become part of the UK[51] and, implicitly, that the sovereignty of Parliament would not extend to them.

Once the Order in Council had been made, however, Parliament decided to extend its revenue legislation so as to bring within the scope of the Taxes Acts any profits or gains from exploration or exploitation activities carried on in the designated areas. This territorial extension of the charge to tax was achieved by the Finance Act 1973.[52]

1.09 The European Union and Brexit

On 1 January 1973, the UK acceded to the Treaty of Rome which had come into effect on 1 January 1959 and had provided for the establishment of a European Economic Community. The Treaty on the Functioning of the European Union (TFEU) is now a foundation instrument for the European Union.

47 29 April 1958.
48 See **1.07** above.
49 Orders have been made in relation to the sea around the Orkneys and Shetlands, the sea west and north-west of the Shetlands, the sea off the west coast of Scotland, the Irish Sea, St George's Channel, the Bristol Channel, the sea south of Cornwall, the south-western approaches to the English Channel, the English Channel, the North Sea and the southern North Sea.
50 Continental Shelf Act 1964 s 1(7).
51 Continental Shelf Act 1964 s 1(1).
52 FA 1973 Sch 15.

In a legally non-binding, advisory referendum on 23 June 2016, a narrow majority of voters expressed the view that the UK should leave the EU. The Government gave notice to this effect on 29 March 2017 pursuant to Article 50 of the TFEU. The Withdrawal Agreement concluded between the UK and the EU extended the application of EU law to the UK until 31 December 2020.

The Court of Justice of the EU has ruled that discrimination on the basis of residence can amount to covert discrimination by reason of nationality which is forbidden by Article 18 of the TFEU.[53] British subjects automatically ceased to be European citizens under TFEU Article 20(1) and no longer benefit from the rights that European citizenship offers, or other rights under EU law in the field of discrimination. British citizens, companies and businesses shorn of their EU rights will have their rights in EU Member States determined by the laws of those states and EU nationals resident in the UK will henceforth be governed by UK law. Readers are directed to Chapter 10 of the 20th edition of this work for discussion on residence, nationality and discrimination in the European Union and the specific implications of Brexit.

Determinants of chargeability

1.10 Residence

Residence is the central pillar of personal taxing jurisdiction in the UK. It is the common thread found in relation to all taxes identified in this work. It is applied to natural persons (individuals), legal persons (companies) and notional persons (trusts or settlements). The task of giving meaning to the expression was largely left to the courts, with legislation addressing only limited issues for more than two centuries. Codification of the residence of trusts and estates was undertaken in 2006. These rules are analysed in Chapter 5. The residence of individuals was largely codified in 2013. The residence of individuals from 6 April 2013 is addressed in Chapter 2. The residence of individuals who come to and depart from the UK is discussed in Chapter 3. The residence of companies remains a mixture of case law and statute and is examined in Chapter 6. The residence of trusts and estates is explained in Chapter 6, and that of partnerships is considered in Chapter 7. An entirely separate meaning is given for all persons only for purposes of Stamp Duty Land Tax and examined in Chapter 8.

The overall effect of the regime introduced by Schedule 45 to the Finance Act 2013 was to establish the following categories of individuals with residence-related fiscal connections to the UK:

53 *Giovanni Maria Sotgiu v Deutsche Bundespost* (Case C-152/73) [1974] ECR 153.

- UK residents: UK residents are liable to income tax and capital gains tax on income and capital gains wherever they arise, whether in or outside the UK.[54]
- Non-residents: non-residents are liable to income tax on income from sources within the UK and certain capital gains on the disposal of assets situated in the UK.
- UK residents with split-year treatment: such individuals are not taxed as fully resident nor as fully non-resident individuals. Instead, they are liable to income tax and capital gains tax in accordance with a lengthy list of amendments to the tax system where certain items qualify for special treatment.
- Temporary non-residents: these are individuals who are not resident in the UK but whose liability to tax on certain income and gains on a worldwide basis is suspended and conditional, pending their possible return to the UK within five years of having departed.

Two further categories of resident were introduced by Finance Act 2025:

- New residents: certain individuals who move to the UK may benefit from exemption from tax on certain foreign income and gains.
- Long-term UK residents: individuals who are UK resident for a sufficient number of years are liable to inheritance tax on worldwide assets.

1.11 Ordinary residence

From 6 April 2013, ordinary residence was generally abolished as a connecting factor for taxation but continues to apply in relation to national insurance contributions and tax credits.[55] Ordinary residence had previously only applied to individuals for the purposes of income tax, capital gains tax and national insurance contributions. In some cases, it may have served to extend taxing jurisdiction. Liability to capital gains tax was expressed to arise where the individual is either resident or ordinarily resident in the UK.[56] In other cases it limited taxing jurisdiction. The anti-avoidance provisions of ITA 2007 relating to transfers of assets only applied to individuals ordinarily resident in the UK.[57] It has an uneasy relationship with simple residence, requiring as it does a degree of settled purpose. Ordinary residence is considered in Chapter 4.

---

54 At the time, a subcategory of UK residents were those who are resident but not domiciled in the UK and whose foreign income and gains may be taxed on the remittance basis. This was abolished by Finance Act 2025 Pt 2 Ch 2.

55 Finance Act 2013 Sch 46; Tax Credits (Residence) Regulations 2003, Reg 3(1).

56 TCGA 1992 s 2.

57 ITA 2007 Pt 13 Ch 2.

1.12 Domicile and long-term residents

Domicile is frequently used to identify the personal law applicable to an individual. It may be described as the country in which the person has his 'permanent home'. It is universally recognised that, though a person may change his shores, this personal law remains the same – except in certain extreme circumstances.

Questions of status and succession are determined according to the law of the domicile, and it has been adopted as the criterion for determining the chargeability of a person to inheritance tax on a worldwide basis. The use of this ultimate, long-term connecting factor as a determinant of liability to income tax and capital gains tax has been a key factor in making the UK attractive to foreigners as a place to live and work. It has been widely regarded as an important contributor to the success of the UK, and London in particular, as the centre of international trade finance, investment, and of artistic and scientific creativity. The scope of domicile as a determining factor for tax purposes was dramatically narrowed by the Finance Act 2008 Schedule 7.

A comprehensive time limit was finally enacted in Finance(No 2)A 2017 which was received with effect from 6 April 2017.

Domicile as a connecting factor for tax purposes was abolished by Finance Act 2025 for tax years from 6 April 2025. It was replaced for inheritance tax purposes with a new residence-based concept of long-term residence. Domicile will continue to be relevant to the income and capital gains taxation of the foreign income and gains accrued to individuals who were not domiciled in the UK up to that date and for certain estate and gift tax treaties.

The concept of domicile is examined in Chapter 9 and long-term residence in Chapter 2.

1.13 Nationality

Nationality now has no impact on taxing jurisdiction of individuals. It is a factor in resolving dual residence of individuals for the purpose of the application of tax treaties.[58] This is considered at **2.45**. Citizenship of the EU is conferred on nationals of all Member States by Article 21 of the TFEU. EU citizenship rights no longer apply to UK nationals following Brexit. See **1.09**.

1.14 Personal connection and UK source income

A person's 'usual place of abode' has been a determinant of liability of payers to withhold tax on certain payments such as interest, royalties or other similar

58 See OECD Model Double Taxation Convention, Art 4(2)(c).

amounts. This expression is discussed in Chapter 10, para **10.03**. New terms have been used to classify the source of income in the context of the modern economy where much value is based on intangible assets and the related digitalisation of the economy. These terms have not been examined by the courts or tribunals.

A digital services tax, enacted by Finance Act 2020 applies to certain digital services supplied to a 'UK user'.[59] A 'UK user' means any user of the service who it is reasonable to assume: (a) in the case of an individual, is 'normally in the United Kingdom'; and (b) in any other case, is 'established in the United Kingdom.' Here HMRC observe[60] that the legislation does not define what 'normally located' means.[61] They say that 'it is not as prescriptive as concepts like citizenship or those used in other taxes like residence or domicile. Rather, it simply tests where the user is located most of the time. In most cases, this will be synonymous with the jurisdiction where the user lives.' Thus, 'the user's location is based on their normal location, rather than their location at the time of the transaction giving rise to the Digital Services revenues.'

1.15 The remittance basis

Until 6 April 2025 some individuals were charged to income tax and capital gains tax on certain kinds of income and gains on the remittance basis; tax was charged only on the income and gains which were remitted to the UK.[62] Usually, the remittance basis applied where the income or gains arise outside the UK and where the individuals are not domiciled and, in some cases, not ordinarily resident in the UK. The remittance basis dated from 1803 and remained largely unchanged over the last century. The meaning of remittance was the subject of detailed and lengthy statutory provisions introduced by Finance Act 2008 Schedule 7 and again by Finance Act 2025 Schedule 9.[63] Remittance will continue to be relevant for individuals who were resident but not domiciled in the UK up to 5 April 2025 and who had unremitted foreign income and gains that had not been remitted to the UK by the end of the 2024/25 tax year. Former remittance basis taxpayers may have such amounts remitted and taxed in the future. In addition, such taxpayers may elect to apply a temporary repatriation facility provided in Finance Act 2025 Schedule 10. This permits them to either remit such amounts or treat them as remitted and to pay tax at preferential rates. The rate is 12% for 2025/26 and 2026/27 and 15% for 2027/28.[64]

---

59 FA 2020 Pt 2.

60 DST32000 – *UK Users*.

61 FA 2020 s 44(3).

62 For the history of previous amendments to the remittance basis, see earlier editions of this work.

63 Contained in ITA 2007 Pt 14 Ch A1.

64 FA 2025 Sch 10 para, 8.

The stated policy objective was 'addressing unfairness in the tax system, so that everyone who is long-term resident in the UK pays their taxes here. The government will therefore remove the outdated concept of domicile status from the tax system and implement a new residence-based regime which is internationally competitive and focused on attracting the best talent and investment to the UK.'[65]

1.16 Foreign income and gains (FIG) regime

From 6 April 2025, the foreign income and gains (FIG) regime provides for exemption from income tax on certain foreign-source income and capital gains tax on the disposal of certain foreign-situated assets for qualifying new residents in their first four years of UK tax residence.[66] The exemption must be claimed on the individual's self-assessment tax return for each item of income and gain sought, giving details of the income and gain in question.[67] A separate election is provided for exemption for qualifying foreign employment income.[68] The exemption can only be claimed for 'qualifying foreign income' identified in ITTOIA 2005 section 845H and cannot include 'disqualified income' listed in section 845I. Similarly, exemption can only be claimed for the types of gains listed in TCGA 1992 Schedule D1. An individual who claims any exemption automatically loses entitlement to any personal allowances[69] and to the capital gains tax annual exempt amount[70] for the tax year in relation to which the claim is made.

1.17 Codification of the residence of individuals

A chain of events started in 2001 with the publication of a Tax Bulletin article on mobile workers, followed by a considerable amount of litigation on individual residence,[71] culminating in the hearing of the *Davies* and *Gaines-Cooper* judicial reviews of HMRC practice in the area.[72] The withdrawal of

65 HM Treasury: Policy paper – Changes to the taxation of non-UK domiciled individuals. Updated 8 August https://www.gov.uk/government/publications/2024-non-uk-domiciled-individuals-policy-summary/changes-to-the-taxation-of-non-uk-domiciled-individuals (accessed 2 July 2025); 2024 HMRC: Policy paper – Reforming the taxation of non-UK domiciled individuals. Published 30 October 2024 https://www.gov.uk/government/publications/tax-changes-for-non-uk-domiciled-individuals/reforming-the-taxation-of-non-uk-domiciled-individuals (accessed 2 July 2025).

66 See Chapter 3, **3.14** for the meaning of 'Qualified new resident'.

67 ITTOIA 2005 s 845A; TCGA 1992 Sch D1 paras 1 and 2.

68 TEPA 2003 ss 41M and 41P.

69 ITTOIA 2005 ss 845E and 845G.

70 TCGA 1992 s 1K(6)(b).

71 See **3.18**.

72 See **3.27**.

IR20 and two versions of HMRC6 in as many years gave rise to pressure to end the uncertainty in such an important area of tax law. The government announced that it proposed to enact a statutory residence test at Budget 2011 and a consultation document was issued on 17 June 2011 by HM Treasury and HM Revenue & Customs setting out their proposals to put the meaning of residence on a statutory basis. It was intended to supersede all existing legislation, case law and guidance for tax years following its introduction.[73] A further consultation document was issued on 21 June 2012 in response to the consultation including draft legislation.[74] A further draft of the legislation along with draft HMRC guidance was published in December 2012.[75] This was followed by the Finance Bill 2013 and amended draft HMRC guidance in May 2013.[76] The statutory residence test, enacted in FA 2013 Schedule 45 is examined in detail in Chapter 2.

The government also announced at Budget 2012 its decision to abolish the concept of ordinary residence for tax purposes generally from 6 April 2013, which was accomplished by FA 2013 Schedule 46.

The stated aim of the statutory residence test was to provide a simple process and clear outcome for the vast majority of people whose circumstances are straightforward[77] and to provide a fair way of determining residence for those with more complicated affairs.[78] The first Consultative Document asserted that, in broad terms, the proposals reflect the HMRC interpretation of the case law with modifications. Thus, it was proposed to take into account both the amount of time the individual spends in the UK and the other connections they have with the UK. However, to avoid the complexity of the case law examination of all facts and circumstances, the test was not proposed to take into account a wide range of connections in the belief that the relevant connections should be simply and clearly defined and the weight and relevance of each connection should be clear.[79] The first Consultative Document expressed the belief that individuals would be able to assess their residence status simply and without the need to resort to specialist advice. Sixty-seven pages of legislation and over one hundred pages of guidance may make this something of a challenge.

Schedule 45 to the Finance Act 2013 is unlikely to be the end of the history of the law of tax residence. HM Treasury Tax Information and Impact Notes for the SRT, published on 11 December 2012, included a commitment that 'this measure will be kept under review through communication with affected

---

73 HM Treasury and HM Revenue & Customs, *Statutory definition of tax residence: a consultation* (17 June 2011) (in this book the 'Consultative Document').

74 HM Treasury and HM Revenue & Customs, *Statutory definition of tax residence and reform of ordinary residence: a summary of responses* (21 June 2012) (in this book the 'Second Consultative Document').

75 HM Revenue & Customs, Guidance Note: Statutory Residence Test (SRT) (December discussion draft) (18 December 2012).

76 HM Revenue & Customs, Guidance Note: Statutory Residence Test (SRT) (May 2012).

77 Consultative Document para 3.2.

78 Consultative Document para 3.4.

79 Consultative Document para 3.4.

taxpayer groups'. On 3 December 2013 the Chartered Institute of Taxation wrote to HMRC recommending that the SRT be formally evaluated in April 2016 (ie, three tax years after the SRT came into force), by an independent review, against its declared objectives, in order to assess whether those objectives are being achieved. No such review has been undertaken or announced.

UK revenue law

1.18 There are four UK direct taxes whose incidence is, to some extent, governed by the residence or domicile status of the person on whom the liability will fall: income tax, corporation tax, capital gains tax and inheritance tax. A detailed consideration of each of those taxes is beyond the scope of this work but, in this and the subsequent paragraphs, the relevance to each of territoriality and of a person's residence and domicile is noted below.

1.19 Income tax

Although income tax is 'one tax, not a collection of taxes essentially distinct',[80] it has, since 1803, been charged in relation to one or another of a number of specified sources each of income. Income tax is now charged in accordance with the Income Tax Act 2007 (ITA), effective from 6 April 2007, the Income Tax (Earnings and Pensions) Act 2003 (ITEPA), effective from 6 April 2003, and the Income Tax (Trading and Other Income) Act 2005 (ITTOIA), effective from 6 April 2005. These Acts were passed by the UK Parliament as part of the Tax Law Rewrite Project, whose aim was to rewrite tax law in plain English and modern legislative drafting structure without changing the law. Some minor changes in the laws have been made but case law which used to appertain to the prior schedular system can still be relevant in interpreting the rewritten legislation.

Income tax is an annual tax, being reimposed for each new year of assessment[81] (ie a year which runs from 6 April in one calendar year to 5 April in the next following calendar year).[82] Thus, in principle, if income is to be charged to tax, it must arise in the year of assessment in question.

The Income Tax (Earnings and Pensions) Act imposes a charge to income tax on employment income, being a charge which is described as a charge on general earnings and a charge on special employment income.[83] Part 2,

80 *A-G v LCC* (1900) 4 TC 265 at 293, per Lord Macnaghten.

81 The continuing structure is preserved by ICTA 1988 s 820, but the tax itself requires an annual parliamentary resolution (invested with statutory authority by PCTA 1968) to keep it alive pending the enactment of the annual Finance Act.

82 ITA 2007 s 4(3) and s 4(5).

83 Income Tax (Earnings and Pensions) Act 2003 ss 1(1), (8), 6, 7.

Chapter 4 of the Act sets out the rules applying to employees who are resident in the UK, while Chapter 5 of the Act sets out the rules applying to employees not resident in the UK. Chapter 5C introduced a new regime for exempting certain foreign employment income of new residents from tax.

The Income Tax (Trading and Other Income) Act 2005 deals with sources of income other than employment and pensions: Partt 2 of ITTOIA 2005 deals with trading profits; Part 3 with property income; Part 4 with saving and investment income; Part 5 miscellaneous income; and Part 8 specifically with foreign income.

The penultimate income tax product of the Rewrite Project is the Income Tax Act 2007, which rewrites and, in some cases, repeals various provisions relating to income tax not dealt with by the two Acts mentioned above. Part 14, Chapter 1 sets out limits on the tax liability of non-residents. Certain international provisions are also contained in the Taxation (International and Other Provisions) Act 2010.

1.20 Corporation tax

The first product of the Rewrite Project for companies was the Corporation Tax Act 2009 (CTA 2009) which generally has effect for accounting periods ending on or after 1 April 2009.[84] Corporation tax is chargeable on the worldwide profits of any company resident in the UK. A non-resident company is, however, chargeable to corporation tax only if it carries on a trade anywhere of dealing in or developing UK land, carries on a trade of dealing in or developing UK land or has other UK property income, carries on a trade in the UK through a permanent establishment in the UK, and, in that event, the profits brought into charge to corporation tax are those sources, including profits arising from loan relationships or derivative contracts relating to those sources of profit or income.[85] The second corporate tax rewrite exercise was the Corporation Tax Act 2010 which includes the definition of permanent establishment.[86]

The profits chargeable to corporation tax are to be arrived at by aggregating with its chargeable gains its income computed on principles similar to income tax but now separately contained in the Corporation Tax Acts.[87]

UK-resident companies are also liable to the controlled foreign companies' charge. This charge is analogous to corporation tax but is imposed by apportioning among UK-resident corporate shareholders with an interest in a non-resident company, the profits of the non-resident company (computed on the basis of it being a company resident in the UK) if that company is controlled by persons resident in the UK, but is resident in a country where its

84 CTA 2009 s 1329(1).
85 CTA 2009 s 5.
86 CTA 2010 Pt 24 Ch 2.
87 See generally CTA 2009 Pts 3 to 10.

profits are subject to a level of taxation lower than that to which they would be subject in the UK.[88] Company residence is examined in Chapter 6.

UK-resident companies (and UK permanent establishments of non-resident companies) that are members of large groups may also be liable to a 'domestic top-up tax' to ensure that their effective corporate tax rate is at least the 15% OECD Global Minimum Tax from 31 December 2024.[89] Such UK resident parent companies may also be liable to a 'multinational top-up tax' designed to apply the Global Minimum Tax to all their profits arising outside the UK.[90]

1.21 Capital gains tax

A charge to capital gains tax arises when a gain accrues to a person on the disposal or deemed disposal of a chargeable asset in a year of assessment during any part of which he is resident in the UK.[91] A chargeable gain accruing to a company is included in its profits for corporation tax purposes.[92]

A disposal occurs whenever the owner of the asset disposes (or is deemed to dispose) of his ownership, absolute and beneficial, of the whole or part of the asset; a chargeable asset is any asset (including incorporeal property) other than, for example, an individual's principal private residence,[93] gilt-edged securities and qualifying corporate bonds,[94] savings certificates and non-marketable securities,[95] life policies, and deferred annuities,[96] tangible moveable assets disposed of for £6,000 or less,[97] private motor vehicles,[98] certain interests under settlements,[99] decorations for valour etc,[100] debts other than debts on a security,[101] and foreign currency for personal expenditure.[102]

Residents are liable to capital gains tax on the disposal of assets wherever they are situated.[103] Non residents of the UK who carry on a trade, profession or vocation in the UK through a branch or agency, are charged tax on gains accruing from the disposal of assets situated in the UK and either held by the branch or used or acquired in connection with the trade profession or

88 TIOPA 2010 Pt 9A. See **7.22** below.
89 Finance(No 2)Act 2023 Pt 4.
90 Finance Act 2025 Pt 3 and Sch 4.
91 TCGA 1992 ss 1 and 2(1).
92 See **1.19** above.
93 TCGA 1992 s 222.
94 TCGA 1992 s 115.
95 TCGA 1992 s 121.
96 TCGA 1992 s 210.
97 TCGA 1992 s 262.
98 TCGA 1992 s 263.
99 TCGA 1992 s 76.
100 TCGA 1992 s 268.
101 TCGA 1992 s 251.
102 TCGA 1992 s 269.
103 TCGA 1992 s 1A(1).

vocation.[104] The charge also applies to disposals of any UK-situated land[105] and of assets, wherever situated, that derive at least 75% of their value from UK land where the person has a substantial indirect interest in that land.[106] Whether an asset is situated outside the UK or not is determined by the provisions of TCGA 1992 section 275.

1.22 Inheritance tax

Inheritance tax is a direct tax on transfers of value made on, or (at a tapered rate) during the seven years preceding, an individual's death;[107] and on transfers by a close company or on certain lifetime transfers by an individual into certain trusts.[108]

Transfers to a spouse are exempt from tax, provided that the spouse is domiciled in the UK,[109] as are gifts of £250 or less,[110] certain gifts in consideration of marriage,[111] and gifts to charities etc.[112] Where lifetime transfers by an individual are chargeable to tax, the amount brought into charge is to be reduced by an annual exemption.

If an individual is a long-term UK resident,[113] then, the transfer, during the last seven years of their life or upon death, of any property to which the individual is beneficially entitled, wherever situated, is within the charge to tax. Only transfers of property situated in the UK will be within the charge in the case of other individuals, even if UK resident.[114] Domicile is now only relevant for the application of double tax treaties that address inheritance tax, and is explained in Chapter 9 below.

1.23 National Insurance Contributions

While not strictly a tax, National Insurance Contributions are often thought of by both those who pay and collect them in the same way as tax. In the international context, they share some of the same jurisdictional issues with income tax. Liability to pay Class 1, Class 1A, Class 1B or Class 2 contributions generally only falls on persons who fulfil prescribed conditions

104 TCGA 1992 ss 1A(3)(a) and 1B.
105 TCGA 1992 s 1A(3)(b).
106 TCGA 1992 ss 1A(3)(c), 1D and Sch 1A.
107 IHTA 1984 Pt I as amended by FA 1986.
108 IHTA 1984 ss 3, 71 and 89; F(No 2)A 1987 s 96(2); FA 2006 Sch 20.
109 IHTA 1984 s 18.
110 IHTA 1984 s 20.
111 IHTA 1984 s 22.
112 IHTA 1984 ss 23–29.
113 See Chapter 3, **3.15** on the meaning of long-term UK resident.
114 IHTA 1984 s 6(1) and (1A).

as to residence or presence in Great Britain.[115] The prescribed conditions refer to both residence and ordinary residence.[116] Chapter 4 discusses the meaning of ordinary residence. Unlike the income tax rules, mere presence by an employed earner at the time of employment may be sufficient to establish liability.[117] These expressions are undefined in the social security legislation and thus the case law on the meaning of those expressions is relevant to this area of law. HMRC guidance indicates that they will apply the case law principles to the expression for National Insurance Contributions purposes.[118]

1.24 Value added tax (VAT)

Member States of the European Union are required to impose value added tax (VAT) under the VAT Directive.[119] Residential concepts are again relevant in determining taxing jurisdiction. While the place of supply of goods for VAT purposes is decided by reference to the goods supplied,[120] the place of supply of services is generally by reference to the location of the supplier or customer.[121] Thus, for example, the place of supply of services is the place where the supplier has established his business or has a fixed establishment from which the service is supplied, or, in the absence of such a place of business or fixed establishment, the place where he has his permanent address or usually resides.[122] UK legislation enacts these rules by referring to where a person 'belongs'.[123]

HMRC practices and concessions

1.25 HMRC guidance and the statutory residence test

Although the Consultative Document expressed the belief that the statutory residence test will allow individuals to assess their residence status simply and without the need to resort to specialist advice, HMRC issued a guidance note (RDR3) in 2013 setting out its views on the operation of the legislation. RDR3 was 105 pages long compared to the previous 86-page HMRC 6. It contains 73 examples to illustrate the application of the SRT and split-year treatment.

115 Social Security Contributions and Benefits Act 1992 s 1(6).
116 Social Security (Contributions) Regulations 2001 (SI 2001/1004) reg 145.
117 Reg 145(1)(a).
118 HMRC National Insurance Manual NIM33555.
119 Council Directive 2006/112 on the common system of value added tax (the VAT Directive).
120 VAT Directive Title V, Chs 1, 2 and 4.
121 VAT Directive Title V, Ch 3.
122 VAT Directive, Art 43.
123 VAT Act 1994 s 7A(2).

The hoped-for simplicity has thus far evaded the legislative drafters. Express limitations on the extent to which the guidance may be relied on suggest that the issues that have dogged guidance on individual residence will not disappear. The latest guidance is in the Residence and FIG Regime Manual.[124] An HMRC online 'Tax Residence Indicator[125] also offers to check whether individuals are considered to be resident in the UK but not whether they meet the requirements for split-year treatment. It does not check the residence status of someone who died in the tax year. The indicator will helpfully perform calculations to deal with the many formulae and numerical thresholds contained in the statutory residence test. It is not authoritative and HMRC cautions that the results given rely on individuals inputting accurate information. In so doing explicit recognition is given of the need to interpret the concepts that constitute the test before any calculations can be made. Tax Residence Indicator invites users to use their guidance in answering the questions posed by the online tool. HMRC recommends that taxpayers should keep the results for future reference in case of enquiry by them.

124 HMRC Residence and FIG Regime Manual RFIG20000, accessed 6 June 2025.
125 See https://www.tax.service.gov.uk/guidance/check-your-UK-residence-status/start/choose-tax-year.

CHAPTER 2

Residence of individuals: the Statutory Residence Test

'An Answer for you?' interrupted Deep Thought majestically. 'Yes, I have.'
'There really is one?' breathed Phouchg.
'To Everything? To the great Question of Life, the Universe and Everything?'
'Yes' said Deep Thought, 'Though I don't think that you're going to like it'
'Forty-two,' said Deep Thought, with infinite majesty and calm.

Douglas Adams, *The Hitchhiker's Guide to the Galaxy*

2.01 Introduction

The 'Statutory Residence Test'[1] (SRT) defines the tax residence of individuals from 6 April 2013.[2] The test is set out in Parts 1 and 2 of Schedule 45 to the Finance Act 2013. It determines the residence of individuals for the purposes of income tax, capital gains tax and, where relevant, corporation tax and inheritance tax.[3] The statutory residence test will determine whether an individual is resident or non-resident in the UK, including those cases where a tax liability of another actual or deemed person depends on the residence of another individual.[4] Thus, for example, the residence of a trust is determined by reference to the residence of the trustees.[5] In such a case the residence of a trust with individual trustees will be determined indirectly by the statutory residence test. It does not apply to National Insurance Contributions or for non-tax purposes.[6]

1 Finance Act 2013 Sch 45 para 1(2). All statutory references in this chapter are to paragraphs of that Schedule unless stated otherwise.
2 See **2.30** for commencement and transitional rules.
3 Sch 45 para 1(2) and (4), 2(1)–(3).
4 Sch 45 para 2(2).
5 See generally, Chapter 6.
6 Sch 45 para 1(4).

The UK, for this purpose, means the United Kingdom including the territorial sea of the United Kingdom.[7] 'Overseas' is defined to mean anywhere outside the UK.[8] The SRT only determines whether an individual is resident in the UK as a whole and not in one of the countries comprising the UK.[9] For 'residence' in Scotland, see **2.43**. The SRT does not apply to individuals whose residential status is expressly dealt with differently in any other statute.[10] It replaces all other tests of residence so that the residential status of individuals is entirely governed by statute.[11]

The background to the adoption of the statutory residence test is considered in Chapter 1.

The overall effect of the statutory residence test and related rules contained in Schedule 45 to the Finance Act 2013 is to establish the following category of persons with residential fiscal connections to the UK:

- ***UK residents***: UK residents are liable to income tax and capital gains tax on income and capital gains wherever they arise whether in or outside the UK.
- ***Non-residents***: non-residents are liable to income tax on income from sources within the UK and certain capital gains on the disposal of assets situated in the UK.
- ***UK residents with split-year treatment***: this is a new legal category of status, rather like the Flying Dutchman who was perpetually between ports. Such individuals are not taxed as fully resident nor as fully non-resident individuals. Instead they are liable to income tax and capital gains tax in accordance with a lengthy list of amendments to the tax system where certain items qualify for special treatment.
- ***Temporary non-residents***: these are individuals who are not resident in the UK but whose liability to tax on a worldwide basis is suspended pending their possible return to the UK within five years of having departed. The list of items on which their liability to tax as a resident is suspended is likewise lengthy.

The abolition of domicile as a connecting factor from 6 April 2026 by Finance Act 2025 also introduced a new category of 'long-term UK resident' as the determinant of worldwide inheritance tax liability.[12] The rules for UK residents

7 Sch 45 para 145. See Chapter 1, paras **1.06** and **1.07** on the territorial extent of the United Kingdom.

8 Sch 45 para 145.

9 Days spent in the UK means days spent anywhere in the UK including within the territorial sea: See Chapter 1 **1.06** to **1.08**. In *Bayard Brown v Burt* (1911) 5 TC 667, an American citizen living on a yacht anchored in the tidal waters off the Essex coast, with no lawful right to be there, was within the UK's territorial waters and the taxpayer was found resident on the basis of presence in the UK.

10 Sch 45 para 2(5). See **2.27** on the residence of members of Parliament and of the House of Lords and **2.28** on the residence of EU officials.

11 Sch 45 para 2(1) and (2).

12 Finance Act 2025 s 44.

with split-year treatment, temporary non-residents and long-term UK residents are examined in Chapter 3.

Drafting of the SRT

The drafting of the statutory residence test and related rules is less than satisfactory. It will be apparent to the reader from different drafting conventions adopted, that different parts of Schedule 45 have been drafted by different individuals and that little attempt has been made to harmonise or reconcile them. Secondly, the legislation has abandoned the clear language of the consultation documents which set out the government policy in favour of bland, uninformative, unmemorable phrases. Thus, for example, 'full-time work abroad' has given way to 'the third automatic overseas test'. 'International transportation workers' has given way to 'P' with a 'relevant job on board a vehicle, aircraft or ship'. The eight cases of split-year treatment are known by their case numbers. Some individual rules have lost conceptual coherence as the draft legislation developed. Whether this is a product of policy or drafting is far from clear. Words such as 'somewhere' in relation to a home or 'something' in relation to work, may leave the reader with the feeling that the drafters sought to evade rather than ensure the clarity and certainty that the statutory residence test was intended to produce. HMRC guidance was contained in a publication entitled *HMRC Guidance Note: Statutory Residence Test (SRT)* ('RDR3'), which was revised several times. Following Finance Act 2025, detailed explanation of the HMRC view is contained in the HMRC internal manual: Residence and FIG Regime Manual.[13]

This chapter aims to explain and analyse the statutory test using ordinary language. Rather than speculating about the meaning of every ambiguous expression, a general caution about the precise meaning of the SRT is appropriate, until the tribunals and courts have had an opportunity to consider them in practice. The legislation remained unexamined by the courts or tribunals until 2022 and since then, only once.[14]

Consistent with the HMRC view of the case law, that residence should have an adhesive nature, the legislation aims to ensure that resident individuals cannot become and remain non-resident without significantly reducing the extent of their connection with the UK.[15] The legislative test has thus been designed to make it significantly harder to become non-resident when leaving the UK after a period of residence than it is to become resident when an individual comes to the UK. Once an individual has become resident and built up connections with the UK, they will be required to scale back their ties to the

13 HMRC Residence and FIG Regime Manual RFIG20000 accessed 6 June 2025.

14 See **2.03**: *A Taxpayer v HMRC* [2025] EWCA Civ 106.

15 HM Treasury and HM Revenue & Customs, Statutory definition of tax residence: a consultation, 17 June 2011 (the 'Consultative Document') para 3.5.

UK significantly or spend far less time here or a combination of the two before they can relinquish tax residence. On the other hand, individuals should not be resident if they have little connection with the UK.[16] In line with this approach, a distinction is made between:

- individuals who were not UK resident in all of the previous three tax years; and
- individuals who were resident in one or more of the previous three tax years.

2.02 Basic rule

The basic rule of the statutory residence test is that an individual is resident in the UK for a tax year if, for that year, either (a) the automatic residence test, or (b) the sufficient ties test is met.[17] The basic rule is modified by the automatic residence test itself. The automatic UK test only applies if none of the automatic overseas tests is met. It is a requirement of the sufficient ties test that none of the automatic UK tests and none of the automatic overseas tests are met.[18]

The automatic residence test contains conclusive connecting factors that would each be sufficient in themselves to make an individual resident. The sufficient ties test contains other connecting factors and day counting rules which, taken together, may make an individual resident. If an individual satisfies neither of these two tests for a tax year, he will definitely be not resident in that tax year.

By this convoluted and circular route, a hierarchy for the application of the three parts of the statutory residence test is established. Firstly, if any of the automatic overseas tests are satisfied, that would be sufficient to make an individual not resident. Secondly, if an individual satisfies any of the automatic UK (residence) tests, but none of the automatic overseas tests, that would itself be sufficient to make an individual resident. Thirdly, if none of the automatic UK tests and none of the automatic overseas tests are satisfied, then the sufficient ties test is engaged. The sufficient ties test contains other connecting factors and day counting rules which will need to be considered only by those whose residence status is not determined by the automatic tests.

The tests

There are four automatic UK tests, five automatic overseas tests and the sufficient ties test, summarised as follows:

16 Consultative Document para 3.6.
17 Sch 45 para 3.
18 Sch 45 para 5.

Automatic UK tests:

- spending 183 days or more in a tax year in the UK (the 'first automatic UK test');[19] or
- having a home in the UK at which sufficient time is spent (and either having no home overseas or spending insufficient time at overseas homes) (the 'second automatic UK test');[20] or
- working sufficient time in the UK over a period of 365 days (the 'third automatic UK test');[21] or
- dying in a year after having been resident in the UK under the automatic UK residence test for each of the previous three tax years and having a home in the UK (the 'fourth automatic UK test').[22]

Automatic overseas tests:

- residence in the UK for one or more of the three tax years preceding the year, and spending less than 16 days in the year in the UK (the 'first automatic overseas test');[23] or
- residence in the UK for none of the three tax years preceding the year and spending less than 46 days in the year in the UK (the 'second automatic overseas test');[24] or
- working sufficient time overseas for the year, spending less than 91 days in the year in the UK and having no more than 31 days in the year on which the individual does more than three hours' work (the 'third automatic overseas test').[25]
- Dying in a year after having been UK resident for neither of the two preceding year tax years (or not UK resident in the previous year and the tax year before that was a split year in certain cases) and having spent less than 46 days in the UK in that year (the 'fourth automatic overseas test').[26]
- Dying in a year after having been UK resident for neither of the two preceding year tax years because of full-time work overseas in certain cases (the 'fifth automatic overseas test').[27]

Sufficient ties test

The sufficient ties test is met by spending the prescribed number of days in the UK in a tax year in conjunction with the following UK ties:

19 Sch 45 para 7. See **2.06.**
20 Sch 45 para 8. See **2.07**.
21 Sch 45 para 9. See **2.12.**
22 Sch 45 para 10. See **2.17**.
23 Sch 45 para 12. See **2.05**.
24 Sch 45 para 13. See **2.06**.
25 Sch 45 para 14. See **2.13**.
26 Sch 45 para 15. See **2.16**.
27 Sch 45 para 16. See **2.16**.

- a family tie;
- an accommodation tie;
- a work tie;
- a 90-day tie; and
- a country tie.[28]

The automatic tests turn on the application of four factors: physical presence in the UK; having and using a home in the UK; full-time work either in the UK or overseas; and death. In this chapter, each factor is discussed in turn as a determinant of residence rather than simply following the list of tests in the numerical order as set out in the legislation.

2.03 Physical presence: counting days

Physical presence in the UK is a central theme in the statutory test. A living individual who is not physically present in the UK at all in a tax year cannot satisfy any of the tests to qualify as a UK resident. All tests, other than the death-related automatic tests, expressly or by necessary implication require such presence. It is also a specific requirement throughout the split-year rules.

A uniform manner of determining the number of days spent in the UK applies to all measures of physical presence in the UK for purposes of the SRT, but one.[29] Different rules, however, apply to determine time spent working,[30] at home or at any other place to live,[31] or seeing children.[32]

Unlike the previous HMRC practice, none of the time periods are averaged. The number of days present in, or absent from, the UK are measured strictly for each tax year concerned. This inflexibility is likely to produce harsh and arbitrary outcomes as few individuals live their lives by the UK tax calendar.[33]

The number of days spent in the UK in a given period is determined by reference to the total number of days spent there, in the aggregate, in that period, whether continuously or intermittently.[34] A day counts as a day spent by an individual in the UK if he is present in the UK at the end of a day. Whether an individual is present in the UK, is a question of fact. The legislation makes explicit that a day does not count as a day spent in the UK if the individual is not present in the UK at the end of that day.[35] Two exceptions are made: in

28 Sch 45 para 16. See **2.18** to **2.26**.
29 Sch 45 para 23(3). See **2.22**.
30 See **2.12** and **2.21**.
31 See **2.07** and **2.20**.
32 See **2.19**.
33 See *Ogden v Revenue & Customs* [2011] UKFTT 212 (TC) for an example under the prior law of the harsh effects of these rules.
34 Sch 45 para 24.
35 Sch 45 paras 22(1) and 23(1).

the case of transit passengers[36] and for circumstances beyond the individual's control.[37]

The first exception is where an individual arrives in the UK as a passenger on a particular day and leaves the UK the next day, and between arrival and departure, the individual does not engage in activities that are to a substantial extent unrelated to his passage through the UK.[38] This is similar to the previous rule introduced by FA 2004 section 24. HMRC regard merely taking dinner or breakfast at a hotel, in the normal course of events, as related to passage. In contrast, enjoying a film at the local cinema or catching up with friends or a brief work-related meeting would be considered substantially unrelated to passage through the UK.[39] See the discussion and examples in RFIG20730.

Secondly, where an individual would not be present in the UK at the end of a day but for exceptional circumstances beyond his control that prevent him from leaving the UK, and the individual intends to leave the UK as soon as those circumstances permit, that day does not count as a day spent in the UK.[40] The relief is tightly drawn. All requirements are cumulative. First, the individual would not otherwise be present in the UK. Second, the circumstances must both be exceptional and beyond the individual's control. Third, and in addition, the circumstances must be such that they prevent the individual from leaving. These expressions are undefined, but the legislation gives examples of circumstances that may be exceptional. They are national or local emergencies such as war, civil unrest or natural disasters, and a sudden or life-threatening illness or injury.[41] HMRC regard only days when a person cannot leave the UK as a result of an 'event' as qualifying. They accept that exceptional circumstances may exist in limited cases where the individual is compelled to come back to the UK.[42] A British national who is evacuated to the UK from a foreign war zone is outside the exception. The same would be true for an individual evacuated to the UK for emergency medical treatment.

HMRC guidance on the subject of exceptional circumstances is circumscribed and dependent on examples rather than general guidance.[43] Whether circumstances can be regarded as exceptional for the purpose of the SRT will always depend on the particular facts, an individual's circumstances and the choices available to them.[44] Exceptional circumstances will normally apply where an individual has no choice concerning the time they spend in the UK or in coming back to the UK.[45] Thus where an individual with serious

36 Sch 45 para 22(3).
37 Sch 45 para 22(4).
38 Sch 45 para 22(3).
39 RFIG20730. Days spent in the UK: Transit days.
40 Sch 45 para 22(4).
41 Sch 45 para 22(5).
42 RFIG22240. What are exceptional circumstances.
43 RFIG22210. Exceptional circumstances introduction (Part of the guidance is also withheld from publication).
44 RFIG22240.
45 RFIG22240.

injury can be removed to hospital outside the UK, the failure to do so will not constitute exceptional circumstances.[46] Some concession appears to be made in very limited circumstances where an individual comes to the UK rather than merely remaining in the UK in circumstances beyond their control: where they are coming back to the UK to deal with a sudden life-threatening illness or injury to a partner or dependent child[47] a passenger (but not a crew member) on a commercial aircraft that is forced to make an emergency landing in the UK and there is no available onward flight to their original destination for two days afterwards[48] evacuation from a ship departing the UK for emergency medical treatment.[49] Where Foreign and Commonwealth Office advice is to avoid all travel to a region because of civil unrest or natural disaster, individuals who return to and stay in the UK while such advice remains at this warning level would 'normally' have days spent in the UK ignored during that period.[50]

HMRC do not consider travel problems, such as a delayed or missed flight due to traffic disruption, train delays or cancellations, or a car breakdown, as exceptional circumstances.[51]

In the view of HMRC, not only must the circumstances be beyond control, they must also be beyond the individual's influence and reasonably unforeseeable.[52] The HMRC view plainly goes beyond the requirements of the statute. No more than 60 days in a year may be excluded from counting as presence in the UK on this ground.[53]

The fact that a day is spent in the UK, detained by exceptional circumstances, does not prevent the day from counting as one spent working in the UK, at home or at any other place to live, or seeing children. Similarly, it does not impact on another day counting rules such as breaks between employments or in the availability of a home or a place to live.[54]

Guidance issued in response to the coronavirus (Covid-19) pandemic was not unequivocal. HMRC emphasises that each case is dependent on particular facts and circumstances. No view was expressed on the requirements of paragraph 22(5) other than that they accept that circumstances are exceptional if the individual is:

- quarantined or advised by a health professional or public health guidance to self-isolate in the UK as a result of the virus;

46 RFIG22240. What are exceptional circumstances, Example 2(a) and (b) (a broken neck).
47 RFIG22240. But see below for other close relatives.
48 RFIG2240. Example 2(b).
49 RFIG22240. Example 1(unconscious and badly burned).
50 RFIG22250. Exceptional circumstances and Foreign and Commonwealth Office (FCO) advice.
51 RFIG22270. Examples of circumstances not normally considered to be exceptional.
52 RRFIG2240. Example 2(b).
53 Sch 45 para 6.
54 RFIG22230. Day counting tests where exceptional circumstances cannot be taken into account when determining number of days spent in the UK. See also RFIG22220 where exceptional circumstances can be taken into account.

- advised by official Government advice not to travel from the UK as a result of the virus;
- unable to leave the UK as a result of the closure of international borders; or
- asked by their employer to return to the UK temporarily as a result of the virus.[55]

A very limited statutory relaxation of the residence rules made in connection with the coronavirus pandemic permitted an individual who came to the UK to work on coronavirus-related matters. It applies to individuals who were not UK resident in the previous tax year but came to the UK either as medical or healthcare professionals for purposes connected with the detection, treatment or prevention of coronavirus or for purposes connected with the development or production of medicinal products (including vaccines), devices, equipment or facilities related to the detection, treatment or prevention of coronavirus.[56] Such individuals could be treated as not resident for either the 2019/20 or 2020/21 years.[57] Days spent in the UK are effectively ignored for various tests that require day counting.[58] The departure of the UK from the EU on 31 January 2020 and the end of the transition period on 31 December 2020 meant that both healthcare professionals and research or engineering professionals were deterred from coming to or left the UK in that period, leaving many roles unfilled.

HMRC's narrow interpretation of exceptional circumstances was rejected by the First-tier Tribunal in *A Taxpayer v HMRC*.[59] At issue was whether the taxpayer was non-resident under the sufficient ties test because she spent less than 46 days or more in the UK.[60] That would be the case if five days in the UK were for exceptional circumstances within paragraph 22(4). In December 2015 and February 2016, she came to the UK to look after her twin sister and her sister's two children. The twin sister was suffering from alcoholism and was suicidal at the time. In finding that the circumstances were indeed exceptional the tribunal said that the purpose of this rule was to prevent the injustice of being unable to leave the UK for reasons out of that individual's control. The rule had to be seen in the context of prescriptive rules by providing a measure of relief against the hard edge of those 'bright line' rules.[61] HMRC's formulation that

---

55 RDRM11005. Coronavirus (COVID-19) published 23 March 2020. The That manual also noted that this guidance could change at short notice as situations change. This application of this policy was further elaborated in RDRM13410 Annex D. International tax clarifications due to coronavirus (Covid 19) – Q&A. Now see RFIG22410 to RFIG22550. Guidance on the invasion of Ukraine implies that HMRC would not regard refugees seeking relief from war and persecution from Ukraine or Russians and Belarussians seeking to evade conscription or political persecution as qualifying for exceptional circumstances: RFIG22260.

56 Finance Act 2020 s 109(4)(8).

57 Finance Act 2020 s 109(1).

58 Finance Act 2020 s 109(3), (4)(b) and (5) to (12).

59 *A Taxpayer v HMRC* [2022] UKFTT 133 (TC). The decision is anonomised, given the very sensitive personal nature of the evidence.

60 Sch 45 para 18, table.

61 *A Taxpayer v HMRC* [2022] UKFTT 133 (TC) at paras 131 and 132.

'The circumstances should be highly exceptional, and not merely 'unusual, not what happens regularly or is expected', but out of the ordinary in the extreme.' was inconsistent with that purpose. The HMRC arguments for a narrow interpretation that were rejected were: First, HMRC submitted that foreseeable circumstances should be excluded because a taxpayer could plan ahead to avoid those circumstances from preventing them from leaving the UK – as well as not being exceptional, the circumstances would also not then be beyond a person's control. Second, exceptional circumstances excluded a person who came to the UK under a moral obligation or an obligation of conscience to care for a family member or other person. Instead, HMRC argued that the test only applied where a person came to and remained in the UK either under a legal obligation or was physically prevented from leaving the UK. Third, HMRC argued that the exception applied only to persons who were already in the UK and, were overtaken by 'exceptional circumstances' which prevented them from leaving. The tribunal said that it was impossible to derive these from the words used by Parliament.[62]

The vigour with which HMRC opposed the conclusion that six days spent in the UK were for exceptional circumstances is remarkable. The Upper Tribunal agreed with HMRC,[63] in particular, that a moral or conscientious obligation could not be exceptional and that evidence to support each element of the statutory test was required for each individual day and that these circumstances were not exceptional.

The Court of Appeal[64] dismissed all the HMRC arguments and upheld the taxpayer's argument that the circumstances were exceptional. Lord Justice Nugee said that:

> 'as a matter of ordinary experience we can distinguish between cases where they are compelled or obliged to stay (and hence are prevented from leaving) and cases where they simply find it more convenient or attractive or otherwise preferable for them to stay.'[65]

In concluding that one of the things that can prevent a person from leaving the UK is a sufficiently compelling moral obligation or obligation of conscience, it was wrong to sharply divide objectively verifiable circumstances and a person's subjective reaction to the circumstances.[66] Thus, a moral or societal obligation which imposes an obligation should be taken into account.[67] Whether circumstances are 'exceptional' is a mixed question of fact and law.[68] Thus, a finding by the First-tier Tribunal on the point may only be disturbed on a further appeal. if 'no person acting judicially and properly instructed

62 *A Taxpayer v HMRC* [2022] UKFTT 133 (TC) at paras 145 to 153.
63 HMRC v A Taxpayer [2023] UKUT 182 (TCC).
64 *A Taxpayer v HMRC* [2025] EWCA Civ 106.
65 At para 46.
66 At paras 49 and 51.
67 At para 63.
68 At para 79.

as to the relevant law could have come to the determination under appeal'[69] or 'no reasonable person could have arrived at the same conclusion as the Commissioners'.[70]

It was uncontentious that the exceptional circumstances test applies to each day. HMRC challenged its application for four specific days. They argued the taxpayer was unable to give a day-by-day account of what happened on each day or to explain why, for example, she was able to leave after the days in question but not before. The Court of Appeal noted that the First-tier Tribunal accepted evidence that if the reason for the Appellant remaining in the UK was the same each day and if that reason constituted exceptional circumstances, that reason remained valid for each relevant day and that it was implicit in their decision that the taxpayer could not leave before she did and that she left as soon as the situation had stabilised.[71] Although there were problems with the evidence, the Court concluded that First-tier Tribunal was entitled to come to the factual conclusion it did based on the evidence before it.[72]

2.04 Day-count hyping

In certain circumstances an individual will be deemed to spend a day in the UK even if that individual is not actually present in the UK at midnight on the day concerned, regardless of the exceptions for transit passengers and circumstances beyond the individual's control. This will be the case for individuals who: (a) have at least three UK ties for a tax year; (b) were resident in the UK for at least one of the three tax years preceding the tax year in question; and (c) are present in the UK at some point in the day but not at the end of the day ('qualifying days') for more than 30 days in a tax year. Such individuals must count any qualifying day in excess of 30 in the tax year as a day spent in the UK.[73]

Day-count hyping (given that the anodyne 'deeming rule' label in the HMRC manual[74] does not apply for the purposes of deciding whether an individual has a 90-day tie or in determining presence in the UK under the full-time work overseas test (the 'third automatic overseas test').[75]

The Second Consultative Document stated that a supplementary rule would apply only to those who are present in the UK on a large number of days without ever being in the UK at midnight on those days to minimise the potential for

69 *Edwards v Bairstow and Harrison* (1955) 36 TC 207 at 229, per Lord Radcliffe.
70 *Pilkington v Randall* (1966) 42 (TC) para 662 at 674, per Salmon LJ.
71 At paras 89 and 90.
72 At para 99.
73 Sch 45 para 23(2)–(4).
74 RFIG20720. The SRT: Days spent in the UK: The deeming rule.
75 Sch 45 para 23(5).

manipulation.[76] The stated policy was not to have such a rule affect those who legitimately commute to and from the UK frequently, especially if they do not have other significant ties to the UK. The day-count hyping deeming rule overshoots that objective and is not restricted to 'manipulators' of the normal day-counting rule.

2.05 Counting days: conclusive non-residence

The automatic overseas tests are designed to treat individuals as clearly not tax resident in the UK in certain circumstances without having to take account of the connections they have with the UK. This is the case when individuals are present in the UK for only a small number of days in a tax year. Two tests are almost entirely dependent on physical presence in the UK. An individual is conclusively not resident in the UK for a tax year if he:

- was resident in the UK in all of the previous three tax years and is present in the UK for fewer than 16 days in the current tax year but does not die in that year (the 'first automatic overseas test');[77] or
- was not resident in the UK in one or more of the previous three tax years and is present in the UK for fewer than 46 days in the current tax year (the 'second automatic overseas test').[78]

Different amounts of time that may be spent in the UK depending on previous residence, reflects the HMRC view of the case law, that residence should have an adhesive nature. As a result, resident individuals cannot become and remain non-resident without significantly reducing the extent of their connection with the UK. The test has been designed to make it harder to become non-resident when leaving the UK after a period of residence than it is to become resident when an individual comes to the UK. Once individuals have become resident and built up connections with the UK, they will be required to scale back their ties to the UK significantly or spend far less time here or a combination of the two before they can relinquish residence. On the other hand, individuals should not be resident if they have little connection with the UK. The stated policy was that it is beneficial to encourage individuals to come to the UK and spend a limited amount of time here without necessarily becoming resident, such as investors assessing investment opportunities.[79] A holiday in the UK of little more than six weeks will take the occasional visitor out of automatic non-resident status.

76 HM Treasury and HM Revenue & Customs, Statutory definition of tax residence and reform of ordinary residence: a summary of responses (June 2012) (the 'Second Consultative Document'), para 3.153.

77 Sch 45 para 12.

78 Sch 45 para 13.

79 Second Consultative Document para 3.154.

2.06 Counting days: conclusive residence

If none of the automatic overseas tests applies to treat an individual as conclusively non-resident, then the individual will be conclusively resident for a tax year if he is present in the UK for 183 days or more in a tax year (the 'first automatic UK test').[80] The application of the 183-day rule is neither new nor complex. Its operation is illustrated by the following example:

David and Edward visit the UK and both spend about six months here in one tax year. David comes to the UK for one continuous period and is treated as resident in the UK if he spends 183 days here. Edward visits for the same period but makes a few trips abroad from the UK during the year and is treated as not resident if days present are less than 183 in the tax year (subject to the second, third and fourth automatic UK tests and the sufficient ties test).[81]

It will be apparent that this is the only simple test based on counting days present in the UK. Even the automatic overseas day counting tests described in **2.05** above require determination of residence in prior years under the whole of the SRT or the case law test for years prior to 6 April 2013 for their accurate application.

2.07 UK home: conclusive residence

The principle that an individual is resident where their home is, is enticingly simple. The most obvious cases cause no difficulty. It might be thought that in modern western society, most people have a home and that the vast majority have only one. This straightforward principle has been converted into a complex test that conflates the amount of time an individual needs to be at the home for it to qualify as such, and a mechanism to deal with those individuals who have homes in the UK and overseas.

An individual is automatically resident if: (a) that individual has a home in the UK during all or part of a year; (b) there is at least one period of 91 consecutive days, of which at least 30 days ('sufficient time') in the aggregate fall within the year in which they have no home overseas; and (c) spend at least 30 days in the year at that UK home.[82] If they have one or more homes overseas during that 91-day period, and spend fewer than 30 days ('a permitted amount of time') in the aggregate, in the year at each of those overseas homes, but spend at least 30 days in the aggregate, in the year at the UK home, then the individual is likewise automatically UK resident.[83] The UK home test (the 'second automatic UK test') thus comprises two separate tests that treat an

80 Sch 45 paras 5(b) and 7.

81 Drawn from HM Treasury and HMRC, *Reviewing the residence and domicile rules as they affect the taxation of individuals: a background paper*, April 2003.

82 Sch 45 paras 8(1), (2) and (4).

83 Sch 45 paras 8(1), (3) and (5).

individual as conclusively resident if the automatic overseas tests do not apply: one for those with no home overseas and a second test for those with at least one home overseas.[84]

In each case an individual will spend a day at a home when they are present there for at least some of the time, no matter how short, on that day. Presence at a dwelling only counts when it is a home of the individual, so that presence there on any other occasion is disregarded. Looking round a property with a view to buying it, is given as an example of disregarded presence in the legislation.[85] Mere presence, rather than occupation is sufficient. Brief presence in this context may be contrasted with the accommodation tie which requires a night to be spent at the accommodation.

In the case of multiple overseas homes, presence at only one of them for less than 30 days may be sufficient to engage the UK home test.[86] Thus, individuals who move from one overseas home to another may not meet the UK home test. Individuals with more than one overseas home concurrently but who spend very limited time at one or more will satisfy the UK home test. A generous rule applies to those who have more than one home in the UK. Each UK home must be looked at separately to see if the second automatic UK test is met, and the test is then met provided it is met in relation to at least one of those homes. Consequently, having multiple homes in the UK will not be met if they are at none of them for 30 days.

2.08 What is a home?

However, even the most straightforward and common cases raise the question: 'What is a 'home'?' Does a student who goes to study at an overseas university retain a home if their bedroom is kept available but they do not use it? What if the room is converted to a study by the student's parents? The ordinary meanings offered by the Oxford English Dictionary are:

> '1. The place where a person or animal dwells.
>
> 2. a. A dwelling place; a person's house or abode; the fixed residence of a family or household; the seat of domestic life and interests. Also (chiefly in later use): a private house or residence considered merely as a building;'

Although this question gave rise to significant comment during the consultation process, Parliament declined to attempt a definition of the term. The HMRC response during the consultation was:

---

84 Sch 45 para 5(b).
85 Sch 45 para 8(6)(b).
86 Sch 45 para 8(8).

> 'The only home condition is not intended to set a low bar but is meant to be indicative of an individual who normally lives only in the UK. The vast majority of UK resident taxpayers will have only one place to live and this will be their home. It will typically be where they and their immediate family live for all, or the greater part, of their time.
>
> The Government has carefully considered whether to further define in legislation what is meant by a home. It has concluded that it would be extremely difficult to provide a precise definition given the wide variety of living patterns adopted by individuals and their families. Any detailed definition would run the risk of inadvertently including or excluding certain individuals from the test because of the way in which they choose to live their lives. The Government is confident however, that the vast majority of people will know where their home is and whether that home is in the UK or overseas.'

Thus the question is ducked in the legislation. Instead, the following statutory explanation is provided:

> '(1) A person's home could be a building or part of a building or, for example, a vehicle, vessel or structure of any kind.
>
> (2) Whether, for a given building, vehicle, vessel, structure or the like, there is a sufficient degree of permanence or stability about [the person]'s arrangements there for the place to count as [the person]'s home (or one of [the person]'s homes) will depend on all the circumstances of the case.
>
> (3) But somewhere that [the person] uses periodically as nothing more than a holiday home or temporary retreat (or something similar) does not count as a home of [the person]'s.
>
> (4) A place may count as a home of [the person]'s whether or not [the person] holds any estate or interest in it (and references to "having" a home are to be read accordingly).
>
> (5) Somewhere that was [the person]'s home does not continue to count as such merely because [the person] continues to hold an estate or interest in it after [the person] has moved out (for example, if [the person] is in the process of selling it or has let or sub-let it, having set up home elsewhere).'[87]

Ownership or form of tenancy does not determine whether a place is a 'home'. It may be a home whether or not the individual holds any estate or interest in it. A home may be any place including a vehicle or vessel.[88] The legislation helpfully clarifies that a place that was a home does not continue as such merely because the individual continues to hold an estate or interest in it after having moved out. It also confirms that where an individual is in the process of selling a home, it will not continue to count as a home for the purpose of the test after they have moved out of the property.[89]

---

87 Sch 45 para 25.

88 Sch 45 para 25(1).

89 Sch 45 para 25(5).

The requirement to be present for at least 30 days at a home will exclude some cases at the margins from the UK home test. However, very many individuals who either leave the UK or come to it, giving up their existing homes and acquiring a new home in the process will find themselves automatically resident under this test. Imperfect alignment of this test with the split-year treatment in Schedule 45, Part 3 will result in extended periods of taxation as a resident for them.[90]

Paragraph 25(2) suggests that 'a sufficient degree of permanence or stability about [the person]'s arrangements' is necessary to make a dwelling place count as a home. No indication of the degree is specified. It will depend on all the circumstances of the case. It is unclear how the requisite degree of permanence or stability will be interpreted in the context of the minimal 91-day period over which an individual having a home combined with will fall within this rule. If 91 days is sufficient, then paragraph 25(2) is otiose. On the other hand, if a broader examination of facts and circumstances is necessary and classification as a home during 30 days in a tax year is sufficient, then the 91-day period in paragraph 8(1)(c) is otiose. While residence is an annual attribute, the existence of a home will in many cases take into account facts in more than one tax year. The position is also compounded by the requirement for an accommodation tie which must be continuously available for 91 days in the tax year.[91] Thus, the main difference between the term 'home' for SRT purposes and available accommodation is that accommodation can be relatively transient and does not require the degree of stability or permanence that a home does.[92]

The only qualitative indicator is that periodic use as nothing more than a holiday home or temporary retreat is not a home in this context. If the guideline is 30 days of presence in a tax year, will occupation for longer periods make a 'holiday home' a 'home'? Under the case law test of residence, occupation of a dwelling place for a portion of a year constitutes residence. In *Cooper v Cadwalader*[93] Mr Cadwalader was an American citizen who had a house in New York but spent two months of each year in occupation of, a furnished house in Scotland. Although the vocabulary is not identical, Mr Cadwalader undoubtedly had a home in Scotland, even if it was only used for holidays. Case law on the word 'temporary' indicated that it means casual as distinguished from regular habits of life. 'Temporary purpose' means the opposite of 'continuous purpose'.[94] These cases suggest that periodic use as a regular matter will mean the accommodation is a home while casual use will not. In *Yates v Revenue & Customs*[95] Ms Yates rented a three-bedroom apartment in Estepona, on

90 See **2.30**.

91 Sch 45 para 34(1)(a). See also **2.20**.

92 RFIG22170.

93 *Cooper v Cadwalader* (1904) 5 TC 101.

94 See Chapter 5 at **5.05**.

95 *Lynette Dawn Yates v Revenue & Customs* [2012] UKFTT 568 (TC). HMRC are of the view that 'home' for SRT purposes is not the same as that term in treaty tie-breaker provisions. See RDRM13030 – The second automatic UK test and the context of a 'home'.

the southern coast of Spain, on an 11-month lease, which was renewed until November 2003, when she purchased another three-bedroom apartment in the same development. She stayed in them when living in Spain. HMRC accepted in the context of Article 4(2)(a) of the Spain-UK income tax treaty that these apartments were both permanent and available to her, but would not accept that they were 'homes' because they did not have the quality of being 'the seat of domestic life' inherent in the French word 'foyer', which is used to distinguish a house from a home. Tribunal Judge John Walters QC, however, found, on the facts, that it was clear that the Spanish apartments had the quality of being her 'homes'.[96] The application of the UK home test inevitably raises questions about the boundary between it and the 'place available to live' expression in the 'accommodation tie' test.[97] The accommodation tie test must be applied in conjunction with physical presence as a 'sufficient ties' test. A detailed exposition of what will constitute 'place available to live', the purposes of the 'accommodation tie' as part of the sufficient UK ties test is provided[98] but no statutory explanation on what makes a place available to live a home. A home in the UK will always be a place to live in the UK, but a place to live may not always be a home. Uncertainty in relation to the UK home test will mean that its reliability as an automatic test will be limited to individuals with no place to live overseas or those with no place to live in the UK in a tax year.

Although HMRC assiduously resist a definition of home for this purpose, their views on its application are set out in a lengthy appendix to their guidance on the SRT in the Residence and FIG Regime Manual.[99] HMRC guidance on record keeping in connection with the question indicated a wide-ranging enquiry into the full facts and circumstances of an individual's life going far beyond connection with a particular property.[100] This approach effectively revives the full enquiry into the pattern of living of individuals required by the previous case law and subverts the purpose of the SRT itself. Questions relating to whether an individual 'has a home' within the second automatic UK test in paragraph 8 compared to an accommodation tie in paragraph 34 are destined for early consideration by the tribunals and the courts.

Relevance of having a home

Whether an individual can be said to have a home is critical to the application of the SRT. It forms the basis of the second automatic UK test.[101] It is an element in the fourth automatic UK test (death after having been previously

96 Sch 45 para 116.
97 See **2.20**.
98 Sch 45 para 34.
99 RFIG22110, RFIG22120, RFIG22140, RFIG22150.
100 See RFIG21920.
101 See **2.07**.

resident).[102] Having a home and when an individual starts or ceases to have one is relevant to split-year treatment under Case 2 (the partner of someone starting full-time work overseas),[103] Case 3 (ceasing to have a home in the UK),[104] Case 4 (starting to have a home in the UK only),[105] Case 7 (the partner of someone ceasing full-time work overseas)[106] and Case 8 (starting to have a home in the UK).[107]

2.09 Introduction

Sufficient work, which equates to effectively full-time work in the UK, gives rise to automatic residence (the 'third automatic UK test'),[108] while sufficient work, which equates to full-time work overseas, (the 'third automatic overseas test') means automatic non-residence.[109] The two tests are not symmetrical. The Second Consultation Document confirms that this asymmetry is intentional[110] and that the full-time work in the UK test will cause more employees to be resident in the UK in years of arrival and departure than under prior law.[111] Dying in a year after having been UK resident for neither of the two preceding year tax years because of full-time work overseas in certain cases (the 'fifth automatic overseas test')[112] further extends the relevance of full-time work. The legislation spells out in some detail what is meant by work, where it is done and the nature of working full time.

An individual who does not meet any of the conditions of the work-related automatic overseas test, nor the conditions of the work-related automatic UK test, would need to consider the application of the work-related significant UK ties test.[113]

Full-time work in or out of the UK also engages split-year treatment.[114]

2.10 What is work?

An individual is considered to be working (or doing work) at any time when they are 'doing something' in the performance of duties of their

102 See **2.19**.
103 See **2.34**.
104 See **2.35**.
105 See **2.36**.
106 See **2.39**.
107 See **2.30**.
108 See **2.12**.
109 See **2.11**.
110 Second Consultative Document, paras 3.97–3.105.
111 Second Consultative Document, para 3.99.
112 See **2.16**.
113 See **2.21**.
114 See **2.33, 2.34, 2.37, 2.38** and **2.39**.

employment, or in the course of a trade carried on by the individual, alone or in partnership.[115] This rather amorphous expression, 'doing something', is not defined in the legislation but is elaborated in relation to both employment and trade. In *Charman v Revenue & Customs*,[116] the First-tier Tribunal recognised that what constitutes 'working' for senior executives is less straightforward than for an employee who is working regular hours. Thus, work events which involve building contacts, marketing may also involve a social element such as catching up with friends and the distinction between work time and social time may be blurred for such persons. The same observation is apt for self-employed persons.

'Employment' in this context has the meaning given in ITEPA 2003 section 4.[117] It therefore includes: (a) any employment under a contract of service; (b) any employment under a contract of apprenticeship; and (c) any employment in the service of the Crown. Employment further includes an office within the meaning of ITEPA 2003 section 5(3). It thus includes, in particular, any position which has an existence independent of the person who holds it and may be filled by successive holders. Nonetheless, a voluntary post for which the individual has no contract of service does not count as employment for these purposes.[118]

'Trade' for this purpose, also includes: (a) a profession or vocation; (b) anything that is treated as a trade for income tax purposes; and (c) the commercial occupation of woodlands (within the meaning of section 11(2) of ITTOIA 2005).'[119]

In each case, whether an individual is working (or 'doing something'), is essentially a question of fact to be determined by the terms of the employment relationship or the office and the scope and nature of the trade. This factual determination is supplemented by a hypothetical exercise required by sub-paragraphs 26(2), (3) and (8). In deciding whether 'something is being done' in the performance of duties of an employment, regard must be had to whether:

> 'if value were received by the individual for doing the thing, it would fall within the definition of employment income in section 7 of ITEPA 2003.'[120]

By contrast, in relation to doing something in the course of a trade, regard must be had to whether, if expenses were incurred by the individual in doing the thing, the expenses could be deducted in calculating the profits of the trade for income tax purposes.[121] In each case, for the purposes of sub-paragraphs 26(2) and (3) it must be assumed that the individual is chargeable to income tax

115 Sch 45 para 26.
116 *Charman v Revenue & Customs* [2018] UKFTT 765 at paras 229 and 230.
117 Sch 45 para 145.
118 Sch 45 para 26(8).
119 Sch 45 para 145.
120 Sch 45 para 26(2).
121 Sch 45 para 26(3).

under ITEPA 2003 or ITTOIA 2005. Thus, in assessing whether any activity undertaken by an individual is work, the individual must first be engaged in hypothetical employment or trade within the charge to tax. This hypothesis ensures that activities not giving rise to income and not within the charge to tax (because, for example, they are performed outside the UK by a putative non-resident) are determined under the UK statutory rules. Secondly, the activity in question must be identified. Thirdly, in the case of employment, it must be decided whether the hypothetical employee would be rewarded for the activity. In the case of a trade, the test is not by reference to hypothetical income for the activity but rather by whether, if hypothetical expenses were incurred, they would be deductible trading expenditure.

Time spent working may include being on call or standby, depending on the conditions of employment and the nature of duties. HMRC guidance seems to suggest that HMRC does not accept that a self-employed individual is working when available for work in a similar way.[122] In the author's view, that is inconsistent with the statute.

HMRC says that work includes 'where your employer instructs you to stay away from work, for example while serving a period of notice while you remain on the payroll.'[123] Some workers might be surprised to discover that their notice period spent enjoying the sights of London or the wilds of the Scottish Highlands meant they were working in the UK!

The stated aim of this additional hypothetical approach is to depart from the traditional distinction between incidental duties which are largely ignored in determining the place of performance of duties of employment under ITEPA 2003[124] and other 'substantive' duties.[125] The Second Consultation Document acknowledges that this tightens the existing approach. Activities such as reporting, which have been regarded as incidental, will in future be something done in the performance of duties of employment. Activities that may be necessary such as attending a medical examination, for which, in isolation, an employee may not normally be rewarded, would be excluded. This suggests a very narrow class of activity. Whereas in the case of an employee the test is by reference to remuneration for the activity, in the case of a self-employed trader deductibility is the criterion. In neither case is it necessary for the employee to be actually rewarded for the activity or for the individual to actually be chargeable to income tax or entitled to a trade related deduction in respect of the activity. Training would normally be regarded as an incidental activity for employment. The legislation, however, deems time spent undertaking training as time spent working if the training is provided or paid for by the employer and is undertaken to help the individual in performing duties of the employment.[126] In the case of a trade, deductibility of the cost of

122 RFIG20750, example 4.
123 RFIG20740.
124 ITEPA 2003 s 39.
125 Second Consultative Document, paras 3.22–3.32.
126 Sch 45 para 26(5)(a).

the training in calculating the profits of the trade for income tax purposes is the criterion.[127]

Time spent travelling will also be time spent working according to rules similar to those applicable to training. Thus, if the cost of the journey could, if it were incurred by the individual, be deducted in calculating his earnings from that employment under ITEPA 2003, the journey will itself count as work. In the case of a trade, a journey is treated as work if the cost would be deductible in calculating the profits of the individual's trade under ITTOIA 2005.[128] Furthermore, if the individual does something else during the journey that would itself count as work, then the journey will also count as work.

Modern working life is such that individuals who can keep a clear divide between work and non-work are becoming increasingly rare. 'Work' as defined, would include activities such as dealing with phone calls and emails, reading work-related documents, and even thinking about work. An individual catching up on a laptop or smartphone while en route for a holiday or weekend break would be working while on such a journey.

Economic activities that do not comprise employment or trade such as management of investments or property business[129] are not 'work' in this context.

2.11 Location of work

Normally, identifying the place of performance of employment duties gives rise to little difficulty. The SRT specifies the location of work in detail. Work is deemed to be done where it is actually done, regardless of where the employment is held or the trade is carried on by the individual.[130] Thus, individuals with flexible working patterns or arrangements will find themselves working for these purposes when dealing with emails, engaged on the phone or reading work-related documents undertaken outside specific work-related visits. The stated policy is that using a specific number of hours to define a working day is the best approach to achieve a clear and objective definition for the purposes of the SRT.[131] Thus, the boundary in the work-related tests is drawn not by reference to the nature of the work but to the amount of time consumed by work-related activities.

The place of work by way of, or in the course of, travel, therefore, calls for particular consideration. An arbitrary line is drawn by reference to the point of embarkation. Work done by way of or in the course of travelling by air or sea or via a tunnel under the sea to or from the UK is treated as done overseas,

127 Sch 45 para 26(5)(b).
128 Sch 45 para 26(4).
129 ITTOIA 2005 ss 264 and 265.
130 Sch 45 para 27(1).
131 Second Consultative Document, para 3.31.

including during the part of the journey in or over the UK.[132] Travelling to or from the UK begins when the individual boards the aircraft, ship or train that is bound for a destination in the UK or (as the case may be) overseas, and ends when the individual disembarks from that aircraft, ship or train.[133] The whole journey is however considered by HMRC to be work. Thus a person working overseas who comes to a meeting in the UK will be working from the start until the finish of the journey, including transit time through the airport, travel from the airport to the meeting and the same on the return journey. This would suggest that almost any one-day visit for a meeting in London will inevitably involve work in the UK for at least three hours on that day, regardless of the length of the meeting.[134]

These rules do not apply to international transportation workers who have specific provisions about the location of their work.[135]

2.12 Full-time work

Full-time work is not used as an expression in the SRT legislation (although it does appear in the title of certain cases for split-year treatment and is used in HMRC guidance), but this status is described as whether an individual works sufficient hours in the UK or overseas as the case may be.[136] 'Sufficient hours', means work for 35 or more hours per week, on average, across a relevant reference period.[137] Where an individual holds more than one employment or carries on more than one trade during the reference period, the hours worked with respect to all of them are aggregated in determining whether they work sufficient hours there for the period.[138] Thus, any combinations of employments and self-employments have to be taken into account together for this purpose.

The period over which the 35 hours per week is to be measured may be reduced for several reasons.[139] First, a reduction in the length of the period may be made to take account of reasonable amounts of annual leave taken by the individual during the period.[140] Reasonable amounts of annual leave are to be assessed having regard to (among other things) the nature of the work, and the country or countries where the individual is working.[141] The

132 Sch 45 para 27(2).
133 Sch 45 para 27(3).
134 See RFIG20750. Travel either to or from a temporary workplace. In HMRC's view, the place of the business meeting is a temporary workplace. This will have implication for all the work-related aspects of the residence tests. See also **2.11**.
135 Sch 45 para 27(4). See **2.15**.
136 Sch 45 paras 9(1)(a) and 14(1)(a).
137 Sch 45 paras 9(2) and 14(3). In each case this is only apparent by working through the steps set out in those paragraphs.
138 Sch 45 paras 9(2) Step 2 and 14(3) Step 2.
139 Sch 45 para 28. This is described as the 'Rules for calculating the reference period'.
140 Sch 45 para 285(2)(a).
141 Sch 45 para 128(4).

reduction is by reference to leave taken and not leave entitlement. This will be relatively straightforward for employed individuals who take all their leave and have regular work patterns. It may give rise to difficulties in the case of less bureaucratic employment or self-employed traders who may not take leave in a formal sense or full entitlement, but, instead work fewer hours. While the country where work is performed may influence the reasonableness of the amount of leave, no reduction is made for weekends or public holidays or other non-working days. A non-working day for this purpose is any day of the week, month or year on which the individual is not normally expected to work according to his contract of employment or usual pattern of work, and does not in fact work.[142] The result is that an individual working in a country where there is a high statutory minimum holiday will be permitted a greater reduction in the length of the reference period compared to countries with no legal minimum and, for example, two weeks' holiday is the customary norm. On the other hand, an individual working in a country with many public holidays may need to work longer hours to catch up on hours not worked on those days to meet the 35-hour average. Reasonable amounts of parenting leave may also be excluded. 'Parenting leave' is maternity leave, paternity leave, adoption leave or parental leave (whether statutory or otherwise).[143]

Absences from work during the period when the individual is on sick leave and cannot reasonably be expected to work as a result of the illness or injury also qualify to reduce the length of the period.[144] The rule requires not only that the person be on sick leave but also establishes an objective standard, that the illness or injury ought to prevent working. No other commonly recognised forms of leave, such as compassionate leave or study leave are referred to, although they may be embraced by annual leave.

An arbitrary formula applies to non-working days that are embedded within a period of leave to take into account leave being determined by reference to working days (and therefore in addition to other non-working days, such as weekends and public holidays). Such non-working days only reduce the reference period if there are at least three consecutive days of leave taken before and after the non-working day or series of non-working days in question.[145]

If the individual changes employment during the period any gap of up to 15 days between the two employments may be deducted from the length of the period, but only if the individual does not work at all at any time between the two employments. If there is more than one change in employment during the reference period a maximum of 30 days may be deducted in determining the reference period. No equivalent rule is expressed in relation to individuals engaged in trade who cease to trade and start a new trade.[146]

142 Sch 45 para 28(6).
143 Sch 45 para 28(2)(a).
144 Sch 45 para 128(2)(b).
145 Sch 45 para 28(2)(c) and 28(5).
146 Sch 45 para 128(8) and (9).

The language used to describe the factors that permit a reduction in the reference period reflects an employment-focused perspective. It is less well adapted to a trade or profession carried on by an individual. In relation to an individual who carries on a trade, annual leave or parenting leave means reasonable amounts of time off from work for the same purposes as the purposes for which annual leave or parenting leave is taken.[147]

2.13 Full-time work overseas: conclusive non-residence

The stated intention is that a UK-resident individual who leaves the UK to work abroad full-time should be non-resident for the duration of this work irrespective of the connections with the UK they leave behind, subject to certain conditions.[148]

An individual who works full-time overseas for a tax year is conclusively non-resident if the individual: (a) works sufficient hours overseas, as assessed, over the tax year; (b) has less than 31 days in the year on which they do more than three hours' work in the UK; (c) spends less than 91 days a year in the UK, excluding day-count hyped days; and (d) there are no significant breaks from overseas work during the year (the third automatic overseas test).[149]

No hours worked overseas count, if worked on a day when the individual does more than three hours' work in the UK.[150] Thus, an individual who works overseas all day for seven hours preparing for a meeting in the UK that day that lasts for over three hours, cannot count those hours worked towards the sufficient hours target.

There is a 'significant break from overseas work' if there are at least 31 consecutive days on which the individual does not do more than three hours' work overseas, or would have done more than three hours' work overseas but for being on annual leave, sick leave or parenting leave.[151] These limits are reduced pro rata for the overseas part of a year in which an individual qualifies for split-year treatment.[152] International transportation workers who have at least six cross-border work trips in a year are outside the scope of the third automatic overseas test.[153]

Assessment of whether sufficient hours have been worked overseas is by application of the following formula in paragraph 14(3):

> '(3) Take the following steps to work out whether P[the individual] works "sufficient hours overseas" as assessed over year X[the tax year in question]—

147 Sch 45 para 146.
148 Consultative Document, para 3.16.
149 Sch 45 para 14.
150 Sch 45 para 14(3) Step 1.
151 Sch 45 para 29(2).
152 See **2.33**, **2.37** and **2.38**.
153 Sch 45 para 14(4). See **2.15**.

Step 1

Identify any days in year X on which P does more than 3 hours' work in the UK, including ones on which P also does work overseas on the same day.

The days so identified are referred to as "disregarded days".

Step 2

Add up (for all employments held and trades carried on by P) the total number of hours that P works overseas in year X, but ignoring any hours that P works overseas on disregarded days.

The result is referred to as P's "net overseas hours".

Step 3

Subtract from 365 (or 366 if year X includes 29 February)—

(a) the total number of disregarded days, and

(b) any days that are allowed to be subtracted, in accordance with the rules in paragraph 28 of this Schedule, to take account of periods of leave and gaps between employments.

The result is referred to as the "reference period".

Step 4

Divide the reference period by 7. If the answer is more than 1 and is not a whole number, round down to the nearest whole number. If the answer is less than 1, round up to 1.

Step 5

Divide P's net overseas hours by the number resulting from step 4.

If the answer is 35 or more, P is considered to work "sufficient hours overseas" as assessed over year X.'

Once days have been excluded because of UK work, permitted leave or gaps in employment, the resulting number of days is divided by seven to produce the number of weeks worked. A minimum average of 35 hours a week is required to work sufficient hours overseas. It should be possible to meet this test without the work starting or finishing in the tax year over which it is assessed, although the reference period will at least need to start and finish in that tax year. This feature (measurement over a tax year) distinguishes working overseas under the third automatic non-residence test from working in the UK under the second automatic UK test described in **2.14**.

2.14 Full-time work in the UK: conclusive residence

If one of the automatic overseas tests does not apply to treat an individual as conclusively non-resident, then the individual will be conclusively resident for a tax year if they work full-time in the UK. That is the case if the individual:

(a) works sufficient hours in the UK, as assessed, over a period of 365 days, all or part of which falls within the tax year; (b) does more than three hours' work in the UK on more than 75% of the total number of days in that period on which the individual does more than three hours' work; (c) does more than three hours' work in the UK on at least one day which is both in that period and the tax year; and (d) during that period, there are no significant breaks from UK work (the third automatic UK test).[154]

No hours worked in the UK count if worked on a day when the individual does more than three hours' work overseas on the same day. A 'significant break from work' is a period of 31 days or more where there is no day in the period on which the individual does more than three hours' work in the UK which does not arise because they were on annual leave or on sick leave.[155]

The full-time work in the UK test does not apply to an individual who is an international transportation worker at any time in a year where they have at least six cross-border work trips in a year.[156]

This test equates work exclusively or predominantly in the UK with residence regardless of any other connecting factors. The meaning of full-time work in the UK is not symmetrical with the expression 'full-time work abroad' for the purpose of the automatic overseas test, both in relation to the qualifying period, and the amount of working or other time spent in the UK. No justification for this is offered in either consultation document although the second accepted that this may cause more employees to be UK resident in the year of arrival or departure than under prior HMRC practice.[157]

Assessment of whether sufficient hours have been worked in the UK is similar to that for overseas work described in **2.13** and is by application of the following formula in paragraph 9(3):

> '(3) Take the following steps to work out, for any given period of 365 days, whether P[the individual] works "sufficient hours in the UK" as assessed over that period—
>
> Step 1
>
> Identify any days in the period on which P does more than 3 hours' work overseas, including ones on which P also does work in the UK on the same day.
>
> The days so identified are referred to as "disregarded days".
>
> Step 2
>
> Add up (for all employments held and trades carried on by P) the total number of hours that P works in the UK during the period, but ignoring any hours that P works in the UK on disregarded days.
>
> The result is referred to as P's "net UK hours".

154 Sch 45 para 9(1).
155 Sch 45 para 29(1).
156 Sch 45 para 9(3).
157 Second Consultative Document, para 3.99.

Step 3

Subtract from 365—
(a) the total number of disregarded days, and
(b) any days that are allowed to be subtracted, in accordance with the rules in paragraph 28 of this Schedule, to take account of periods of leave and gaps between employments.

The result is referred to as the "reference period".

Step 4

Divide the reference period by 7. If the answer is more than 1 and is not a whole number, round down to the nearest whole number. If the answer is less than 1, round up to 1.

Step 5

Divide P's net UK hours by the number resulting from step 4.

If the answer is 35 or more, P is considered to work "sufficient hours in the UK" as assessed over the 365-day period in question.'

The stated purpose of the test is to provide a clear answer for individuals coming to the UK to work, including those who come to the UK partway through the tax year. The purpose of the rule is to provide certainty for this group, including the many expatriate employees who come from abroad to work on posts in the UK.[158] Unlike the prior HMRC practice, arrival in the UK for full-time work and split-year treatment are not fully aligned with each other and, while the tests for work-related residence and work-related split-year treatment will dovetail in many cases, there is no guarantee that they will.

Examples

The operation of this rule is illustrated by the following examples.[159]

Fergal

Fergal has his home in the Irish Republic and bases his life and family there. He is employed full-time as a scientist at a research establishment in Northern Ireland. Each morning he crosses the border to work and again in the evening when he returns home. He is conclusively resident in the UK.

158 Second Consultative Document, para 3.100.

159 These are adapted from HM Treasury and HMRC, *Reviewing the residence and domicile rules as they affect the taxation of individuals: a background paper*, April 2003.

Gail

Gail has her home in the United States and bases her life and family there. She works in the human resources department of a New York bank. She is seconded to the London branch to stand in for the head of human resources there during the London head's maternity leave from 1 December to 30 November. She works a 50-hour week in London for 34 weeks to enable her to go home to New York unofficially regularly for a week at a time. At home she does no more than an hour a day's work. Her four-week annual holidays are taken outside the UK. She is conclusively resident in the UK in both the year of her arrival and of departure.

Helene

Helene has her home in France and bases her life and family there. She works in the human resources department of a Paris bank and is required to cover for the head of human resources there during the London head's maternity leave from 1 December to 30 November while continuing her existing responsibilities and she regularly visits London during the week for this purpose so that she spends 75 days working there in the tax year she first visits, and 150 days in the second. On one-third of the days that she works in the UK for at least three hours (including travelling time) she also works for three hours in Paris. She is not conclusively resident in the UK in either year.

2.15 International transportation workers

International transportation workers are singled out for special treatment. International transportation workers are those who have 'relevant jobs on board vehicles, aircraft or ships'.[160] In the case of employees, their duties are relevant if they are to be performed on board a vehicle, aircraft or ship while it is travelling.[161] In the case of self-employed individuals, the activities of their trade consist of work to be done or services to be provided on board a vehicle, aircraft or ship while it is travelling and which require them to be present (in person) on board the vehicle, aircraft or ship while it is travelling.[162] Substantially all of the trips made in performing those duties or carrying on those activities must involve crossing an international boundary at sea, in the air or on land.[163] Any duties or activities of a purely incidental nature are to

160 Sch 45 para 30.
161 Sch 45 para 30(2)(a).
162 Sch 45 para 30(2)(b) and (4).
163 Sch 45 para 30(3).

be ignored in determining the character of the services.[164] A ship includes any kind of vessel (including a hovercraft) for this purpose.[165]

Neither the full-time work in the UK test (the 'third automatic UK test'), nor the full-time work overseas test (the 'third automatic overseas test') applies to an individual who is an international transportation worker at any time in a year in which they have at least six cross-border work trips in a year.[166] Their work in such cases is thus only relevant to the work tie for the sufficient ties test.[167] For that purpose, international transportation workers are assumed to do more than three hours' work in the UK on any day on which they start a cross-border trip that begins in the UK in their international transportation working capacity. They are also assumed to do fewer than three hours' work in the UK on any day on which such a cross-border trip ends in the UK. These assumptions apply whether or not the worker completes the journey on that day, regardless of how late in the day the journey begins, and whether or not the worker also starts other international journeys on the same day that begin overseas.[168]

Any day on which an international transportation worker has a trip that starts in the UK is deemed to be one on which the worker is assumed to do more than three hours' work in the UK and a trip that ends in the UK is assumed to be a day with less than three hours of work in the UK.[169]

A cross-border trip to or from the UK that is undertaken in stages is deemed to begin or end, as the case may be, on the day the UK border crossing begins or ends. Accordingly, any day on which a stage is undertaken solely within the UK must be counted separately as a day on which the worker does more than three hours' work in the UK, if the trip lasts for more than three hours.[170]

2.16 Death: conclusive non-residence

The effect of death on residential status has neither been canvassed by the courts nor considered in previous HMRC published practice. Three automatic tests that deal with death are included in the SRT. Two confer non-residence status and one confers UK residence. The first automatic overseas test, under which an individual is not resident if they have been resident in each of the

164 Sch 45 para 30(5). RFIG20780 gives the example of a pilot whose job consists of making long-haul international flights and who attends a meeting in the UK to hear an announcement about the airline's restructuring, the duties spent at the meeting are incidental to the duties of flying the plane, and so can be ignored. The dividing line in the guidance is not entirely clear. Attending a work-related training course is work.

165 Sch 45 para 145.

166 Sch 45 paras 9(3) and 14(4)

167 See **2.21**.

168 Sch 45 para 36.

169 Sch 45 para 36(3).

170 Sch 45 para 36(7).

three preceding years and spends less than 16 days in the UK, does not apply to a year in which the individual dies.[171] The other automatic tests, that do not concern the death of an individual, may be applicable in the year of death in appropriate circumstances. The work-related automatic tests are more likely to apply to individuals who die towards the end of a tax year, by which time the requirements of those tests may have been met.[172] The UK home test may be met at various times in the tax year.[173] If none of the automatic tests applies, then the sufficient ties test must be applied in the year of death. Mercifully, the legislature has not ventured a definition of death.

Where an individual dies in a tax year, and was not resident in the UK for either of the two tax years preceding the year, and spent less than 46 days in the UK in that year, then the individual is conclusively not resident in the year of death. If such an individual was not resident in the UK for the preceding tax year, and the tax year before that was a split year within Case 1 (starting full-time work overseas), Case 2 (the partner of an individual starting full-time work overseas) or Case 3 (ceasing to have a home in the UK), then the individual is similarly conclusively not resident in the year of death. These two tests together form the fourth automatic overseas test.[174] An individual who dies in a tax year, was not resident in the UK for either of the two preceding tax years under the third automatic overseas test (full-time work overseas) for each of those years and who would have met the third automatic overseas test (modified to take into account the death) for the year of death is conclusively non-resident in the year of death. Similarly, if such an individual was not resident in the UK for the preceding tax year under the third automatic overseas test for that year, and the tax year before that was a split within Case 1 (starting full-time work overseas), the individual is conclusively non-resident in the year of death. The modifications of third automatic overseas test (full-time work overseas) for this purpose, limit the period over which days are disregarded because of work done in the UK and over which net overseas hours worked are calculated, as well as the reference period to start of the year up to the day before the date of death. These two tests together form the fourth automatic overseas test.[175]

2.17 Death: conclusive residence

An individual who dies and is not conclusively non-resident under one of the automatic overseas tests will be UK resident in two circumstances: If an individual dies in a tax year, and was resident in the UK for each of the previous three tax years by meeting the automatic residence test, the previous

171 Sch 45 para 12(c).
172 See **2.13** and **2.14**.
173 See **2.07**.
174 Sch 45 para 15.
175 Sch 45 para 16. See **2.13** for the third automatic overseas test (full-time work overseas) and **2.33** for Case 1 (starting full-time work overseas) split-year treatment.

year was not a split year or would not be a split year even on the assumption that the individual was not resident in the tax year of death, when the individual died, his only home was in the UK, then the individual is conclusively UK resident for that year. Secondly, if, at the time of death, such an individual had more than one home and at least one of them was in the UK, and they were not present at the overseas home on at least 30 days in the year, in the aggregate, for at least some of the time, no matter how short, or was similarly present there for at least some of the time each day of the year up to and including the date of death, then the individual is likewise conclusively UK resident for that year. If the individual had more than one home overseas at the time of death, sufficient presence at each overseas home must be tested separately. Unless the individual was sufficiently present at each of them, they will be UK resident. These tests together form the fourth automatic UK test.[176]

2.18 The sufficient ties test: other connecting factors and day counting

The sufficient ties test applies only to those individuals whose residence is not determined by any automatic UK tests nor by any automatic overseas tests.[177] Under the sufficient ties test, an individual will be resident according to a scale of the number of days spent in the UK in a tax year in conjunction with five connecting factors. Separate scales apply to individuals who were UK resident in any of the three tax years preceding the year in question and to individuals who were not so resident in any of those three years. Individuals who were previously so resident will be UK resident when they spend fewer days in the UK with the same connecting factors as individuals who were not resident in any of the three preceding years. This reflects the principle that it is harder for anyone leaving to relinquish residence than it is for a newly arrived person to acquire it.

These connecting factors are:

- family – the individual's spouse or civil partner or common law equivalent or minor children are resident in the UK (a family tie);
- accommodation – the individual has a place to stay in the UK and makes use of it during the tax year (accommodation tie);
- work – the individual works in the UK for 40 days in the year (work tie);
- UK presence in previous year – the individual spent 90 days or more in the UK in either of the previous two tax years (90-day tie); and
- more time in the UK than in other countries – the individual spends more days in the UK in the tax year than in any other single country (country tie).

176 Sch 45 para 10. See **2.07** and **2.08**.
177 See **2.02**.

The chosen factors are mostly drawn from the previous case law indicators of residence.[178] More time spent in the UK than any other country as a connecting factor is not an established principle. In *Grace v Revenue & Customs*[179] a comparison was made by the First-tier Tribunal between time spent in the UK and South Africa which led to a conclusion of dual residence. In *Gaines-Cooper v Revenue & Customs*[180] an examination of the total travel pattern of Mr Gaines-Cooper was explained by reference to his 'unusual background'.[181] The Special Commissioners did not include the comparison as a factor in coming to their conclusion and none of the cases cited by them was in support of such a proposition. Certainty is increased by limiting the factors only to those specified. The country tie is only a connecting factor for individuals who were UK resident in one or more of the three years preceding the year of arrival.

2.19 Family tie

An individual has a family tie for a year if, in that year, the individual has a 'relevant relationship' with another person who is resident in the UK for that year.[182] Regardless of the number of relevant relationships an individual has, they will only have one family tie. The legislation specifically prohibits the residence of the family member from being tested by reference to the individual whose residence is tested.[183] Thus, the family member with whom the individual has a relevant relationship must be resident in the UK for other reasons. This prevents circularity that might arise if the status of both individuals was mutually dependent on the status of each other.

A 'relevant relationship' is one between a husband and wife or between civil partners if they are not separated at the time, as well as between persons living together as husband and wife or, if they are of the same sex, as civil partners.[184] For this purpose, 'separated' means separated under an order of a court of competent jurisdiction, by deed of separation, or in circumstances where the separation is likely to be permanent.[185]

Whether individuals are legally married or are civil partners is a legal question. Similarly, whether individuals are legally separated by order of a court or by deed of separation is largely legal and relatively easily evidenced by the relevant legal documents.

---

178 For the case law see the previous edition of this work: *Booth and Schwarz: Residence, Domicile and UK Taxation* (21st edn, Bloomsbury) Chapter 3: family – see **3.16**; accommodation – see **3.8** and **3.9**; work – see **3.17**; presence in previous year – see **3.11** and **3.14**.

179 [2011] UKFTT 36 (TC).

180 [2006] UKSPC SPC 568.

181 [2006] UKSPC SPC 568. at para 92.

182 Sch 45 para 32(1).

183 Sch 45 para 33(2).

184 Sch 45 para 32(2)(a) and (b).

185 Sch 45 para 32(5).

On the other hand, whether individuals are living together as husband and wife or as civil partners, not only requires interpretation of that expression but also a detailed examination into intimate elements of the lives of the individuals concerned. The right to equal treatment means that both kinds of relationships are likely to be tested in the same way.[186] A thorough examination of the legally relevant characteristics of cohabitation was undertaken by the Court of Appeal in *Amicus Horizon Ltd v Mabbot & Anor*[187] where Lord Justice Ward said:

> 'One does not have to spend too much time in the Family Division to realise that husbands and wives live their married lives in many and various ways, yet always at its heart marriage is a serious but public commitment to have and to hold the other as one's husband or one's wife and in whatever religious or civil form the promises are made, in essence always to love and to cherish until death us do part. A married couple share their lives and make their home together. They bear equal responsibilities for bringing up their children. They offer each other love, commitment and support. Lord Nicholls of Birkenhead spoke of the "intimate mutual love and affection and long term commitment that typically characterise the relationship of husband and wife" *Fitzpatrick v Sterling Housing Association* Ltd [2001] 1 AC 27 at page 24, and Lord Slynn of Hadley said at page 38: "The hall marks of the relationship were essentially that there should be a degree of mutual inter-dependence, of the sharing of lives, of caring and love, of commitment and support."'[188]

Lord Justice Ward adopted comments in the speech of Baroness Hale in the House of Lords in *Ghaidan v Godin-Mendoza* where she said:

> 'Some people, whether heterosexual or homosexual, may be satisfied with casual or transient relationships. But most human beings eventually want more than that. They want love. And with love they often want not only the warmth but also the sense of belonging to one another which is the essence of being a couple. And many couples also come to want the stability and permanence which go with sharing a home and a life together, with or without the children who for many people go to make a family.'[189]

In *Nutting v Southern Housing Group*,[190] the relationships were described thus:

> 'In my judgment the relationship, to come within this subsection, cannot have a single (or even a simple) definition. Human relationships are too complex and varied for that to be the case. There are, however, indicia. I have chosen to put them by questions, which must be asked in the affirmative as follows:
>
> (a) Have the parties openly set up home together?

186 *Ghaidan v Godin-Mendoza* [2004] UKHL 30, [2004] 3 WLR 113, [2004] 2 AC 557.
187 *Amicus Horizon Ltd v Mabbot & Anor* [2012] EWCA Civ 895.
188 Sch 45 para 16.
189 Sch 45 para 142.
190 *Nutting v Southern Housing Group* [2004] EWHC 2982, [2005] HLR 25.

> (b) Is the relationship an emotional one of mutual lifetime commitment rather than simply one of convenience, friendship, companionship or the living together of lovers?
> (c) Is the relationship one which has been presented to the outside world openly and unequivocally so that society considers it to be of permanent intent—the words 'till death us do part' being apposite?
> (d) Do the parties have a common life together, both domestically (in relation to the household) and externally (in relation to family and friends)?
>
> The above indicia (which may overlap) must principally be objectively assessed by reference to what the outside world can see (albeit that the domestic aspect may not be viewable without visitors) and the indicia at (b) must also be assessed by reference to the viewpoint of the parties themselves, so far as that can be ascertained on evidence. In that regard the relationship of the spouse does have some subjective element to it, but accompanying its subjectivity there must be express or implied communication of one party to the other by way of a demonstration of a lifetime emotional commitment. Whist the length of time which the relationship has been in existence is irrelevant to the above indicia, it may sometimes corroborate them or even, in appropriate cases, be of sufficient length to satisfy a court that they are satisfied that the relationship of spouse exists.'

HMRC practice may be indicated by their approach in relation to similar expressions in relation to tax credits:

> 'These "signposts" are the only indicators to help form a sustainable view of whether two people are living together as husband and wife or as civil partners for the purposes of a tax credits claim. The weight and worth of each indicator will vary from relationship to relationship and an officer of HMRC should conclude their decision on the balance of evidence, based on all the facts.
>
> The signposts include:
>
> - living in the same household
> - stability of the relationship
> - financial support
> - sexual relationship
> - dependent children
> - public acknowledgement.'[191]

A parent of a child under the age of 18 also has a 'relevant relationship' with that child.[192] There are three exceptions to this rule, one relating to seeing the child and two dealing with children in full-time education. Firstly, there will be no family tie for the parent for a year in which the parent sees the child in the UK on fewer than 61 days in total in the year. If the child turns 18 during

191 HMRC Tax Credits Manual TCTM09330 to TCTM09347: The meaning of living together as a married couple or civil partners TCTM09341, last updated 03.02.2025. Previously HMRC indicated that the same test is applied for SRT purposes. See RDRM11530 – Residence: The SRT: Definition of a family tie.

192 Sch 45 para 32(2)(c).

the year, then there will be no family tie for the parent for a year in which the parent sees the child in the UK on fewer than 61 days in total during the part of the year before the day on which the child turns 18.[193] A day on which the parent sees the child counts as a day if the parent sees the child in person for all or part of the day.[194]

Secondly, a child in full-time education in the UK may be ignored for this purpose in certain circumstances. That will be the case if they are resident in the UK for the year, but would not be resident if the time spent in full-time education in the UK in that year were disregarded. Time spent in full-time education is the time spent there during term-time. Furthermore, half-term breaks and other breaks when teaching is not provided during a term are treated as part of term time for this purpose.[195] The whole of the SRT must be applied to the child but in doing so, time spent in full-time education is excluded in determining days present in the UK. The child may well still be UK resident in their own right, but will not be a family tie for a parent.

Thirdly, if the child spends less than 21 days in the UK outside term-time, they are treated as not resident in the UK for the year for this purpose. Full-time education in the UK, for the purpose of the family tie test, must be at a university, college, school or other educational establishment in the UK.[196] In *Barry v Hughes*,[197] a hospital unit for training mentally challenged individuals was not an educational establishment. It was not within the expression 'university, college, school or other educational establishment', because of the word 'educational'. In that context, education was considered to be devoted exclusively to training of the mind and not manual skills.

2.20 Accommodation tie

Accommodation is referred to for the purposes of this tie as a 'place to live' in the UK.[198] An individual is considered to have a 'place to live' in the UK if their home, or at least one of those homes, if there are more than one, is in the UK.[199] Home in this context must have the same meaning as in the 'second automatic UK test' (the 'UK home' test).[200] In addition, an individual is considered to have a 'place to live' in the UK if they have a holiday home or temporary retreat (or something similar) in the UK, or if accommodation is otherwise available to the individual where they can live when in the UK.[201] While the expression

193 Sch 45 para 32(3).
194 Sch 45 para 32(4).
195 Sch 45 para 33(4), (5)(b) and (6).
196 Sch 45 para 33(3).
197 *Barry v Hughes* 48 TC 586; [1973] STC 103, Ch D.
198 Sch 45 para 34(1)(a).
199 Sch 45 para 34(3)(a).
200 See **2.08**.
201 Sch 45 para 34(3)(b) and (c).

is undoubtedly widely drawn, it is not without limits. The individual must be able to live at the place. This would exclude, for example, a sleeping pod at an employer's premises designed only for exceptional overnight stays. A 'place to live' connotes a minimum level of facility to enable human habitation is required.

An individual has an accommodation tie for a year if they have a place to live in the UK that is available to them during the year for a continuous period of at least 91 days.[202] This connotes a degree of entitlement. Accommodation may be available even if the individual holds no estate or interest in it and has no legal right to occupy it.[203] The place must be at the disposal of the individual. Thus a hotel room is not available unless it is booked for sufficient time, or a friend's or family member's home is not normally available without an invitation. Despite this, if there is a gap of fewer than 16 days between periods in the year when a particular place is available to an individual, then that place is to be treated as continuing to be available during that gap.[204] This has a surprising effect for intermittent users of certain kinds of accommodation. An individual who stays at the same hotel or company flat one night every two weeks, will have it available throughout that period. Eight such stays will make it available for 91 days.

The individual must spend at least one night at that place in that year to have an accommodation tie.[205] If the accommodation belongs to a close relative of the individual, then they must spend at least 16 nights at that place in that year.[206] For this purpose, a close relative is a parent or grandparent, a brother or sister, a child aged 18 or over, or a grandchild aged 18 or over, in each case whether by blood or half-blood or by marriage or civil partnership.[207]

While the legislation goes into great detail in prescribing when a day is spent in the UK, at a home or working, it is silent on when a night is spent at a place to live. The ordinary meaning of the expression implies both physical presence there for a significant time from evening to morning as well as its use as a dwelling during that time such as for sleeping. Visiting a grandparent or adult child for dinner would not, for example, qualify as spending a night there.[208] In *R v National Insurance Commissioner, ex parte Secretary of State for Social Services*,[209] Lord Widgery CJ observed that 'night' is one of the commonest English words in its ordinary usage, it does have different shades of meaning and the decision of the correct shade of meaning to give to the word

202 Sch 45 para 34(1).
203 Sch 45 para 34(4).
204 Sch 45 para 34(2).
205 Sch 45 para 34(1)(c).
206 Sch 45 para 34(5).
207 Sch 45 para 34(6).
208 See *Amicus Horizon Ltd v Mabbot & Anor* [2012] EWCA Civ 895, at para 4 for an example of the ordinary use of the expression.
209 *R v National Insurance Commissioner, ex parte Secretary of State for Social Services* [1974] 3 All ER 522, at 526.

in a particular context requires consideration of the context and thus becomes a matter of construction and therefore a matter of law.' He held that the word 'night' does not mean the period between sunrise and sunset but refers to that period of inactivity beginning with the time when, in accordance with its domestic routine, the household in which the disabled person lives closes down for the night in the context of section 42(a) of the National Insurance (Old Persons' and Widows' Pensions and Attendance Allowance) Act 1970, which entitles a disabled person to an attendance allowance if he requires, *inter alia*, prolonged or repeated attention during the night.

2.21 Work tie

An individual has a work tie for a year if they work in the UK for at least 40 days (whether continuously or intermittently) in the year. Working in the UK for a day means doing more than three hours' work in the UK on that day.[210] For the meaning of work, see **2.10** and for the place where work is undertaken, see **2.11**. The special rules that apply to the work of international transportation workers are discussed at **2.15** above.

Eight five-day weeks of working under half a day in the UK may result in a work tie. The effect of this rule may also be illustrated by the following example:

Ian and Isobel, who live and work in the Netherlands, are sent to work on a project in the UK. They both work in the UK for 130 hours on the project in a year. Ian works for three-and-a-quarter hours on each of 40 days in the UK. He has a work tie. Isobel works six and a half hours on each of 20 days in the UK and has no work tie.

2.22 90-day tie

An individual has a 90-day tie for a year if they have spent more than 90 days in the UK in the tax year preceding the year in question, the tax year before that preceding year, or in each of those tax years.[211] Thus, while there is no mechanism for averaging presence in the UK over a period of time, an individual who has spent 91 days or more will find themselves put into a category where they will either need to spend much less time in the UK or eliminate other factors. For example, an individual who was not resident in the previous two years, spent 91 days in the UK in a year and who otherwise has two connecting factors could only spend 45 or fewer days in the UK for three years thereafter without becoming UK resident. The 90-day tie is applied in

210 Sch 45 para 35.
211 Sch 45 para 37.

mechanical fashion. Thus, an individual who was resident in the UK in the two previous years on a basis that is not by reference to time spent, such as having a UK home will still need to count days spent in the UK for this purpose. The day-count hyping rule described in **2.04** does not apply to determine whether an individual has a 90-day tie.

2.23 Country tie

An individual has a country tie for a year if the country in which they spend the greatest number of days in the year is the UK. If the individual spends the same number of days in two or more countries in a year, and that number is the greatest number of days spent by them in any country in the year, the individual has a country tie for the year if one of those countries is the UK.[212]

Presence in a country at the end of a day means that a day is spent in that country.[213]

A 'country' as defined for this purpose 'includes a state or territory'.[214] This raises the question of the operation of this tie in relation to federal systems. In relation to the United States of America, for example, is each state in the Union a 'country' for the purpose of this tie? The answer may have a significant impact on the existence of a country tie. An individual who spends a quarter of the year in each of say, New York, Florida and the UK, with the balance in a variety of places around the world, would have a country tie if New York State and Florida are each counted as separate countries but would not if the United States of America as a whole is the relevant country. Would the question be answered differently if the three jurisdictions were the Netherlands, the UK and Spain? No official guidance is given on this important question. Any answer is likely to produce anomalous results with individuals in similar circumstances being treated differently as a result of widely differing constitutional systems. The UK is treated as one country for the purpose of this rule, but the legal ties that bind its constituent countries of England and Wales, Scotland and Northern Ireland together provide no clear test for comparing other jurisdictions. HMRC, however, express the view that 'presence at midnight in any state, territory or canton into which a country is subdivided is regarded as presence at midnight in that country.'[215]

212 Sch45 para 38.

213 Sch 45 para 38(3). For some inexplicable reason, the drafter of this part of the Schedule has chosen to call this the 'midnight test'. This is defined to mean the end of the day!

214 Sch 45 para 145.

215 RFIG20580.

2.24 The sufficient ties test: day counting for former non-residents

The residence status of individuals who were not resident in any of the previous three tax years[216] is judged by reference to combinations of four ties, namely, a family tie, a work tie, an accommodation tie and a 90-day tie.

Connecting factors combine with days spent in the UK to determine residence[217] as follows:

Fewer than 46 days	Always non-resident (the second automatic overseas test)
46–90 days	4 ties – resident
91–120 days	3 or more ties – resident
121–182 days	2 or more ties – resident
183 days or more	Always resident (the fourth automatic UK test)

2.25 The sufficient ties test: day counting for former residents

The residence status of individuals who were resident in one or more of the previous three tax years[218] is judged by reference to combinations of five ties, namely, a family tie, a work tie, an accommodation tie, a 90-day tie and a country tie. Connecting factors combine with days spent in the UK to determine residence[219] as follows:

Fewer than 16 days	Always non-resident (the second automatic overseas test)
16–45 days	4 or more ties – resident
46–90 days	3 or more ties – resident
91–120 days	2 or more ties – resident
121–182 days	1 or more ties – resident
183 days or more	Always resident (the fourth automatic UK test)

216 Sch 45 para 19.

217 The day counting automatic overseas tests and the automatic UK test are included here to set the day counting for the sufficient ties test in context, but do not form part of the test.

218 Sch 45 para 18.

219 The day counting automatic overseas tests and the automatic UK test are included here to set the day counting for the sufficient ties test in context, but do not form part of the test.

2.26 The sufficient ties test: day counting in the year of death

If residence is not determined by any of the automatic tests, the sufficient ties test will apply in the year of death. Death in a year changes the number of days of UK presence that make the individual resident. The ties will be determined in the normal way in the year of death, although the death may affect the existence of a tie. There is no reduction in the number of days in any of the ties by reason of death. Any individual spending less than 46 days in the UK will require four factors to be resident.[220]

In addition, if the death occurs before 1 March the number of days presence required is reduced by multiplying the number of days, in each case, by the number of whole months in the year after the month in which the individual died, divided by 12. If, the result is not a whole number, it is rounded up if the result is 0.5 or more, and, otherwise, down.[221]

HMRC have produced the following tables to show the application of the tests by reference to the date of death of the individual.[222] In each case, the number of days shown will result in UK residence:

Individuals who were not resident in any of the previous three tax years before the year of death

Date of death	All 4 ties	At least 3 ties	At least 2 ties
6–30 April	4–7	8–10	over 10
1–31 May	8–15	16–20	over 20
1–30 June	11–22	23–30	over 30
1–31 July	15–30	31–40	over 40
1–31 Aug	19–37	38–50	over 50
1–30 Sep	23–45	46–60	over 60
1–31 Oct	27–52	53–70	over 70
1–30 Nov	31–60	61–80	over 80
1–31 Dec	34–67	68–90	over 90
1–31 Jan	38–75	76–100	over 100
1–29 Feb	42–82	83–11-	over 110
1 Mar–5 April	46–90	91–120	over 120

220 Sch 45 para 20.
221 Sch 45 para 20(4).
222 RFIG20970 Table C.

Individuals who were resident in one or more of the previous three tax years before the year of death

Date of death	At least 4 ties	At least 3 ties	At least 2 ties	At least 1 tie
6–30 April	not more than 4	5–7	8–10	over 10
1–31 May	not more than 7	8–15	16–20	over 20
1–30 June	not more than 11	12–22	23–30	over 30
1–31 July	not more than 15	16–30	31–40	over 40
1–31 Aug	not more than 19	20—37	38–50	over 50
1–30 Sep	not more than 22	23–45	46–60	over 60
1–31 Oct	not more than 26	27–52	53–70	over 70
1–30 Nov	not more than 30	31–60	61–80	over 80
1–31 Dec	not more than 34	35–67	68–90	over 90
1–31 Jan	not more than 37	38–75	76–100	over 100
1–29 Feb	not more than 41	42–82	83–110	over 110
1 Mar –5 Apr	not more than 45	46–90	91–120	over 120

2.27 Residence of MPs and members of the House of Lords

The residential status of members of Parliament and the House of Lords is not governed by the SRT. Individuals who, for any part of a tax year are members of the House of Commons and of the House of Lords are treated as resident in the UK for the whole of that tax year. This treatment applies for the purposes of income tax, capital gains tax, and inheritance tax.[223]

For this purpose, an individual becomes a member of the House of Commons when (having been elected to that House) they make and subscribe the oath required by the Parliamentary Oaths Act 1866 (or the corresponding affirmation), and cease to be a member of that House when the Parliament to which they were elected is dissolved, or the individual's seat is otherwise vacated.[224] An individual is a member of the House of Lords if the individual is entitled to receive writs of summons to attend that House except in the case of an archbishop or bishop.[225]

223 Constitutional Reform and Governance Act 2010 s 41.

224 S 41(4).

225 S 41(5) and (6).

2.28 EU officials

Employees of European Union institutions are subject to deemed residence rules for tax purposes under Article 13 of the 7th Protocol on the Privileges and Immunities of the European Union annexed to the Treaty on European Union. Officials and servants of the EU who establish their residence in the territory of a Member State other than their country of residence for tax purposes at the time of entering the service of the Union, solely by reason of the performance of their duties in the service of the Union, are deemed to be tax resident in their home Member State. This deemed residence applies both in the country of their actual residence and in their home Member State, spouses have the same deemed tax residence, to the extent that they are not separately engaged in a gainful occupation, as do dependent children.

Following Brexit, this treatment continues for those persons who entered the service of the EU before the end of the transition period on 31 December 2020, as well as, irrespective of their nationality, their spouses who not separately engaged in a gainful occupation, and their dependents.[226]

2.29 An annual attribute

The rule that residence in the UK means residence for the whole tax year is codified in the statutory residence test. Thus an individual who, in accordance with the statutory residence test, is resident (or not resident) in the UK for a tax year is taken for the purposes of any enactment relating to a relevant tax to be resident (or not resident) there at all times in that tax year.[227]

2.30 Dual residence

The concept of dual residence has disappeared as a matter of domestic law under the statutory residence test. The legislation only determines whether an individual is resident in the UK and provides no basis for determining whether an individual is also resident elsewhere. Dual residence will therefore only arise and be relevant where an individual is resident in another country for the purposes of that country's tax system. Where the other country is a party to a tax treaty with the UK, then dual residence may be resolved for the purposes of the application of that treaty, at least in treaties patterned on the OECD and UN models.[228]

---

226 Agreement on the withdrawal of the United Kingdom of Great Britain and Northern Ireland from the European Union and the European Atomic Energy Community (2019/C 384 I/01), European Union (Withdrawal) Act 2018 s 7A.

227 Sch 45 para 2(3).

228 See **2.33.**

A glaring omission from the legislation is treating individuals who are resident in another contracting state under a tiebreaker as non-UK resident for all purposes in the same way that companies are so treated under CTA 2009 section 18.[229] The application of this principle to individuals would bring coherence and consistency to the UK tax system. It would also help to reduce some of the harsh and surprising results of the current legislative proposals.

2.31 Commencement and transitional rules

The statutory residence test and the statutory split-year treatment generally have effect for determining whether individuals are resident or not and in calculating an individual's liability to income tax or capital gains tax for the tax year 2013/14 or any subsequent tax year. The split-year treatment and the temporary non-residence rules have effect if the year of departure is the tax year 2013/14 or a subsequent tax year.[230]

Transitional rules apply for a limited period. If it is necessary to determine whether an individual was resident or not resident in the UK for a tax year before the tax year 2013/14 (a pre-commencement tax year) for the purpose of determining residence in 2013/14, 2014/15 or 2015/16 then the existing case law and statutory rules described in Chapters 3 and 5 apply. However, an individual may elect, in respect to one or more pre-commencement tax years, for the question to be determined instead in accordance with the statutory residence test by notice in writing to HMRC. Such a notice must be given no later than the first anniversary of the end of year for which the question is relevant and is irrevocable.[231]

Where such an election is made, the SRT rules are modified in their application to years before 2013/14. In applying the fourth automatic UK test to an individual, residence on any basis, and not only automatic residence will govern. In applying the fifth automatic overseas test, the deceased individual must have been non-resident in those previous tax years (the earlier year will meet this condition if ESC A11 applied to a departure from the UK that year).[232] Split-year treatment in the earlier years under the relevant Extra-Statutory Concessions is given statutory effect by reference to the actual or deemed departure.[233] The existing temporary non-resident provisions, as in force immediately before the day on which the Finance Act enacting the statutory residence test is passed, continue to have effect on and after that day in any case where an individual's year of departure is a tax year before the tax year 2013/14.[234] The existing temporary non-resident provisions are:

---

229 See **7.18**.
230 Sch 45 para 153.
231 Sch 45 para 154.
232 Sch 45 para 154(5).
233 Sch 45 paras 155 and 156. See **3.02**.
234 Sch 45, para 158.

- section 10A of TCGA 1992 (chargeable gains);
- section 576A of ITEPA 2003 (income withdrawals under certain foreign pensions);
- section 579CA of ITEPA 2003 (income withdrawals under registered pension schemes); and
- section 832A of ITTOIA (relevant foreign income charged on remittance basis).[235]

Where those provisions continue to have effect, the question of whether a person is or is not resident in the UK for the tax year 2013/14 or a subsequent tax year is to be determined in accordance with the statutory residence test, but the effect of the new statutory split-year treatment is to be ignored. Whether an individual met the requirements for UK residence four out of the seven years preceding departure is determined for earlier years under the prior law.[236]

2.32 Scottish and Welsh taxpayers

Scotland and Wales are both countries within the UK that each have an element of autonomy in relation to income tax.

A 'Scottish taxpayer' may be liable to the Scottish rate of income tax under Part 4A, Chapter 2 of the Scotland Act 1998. The expression 'Scottish taxpayer' is used rather than 'Scottish resident' although the definition bears the hallmarks of residence.

A Scottish taxpayer is an individual who is resident in the UK for income tax purposes and meets any one of three conditions.[237]

The first condition applies to an individual who has a closer connection with Scotland than with any other part of the UK for any year. This will be the case if in that year they have only one place of residence in the UK and that place is Scotland provided they live at that place for at least part of the year.[238] An individual who has two or more places of residence in the UK, is a Scottish taxpayer if their main place of residence in the UK is in Scotland for at least part of the year and they live at a place of residence in Scotland for at least part of the year. In addition, the times in the year when their main place of residence is in Scotland must comprise (in aggregate) at least as much of the year as the times when their main place of residence is in any one other part of the UK.[239] A 'place' includes a place on board a vessel or other means of transport.[240]

235 Sch 45 para 157.
236 See Chapters 3 and 5.
237 Scotland Act 1998 s 80D.
238 Scotland Act 1998 s 80E(2).
239 Scotland Act 1998 s 80E(3).
240 Scotland Act 1998 s 80E(4).

HMRC guidance[241] on the application of these tests is hardly unequivocal. HMRC consider that an individual's 'place of residence' is 'a place that a reasonable onlooker, with knowledge of the material facts, would regard as the dwelling in which that person habitually lives: in other words his or her home.'[242] Where, in a tax year, an individual has two or more 'places of residence' in the UK, HMRC say that:

> 'A "main place of residence" is not necessarily the residence where the individual spends the majority of their time, although it commonly may be. A "main place of residence" is the "place of residence" with which the individual can be said to have the greatest degree of connection.'

This is a matter of fact and all of the facts and circumstances of the particular case must be considered.[243] An individual's election of 'main residence' for CGT purposes will not determine 'main place of residence' for Scottish taxpayer purposes.[244] The factors that HMRC regard as indicative are similar to their approach to the meaning of 'home' for purposes of the Statutory Residence Test.[245]

Scottish taxpayer status will be dependent on whether a 'close connection' with Scotland or another part of the UK exists. Central to that test is establishing an individual's 'main place of residence'.

The second condition is that the individual spends more days of a year in Scotland than in any other part of the UK. A day spent in Scotland or elsewhere in the UK is spent there only if the individual is there at the end of the day. An individual is not treated as being in the UK at the end of a day if on that day they arrive in the UK as a passenger and departs from the UK on the next day, and during the time between arrival and departure does not engage in activities which are to a substantial extent unrelated to their passage through the UK.[246]

Thirdly, members of Parliament for constituencies in Scotland, and members of the Scottish Parliament are all Scottish taxpayers.[247]

In the same way, Welsh taxpayers are liable to pay the Welsh rate of income tax determined by the Senedd Cymru (the Welsh Parliament).[248] The meaning of Welsh taxpayer is the same as the definition of Scottish taxpayer as applied to Wales.[249]

However, in the case of elected parliamentarians, a person who would otherwise qualify as a Welsh taxpayer, is not a Welsh taxpayer if they represent

241 HMRC, Scottish Taxpayer Technical Guidance Manual (3 November 2015).
242 HMRC, Scottish Taxpayer Technical Guidance Manual STTG3400.
243 HMRC, Scottish Taxpayer Technical Guidance Manual STTG3700.
244 HMRC, Scottish Taxpayer Technical Guidance Manual STTG3100.
245 See **2.08** and STTG3700 and STTG5000.
246 Scotland Act 1998 s 80F.
247 Scotland Act 1998 s 80D(4).
248 Government of Wales Act 2006 Pt 4A.
249 Government of Wales Act 2006 ss 116E to 116H.

a Scottish constituence or are a member of the Scottish Parliament.[250] Persons who otherwise would qualify as Scottish taxpayers are similarly excluded from that status if if they represent a Scottish constituence or are a member of the Senedd Cymru.[251]

2.33 Residence for tax treaty purposes

It will be apparent that an individual may be resident in the UK for tax purposes although also living elsewhere. In most, but not all cases, residence in another country will entail a liability to tax in that country as well. The UK has entered into over 120 treaties with the objective of the prevention of, or relief from, double taxation (ie the taxation of the same income or gains by both the UK and the foreign state concerned).[252] A double tax treaty generally protects a person against double taxation by allocating taxing jurisdiction between the contacting states and providing that income arising in one state is not to be charged to tax in the hands of a resident of the other state, or affords them relief by providing that, where they are charged to tax on income accruing to them in the source state, they are to be given exemption or a credit for that tax in the state of which they are resident.

Included in the mechanisms for allocating taxing jurisdiction are rules for determining which residence status of the two is to prevail for the purposes of the treaty where both states claim taxing rights on the basis that the taxpayer is resident in each state.

Most modern treaties to which the UK is a party follow the Model Double Taxation Convention on Income and Capital published by the Organisation for Economic Co-operation and Development, Paris. Although the model has been amended several times, the provisions dealing with residence have in essence remained constant since the 1963 OECD Draft Double Taxation Convention. The current form, as it applies to individuals reads as follows:

'**Article 4:** Residence

(1) For the purposes of this Convention, the term "resident of a Contracting State" means any person who, under the laws of that State, is liable to tax therein by reason of his domicile, residence, … or any other criterion of a similar nature; the term does not include any person who is liable to tax in that Contracting State only if he derives income or capital gains from sources therein.

(2) Where by reason of the provisions of paragraph (1) of this Article an individual is a resident of both Contracting States, then his status shall be determined in accordance with the following rules:

---

250 Government of Wales Act 2006 s 116E(5) and (6).

251 Scotland Act 1998 s 80DA.

252 Such treaties are given effect in domestic law by Order in Council made under the authority of TIOPA 2010 s 2.

(a) he shall be deemed to be a resident of the Contracting State in which he has a permanent home available to him; if he has a permanent home available to him in both Contracting States, he shall be deemed to be a resident of the Contracting State with which his personal and economic relations are closer (centre of vital interests);

(b) if the Contracting State in which he has his centre of vital interests cannot be determined, or if he has not a permanent home available to him in either Contracting State, he shall be deemed to be a resident of the Contracting State in which he has an habitual abode;

(c) if he has an habitual abode in both Contracting States or in neither of them, he shall be deemed to be a resident of the Contracting State of which he is a national;

(d) if he is a national of both Contracting States or of neither of them, the competent authorities of the Contracting States shall settle the question by mutual agreement.'

In *Hankinson v HMRC*[253] the First-tier Tribunal found the taxpayer was resident and ordinarily resident in the UK during 1998/99. Mr Hankinson had entered into a service agreement with a Dutch subsidiary of a company that he was indirectly interested in, to work in the Netherlands from 23 February 1998 for a period of a minimum of 15 months, while remaining as non-executive chairman of the parent company. On 2 January 1999 he became ill on a flight to Barbados where he had booked a holiday from 2 to 30 January 1999. He returned to the UK on 30 April 1999 but did not return to work in the Netherlands again, and retired from the service of the Dutch company on about 15 August 1999 and from his non-executive chairmanship of the parent company on 31 August 1999. He contended, somewhat optimistically, that he was nonetheless resident in the Netherlands for the purposes of the UK-Netherlands tax treaty. The case concerned a capital gain made in March 1999 which falls within the UK tax year 1998/99 and the Dutch tax year 1999. The overlap of tax years was from 1 January to 5 April 1999.

The only evidence before the tribunal on residence in the Netherlands was advice from Mr Hankinson's Dutch accountants that residence in principle is a question of facts and circumstances and that in view of Mr Hankinson's wife not living in the Netherlands while he was working full-time (as they were instructed) in the Netherlands, 'it is not very likely that Dutch tax authorities will regard you as a resident of the Netherlands'. During 1999 he spent only five days in the Netherlands to collect his belongings from the apartment after the employment contract had apparently been terminated. The tribunal had no hesitation in deciding as a fact, even in the absence of any expert evidence on Dutch law, that the Dutch authorities would not regard him as a resident of the Netherlands. Accordingly Mr Hankinson was held to be a resident of the UK and not of the Netherlands for the purpose of Article 4(1) of the treaty.[254]

253 *Hankinson v HMRC* [2009] UKFTT 384 (TC).

254 At para 63.

Consequently, it was unnecessary to determine his status under the tie-breaker in Article 4(2) of the treaty. Nonetheless, the tribunal examined the tie-breaker as if Mr Hankinson were also a resident of the Netherlands. Each of the rules listed in Article 4(2) is to be applied sequentially.[255]

The first of these is that he is deemed to be a resident of the state in which he has a permanent home available to him. According to the OECD Commentary to the Model Convention 'any form of home may be taken into account (house or apartment belonging to or rented by the individual, rented furnished room).[256] If that is to be so, 'home', in the context of Article 4(2)(a), may be taken to be similar to 'place of abode' as described at **2.08** to **2.09** above.[257] Permanence is however essential. According to the commentary, this means that 'the individual must have arranged to have the dwelling available to him at all times, continuously, and not occasionally and retained [the home] for his permanent use as opposed to staying at a particular place under such conditions that it is evident that the stay is intended to be of short duration'. This rules out the possibility that a house, etc which is let between visits might be a 'permanent home' for tie-breaker purposes.

In *McCabe v HMRC*,[258] the taxpayer transferred ownership of the family home to his wife, removed his possessions and handed over his keys to her. He did not spend a single night at the property during the years in question and stayed in hotels when he came to the UK. The Upper Tribunal held that these steps were irrelevant, as he could have stayed there whenever he wanted to, as his wife would have given permission if asked. Availability, rather than actual use, is the test.

If a person has a permanent home in both states (but not if they have a permanent home in neither), then they shall be deemed to be a resident of the state with which their personal and economic relations are closer (centre of vital interests).

The meaning of the words in parentheses is by no means clear, but the OECD Commentary provides some guidance by stating that:

---

255 Although unnecessary for the decision, the judge in *Hankinson* set out his views *obiter* on the operation of the tie-breaker in Art 4(2). Another case in the UK where the residence tie-breaker provisions of Art 4(2) were invoked is *Squirrell v Revenue & Customs* [2005] UKSPC SPC 00493 (23 June 2005). The taxpayer left the UK on October 2000, moving to the US where he was treated as resident for the whole of 2000. He was resident in the UK in the tax year 1999–2000 when he received a termination payment from his UK employer. Although Art 4(2) of the US-UK treaty was referred to, no claim had been made in either country to determine his residence status for the purposes of the treaty by going through the tie-breaker provisions in turn. In any event the Special Commissioner concluded that the taxpayer's UK tax treatment was the same regardless of where he was resident for purposes of the treaty. See generally Jonathan Schwarz, *Schwarz on Tax Treaties* (7th edn, Wolters Kluwer, 2025), Ch 6 on treaty residence.

256 Commentary to Art 4, para 13.

257 It is interesting to note that, in *R v Hammond* (1852) 17 QB 772, Lord Campbell CJ said (at 780 and 781) that 'a man's residence, where he lives with his family and sleeps at night, is always his place of abode in the full sense of that expression'.

258 *McCabe v HMRC* [2024] UKUT 280 (TCC).

> '... regard will be had to his family and social relations, his occupations, his political, cultural or other activities, his place of business, the place from which he administers his property etc ... but ... considerations based on the personal acts of the individual must receive special attention'.[259]

If a person's centre of vital interests are divided equally between the two states concerned, or if the person concerned has no permanent home, then the person is to be regarded as resident in the state 'in which he has an habitual abode'. The OECD Commentary suggests that the place where they spend more time tips the balance in favour of that state.[260] Furthermore, the French version of the text is '*où elle séjourne de façon habituelle*', which indicates that what is being referred to is the state in which a person habitually *stays*.

Where, even after the application of these tests, the question of a person's residence remains unresolved, nationality becomes the deciding factor. If the person is a national of both states or of neither of them, then the competent authorities of the contracting states are required to settle the question by mutual agreement.

A more extensive application of the tie-breaker was necessary in *Yates v Revenue & Customs*.[261] Ms Yates was found to be resident in both the UK and Spain under their respective domestic tax laws in each of 2003/04, 2004/05 and 2006/07 when certain capital gains were realised. Prior to moving to Spain, she lived together with her husband in a jointly purchased residential property, near Nottingham ('Kingston Hall'). In March 2000, Ms Yates rented a three-bedroom apartment, on the southern coast of Spain on an 11-month lease which was renewed until November 2003. She then purchased another three-bedroom apartment in the same development. In applying the tie-breaker in Article 4(2)(a) of the Spain-UK Income tax treaty, the tribunal found that she had permanent homes in both states. Therefore, it was necessary to examine whether in the relevant years Ms Yates's personal and economic relations (centre of vital interests) were closer to Spain or to the UK.

The tribunal concluded that her centre of vital interests was retained in the UK. Her husband, who remained UK resident throughout, was the centre of her vital interests. He was unable to join her in Spain while she was there (except for occasional but regular visits) because of his business commitments in the UK. Other significant relationships were with her parents, who lived in the UK, and her siblings, who lived in the UK, except for a sister in Italy. They far outweighed in significance and importance any social ties she may have formed in Spain. The main factor connecting Ms Yates to Spain was the desirability of residence there for health reasons. This, the tribunal ruled, was not a factor of importance to consider in locating Ms Yates's centre of vital interests. Her economic relations were also with the UK as she was financially

259 Commentary to Art 4 para 15.
260 Commentary to Art 4 para 17.
261 *Lynette Dawn Yates v Revenue & Customs* [2012] UKFTT 568 (TC).

dependent on her husband. As a result, she was a resident of the UK and not Spain for treaty purposes. The tribunal observed, *obiter*, that, had it been necessary to apply the habitual abode test in Article 4(2)(b) of the treaty, she would probably have had an habitual abode in Spain, and not the UK, having regard to the day-count. Both the *Hankinson* and *Yates* decisions emphasise that the tie-breaker is a series of successive tests. If one is satisfied then, the later tests do not apply.

Oppenheimer v HMRC,[262] concerned the application of the tie-breaker in Article 4(2) of the South Africa-UK Double Tax Treaty to a very high net worth individual with a peripatetic lifestyle. Mr Oppenheimer was a resident of both the UK and South Africa, with very extensive residential and other connections in several countries, most notably the United States during the six years in dispute. It was agreed that the taxpayer had a permanent home available in both states and was a citizen of South Africa. Nearly 3,000 pages of documentary evidence and testimony of six witnesses focused on where his centre of vital interests lay and whether he had an habitual abode in either state. The judge ruled that personal and economic relations is a comparative, composite test and is a matter of fact and degree. In concluding that Mr Oppenheimer's centre of vital interests was in South Africa, the tribunal decided that personal and economic connections in third countries should be excluded. Economic interests that were not owned personally were however included. 'Relations' the judge said, simply means the way people or things are connected. Over the six years, the taxpayer spent more than twice the time in the UK than in South Africa and as much time in other countries, mostly the United States as he spent in South Africa. It was common ground that he had an habitual abode in the UK. The tribunal decided that he also had an habitual abode in South Africa because his stays there were both part of the settled routine of his life and were of sufficient frequency, duration and regularity. While the OECD Commentary was considered, the judge concluded that it contemplated much simpler circumstances and was, as a result, of only limited assistance.

262 *Jonathan Oppenheimer v Revenue & Customs* [2022] UKFTT 112 (TC).

CHAPTER 3

Individuals coming to and departing from the UK

They sailed away for a year and a day,
To the land where the Bong-tree grows.

Edward Lear *The Owl and the Pussy-Cat*

3.01 Introduction

While it is self-evident that an individual who never leaves the UK is always resident and that an individual who never comes to the UK is never resident, the degree and nature of movement between those extremes that may give rise to a change in tax status form the subject matter of this chapter. Historically the residence rules for individuals coming to and leaving the UK attracted little legislative attention. The ability of individuals who move to or from the UK to divide the tax year of arrival and departure into periods of residence and non residence for certain tax purposes was put on a statutory footing from 2013/14.[1] Individuals who cease to be resident but return within five years of leaving are classified as Temporary Non Residents under legislation introduced in 1998.[2] The criteria for temporary non-residence changed, and its significance was enlarged by Finance Act 2013.[3] In 2025 a new category of person coming to the UK was introduced: 'New residents' who may benefit from temporary exemption from tax on certain foreign income and gains.[4] Abolition of the remittance basis for non-domiciled UK residents from 6 April 2025 also brought with it the category of 'Long-term UK residents' as a determinant of inheritance tax liability.[5]

1 Sch 45 Part 3.
2 Finance Act 1998 s 127.
3 Sch 45 Pt 4.
4 ITTOIA s 845B Inserted by Finance Act 2025 s 37(1).
5 IHTA s 6A Inserted by Finance Act 2025 s 44(3).

Because all the current residence rules for individuals coming to and leaving the UK have a look-back element, it may, in some cases, be necessary to look back to the law and HMRC practice years including prior to the commencement of the statutory residence test for the 2013/14 tax year to determine a current liability to UK tax. Since the 2013/14 tax year, detailed rules apply to individuals coming to or leaving the UK part way through a tax year, and may qualify for split-year treatment from 6 April 2013.

Split-year treatment

3.02 Introduction

Under the SRT, an individual is either resident or not resident in the UK for the whole of a tax year. However, in reality, individuals become and cease to reside in the UK at different times during the year. In principle this leads to a situation where an individual is liable to UK tax on worldwide income and gains as well as the other tax consequences of UK residence for the whole tax year even though in ordinary terms they are not resident or living in the UK. Statutory split-year treatment is set out in Part 3 of Schedule 44 to the Finance Act 2013.

Meaning of split year

A tax year is a 'split year' for an individual who is resident in the UK for that year, and falls within one of the prescribed cases involving either their actual or deemed departure from the UK or their actual or deemed arrival in the UK.[6] The first three cases apply to departures from the UK and the last five apply to arrivals in the UK. The cases are:

Case 1 (starting full-time work overseas);[7]
Case 2 (the partner of someone starting full-time work overseas);[8]
Case 3 (ceasing to have a home in the UK);[9]
Case 4 (starting to have a home in the UK only);[10]
Case 5 (starting full-time work in the UK);[11]
Case 6 (ceasing full-time work overseas);[12]

6 Sch 45 para 43(1).
7 Sch 45 para 44. See **2.33**.
8 Sch 45 para 45. See **2.34**.
9 Sch 45 para 46. See **2.35**.
10 Sch 45 para 47. See **2.36**.
11 Sch 45 para 48. See **2.37**.
12 Sch 45 para 49. See **2.38**.

Case 7 (the partner of someone ceasing full-time work overseas);[13]
Case 8 (starting to have a home in the UK).[14]

The cases are closely connected with certain of the automatic tests both for UK and overseas residence. Thus, split-year treatment is available for individuals who start or cease full-time work overseas and their accompanying spouses and civil partners. These relate to the 'third automatic overseas test'.[15] Individuals who start full-time work in the UK and their accompanying spouses and civil partners may likewise qualify. These relate to the 'third automatic UK test'.[16] There are no automatic tests of residence for accompanying spouses and civil partners whose status must be determined by other tests. As a result, the split-year cases for such individuals are more complex.

Individuals who move to or from the UK in non-work related circumstances may also qualify for split-year treatment if they start or cease to have a home in the UK or if they start or cease to have their only home in the UK. These cases are all closely connected with the 'second automatic UK test'.[17]

No split-year treatment is available in respect of the automatic tests that operate by reference to physical presence only,[18] nor where the sufficient ties test determines residence.[19] In addition, individuals who meet the related automatic tests will still need to meet the detailed particular conditions of the case in question.

3.03 The effect of a split year

A split year is divided into a UK part and an overseas part. Intuition might lead one to regard the individual as UK resident for the UK part and not-resident for the overseas part. This is not, however, the case. The effect of a tax year being a split year is to 'relax' the effect of treating individuals who are UK resident 'for' a tax year as being UK resident at all times in that year.[20] This is achieved by the special charging rules introduced by the amendments made to TCGA 1992, ITEPA 2003 and ITTOIA 2005 by paragraphs 57–101 of Schedule 45 so as to alter the incidence of taxation of certain sources of income and gains. There is no comprehensive split-year treatment for all sources other than as specifically introduced by these amendments. In all other respects, individuals with split-year treatment remain to be taxed as residents.[21]

13 Sch 45 para 50. See **2.39**.
14 Sch 45 para 51. See **2.40**.
15 See **2.13**.
16 See **2.14**.
17 See **2.07**.
18 See **2.05** and **2.06**.
19 See **2.18**.
20 Sch 45 para 40(1).
21 Sch 45 para 40(3).

Somewhat obscurely, this status is reinforced by paragraph 42 which states that 'The existence of special charging rules for cases involving split years is not intended to affect any question as to whether an individual would fall to be regarded under double taxation arrangements as a resident of the UK.'

Although the statutory residence test determines whether an individual is resident or non-resident in the UK, including where a tax liability of another actual or deemed person depends on the residence of another individual, this rule is disapplied in the case of split years. Thus, split-year treatment does not apply in determining the residence status of personal representatives.[22] Split-year treatment applies in determining the residence status of the trustees of a settlement only to the extent that section 475 of ITA 2007 and section 69 of TCGA 1992 are amended by paragraphs 102 and 103 of Schedule 43.[23]

'The UK part' of a split year is the part of a year that is not 'the overseas part'.[24] Because the special charging rules do not simply exclude foreign income and gains during the overseas part of the year, an elaborate and convoluted definition of the overseas part by reference to the period before arriving in the UK or after leaving, as the case may be, linked to each of the cases.[25] Identification of the overseas part follows analysis of the cases which give rise to split years. These are each discussed below.

3.04 Which split-year case applies?

Individuals who move to or from the UK may well qualify for split-year treatment under more than one case. Since the division of the year into UK and overseas parts is by reference to different criteria, a hierarchy is established for the application of the cases. For individuals leaving the UK, Case 1 (starting full-time work overseas) takes priority followed by Case 2 (the partner of someone starting full-time work overseas) and then Case 3 (ceasing to have a home in the UK).[26]

A complex hierarchy applies to individuals moving to the UK. Firstly, where an individual works overseas and moves to work in the UK, then if Case 6 (ceasing full-time work overseas) and Case 5 (starting full-time work in the UK) both apply and the split-year date in relation to Case 5 is earlier than the split-year date in relation to Case 6, Case 5 has priority. Otherwise, Case 6 has priority.[27]

Secondly, where a non-working spouse overseas starts to work full time in the UK, then if Case 7 (the partner of someone ceasing full-time work overseas) (but not Case 6 (ceasing full-time work overseas)) applies and if

22 Sch 45 para 41(a).
23 Sch 45 para 41(b). See Chapter 5, para **5.06**.
24 Sch 45 para 56.
25 Sch 45 para 53.
26 Sch 45 para 54.
27 Sch 45 para 55(1).

Case 5 (starting full-time work in the UK) also applies and the split-year date in relation to Case 5 is earlier than the split-year date in relation to Case 7, Case 5 has priority. Otherwise, Case 7 has priority.[28]

Thirdly, if two or all of Cases 4 (starting to have a home in the UK only), 5 (starting full-time work in the UK) and 8 (starting to have a home in the UK) apply but neither Case 6 (ceasing full-time work overseas) nor Case 7 (the partner of someone ceasing full-time work overseas), the Case which has priority is the one with the earliest split-year date.[29] But if, in these circumstances, two or all of the cases which apply share the same split-year date and that date is the only, or earlier, split-year date of the cases which apply, the cases with that split-year date are to be treated as having priority.[30]

3.05 Case 1: Starting full-time work overseas

Split-year treatment is available in the year in which an individual starts working full-time overseas. In order to qualify for split-year treatment in a year when the individual starts full-time work overseas, they must, firstly, have been resident in the UK for the previous tax year for any reason (whether or not it was a split year),[31] and, secondly, also not be resident in the UK for the next tax year by reason of the full-time work abroad (third automatic overseas) test.[32] The second requirement, although inherent in the case raises practical difficulties for taxpayers in filing returns by the deadline of 31 January in the year after the tax year ends. Taxpayers will only know that they have met this requirement by the following 6 April and amended returns may be required.

The third requirement is that there is a period in the year which starts on the day the individual does more than three hours' work overseas and ends on the last day of the tax year during which the individual meet the requirements for full-time work overseas.[33] This means working sufficient hours overseas assessed over that period without any significant breaks from overseas work and not exceeding the permitted limit for days on which more than three hours' work is done in the UK.[34] Whether sufficient hours are worked overseas is determined in the same way as for the third automatic overseas test by reference to the number of days from the date on which overseas work starts to the end of the tax year. The normal permitted limit for work in the UK of 30 days a year under the third automatic overseas test is reduced by the proportion of the year before starting full-time work overseas. Similarly, the permitted limit for days spent in the UK (90 days a year under the third automatic overseas

28 Sch 45 para 55(3).
29 Sch 45 para 55(4) and (5).
30 Sch 45 para 55(6).
31 Sch 45 para 44(2).
32 Sch 45 para 44(4).
33 Sch 45 para 44(3).
34 Sch 45 para 44(5).

test) is reduced by the same proportion.[35] This proportion is determined by reference to the number of whole months in the year before the day full-time work overseas starts.[36]

HMRC have produced the following table[37] to show the permitted limits for Case 1:

Date	**Permitted limit on days where you can work more than 3 hours and maximum number of days that can be subtracted for gaps between employments**	**Permitted limit on days spent in the UK**
6–30 Apr	30	90
1–31 May	27	82
1–30 Jun	25	75
1–31 Jul	22	67
1–31 Aug	20	60
1–30 Sep	17	52
1–31 Oct	15	45
1–30 Nov	12	37
1–31 Dec	10	30
1–31 Jan	7	22
1–29 Feb	5	15
1–31 Mar	2	7
1–5 Apr	0	0

The overseas part of a split year for Case 1 is the period from when full-time work overseas starts to the end of the year. If there is more than one period of full-time work overseas (without significant breaks), the overseas part starts at the part beginning of the longest of those periods.[38]

3.06 Case 2: Spouse or partner of someone starting full-time work overseas

A spouse or civil partner of an individual who qualifies for split-year treatment under Case 1 (starting full-time work overseas) by accompanying the working

35 Sch 45 para 44(5).
36 Sch 45 para 44(8) and (9).
37 RFIG21070. Residence: Split year treatment: Case 1: Calculating whether individual works full-time overseas in the relevant period.
38 Sch 45 para 53(2).

spouse or civil partner overseas may also qualify for split-year treatment.[39] An individual qualifies for split-year treatment in this case firstly, if they were resident in the UK for the previous tax year (whether or not it was a split year) for any reason and, secondly, are not resident in the following year under any part of the SRT. Thirdly, the individual must have a partner who qualifies for split-year treatment under Case 1 for either the relevant year or the previous tax year.[40]

Fourthly, the individual must move overseas on a particular day in the year so they can continue to live together while their spouse or civil partner is working overseas.[41] When an individual 'moves' overseas it may give rise to difficulties of interpretation and application in practice. In *R (on the application of Davies & Anor) v Revenue & Customs Commissioners; R (on the application of Gaines-Cooper) v Revenue & Customs Commissioners*,[42] the Supreme Court spent some time considering whether a taxpayer 'left' the UK within the meaning of Booklet IR20. Lord Wilson, speaking for the majority of the Court, concluded that the individual 'was required to "leave" the UK in a more profound sense than that of travel, namely permanently or indefinitely or for full-time employment.'[43] and Lord Hope agreed that a distinct break with the UK was required.[44] Even if a mere departure meets the statutory requirement, in many cases further evidence of the context of a particular departure may be required to show which of several departures constituted the 'move'. Fifthly, the individual must either have no home in the UK at any time, or spend the greater part of the time living in the overseas home where the individual has homes in both the UK and overseas during the period from the 'deemed departure day' to the end of the year.[45] Identification of the date of the move may cause difficulties given modern travel patterns as illustrated by *Kimber v HMRC*[46] where the taxpayer arrived and departed physically several times for different purposes in the course of moving from one country to another. Mr Kimber, who had previously lived in Japan, disposed of shares on 12 August 2005. Was he UK-resident on that date? It was agreed that he was non-UK resident between the years 1989 and 1994 and also from 17 September 1997 until at least 17 July 2005. He was in the UK between 17 and 30 July 2005, for the regular holiday he and his family had taken during all the years when he had been non-resident. During that period the family stayed in Kent with his mother. On 30 July, he and his family then flew to Italy for a four-week holiday booked months before, when he had been living in Japan. On 28 August, he

39 Sch 45 para 45.
40 Sch 45 para 45(3).
41 Sch 45 para 45(4).
42 *R (on the application of Davies & Anor) v Revenue & Customs Commissioners; R (on the application of Gaines-Cooper) v Revenue & Customs Commissioners* [2011] UKSC 47.
43 Sch 45 para 45.
44 Sch 45 para 63.
45 Sch 45 para 45(5).
46 *Kimber v HMRC* [2012] UKFTT 107 (TC).

and his family returned to the UK from Italy. While on holiday he found a property available to rent on a furnished basis in Norfolk near to where his children were to start school as arranged while he was living in Japan. The lease was to commence on 1 September 2005. Although it was unclear when he had signed it, a printed date at the bottom of the first page of the lease, which contained the names and address in Kent of the appellant and his wife, was 27 July 2005.

The First-tier Tribunal decided that at some time before 30 July, even if not on 17 July, Mr Kimber formed the intention to stay in the UK permanently and then became resident.[47] Alternatively, when he and his family arrived in the UK on 17 July, he was not coming to the UK for a temporary purpose, but knew that, with the interval of a pre-booked holiday in Italy apart, he and his family were returning to the UK, and very specifically to Norfolk.[48] Although the decision was based on the pre-2013 law, it may also illustrate the difference between a place to stay (the home of Mr Kimber's mother) and a 'home' (the property rented near where his children would go to school).

Sixthly, the individual may spend no more days in the UK than the permitted limit during the period from the deemed departure date to the end of the year. The permitted limit for days spent in the UK is 90 days a year reduced by the proportion of the year before the deemed departure day. This proportion is determined by reference to the number of whole months in the year before the deemed departure day.[49]

The 'deemed departure day' depends on whether the working spouse or civil partner qualifies for split-year treatment under Case 1 for the year of departure, or the previous tax year of the accompanying spouse or civil partner. If it is in the year of departure, the 'deemed departure day' is the later of the day the individual moves overseas and the first day of the overseas part of the relevant year for the working spouse or civil partner under Case 1. If it is the previous tax year, the 'deemed departure day' is the day the individual moves overseas.[50]

The overseas part of the split year is the part beginning with the deemed departure day.[51]

3.07 Case 3: Ceasing to have a home in the UK

Although Case 3 is headed 'ceasing to have a home in the UK', it may be more accurately described as leaving the UK to live overseas, given the requirements of the Case.[52] In order to qualify for split-year treatment in a year under Case 3, an individual must, firstly, have been resident in the UK for the previous tax

47 At para 23.
48 At para 23.
49 Sch 45 para 45(5)(c) and (9).
50 Sch 45 para 45(7) and (8).
51 Sch 45 para 53(3).
52 Sch 45 para 46.

year for any reason (whether or not it was a split year), and, secondly, also not resident in the UK for the next tax year for any reason.[53] Thirdly, at the start of the relevant year, the individual must have had one or more homes in the UK but ceased to have any home in the UK on a day in the relevant year and thereafter have no home in the UK for the rest of that year.[54] A day must be found when the individual no longer has a home in the UK. In straightforward cases this may entail a sale, lease, removal of furniture and belongings or simply leaving. The scheme of the SRT clearly contemplates that a UK home may be downgraded to a place to stay. Similarly, a place to stay may become upgraded to a home. HMRC's view is that mere accommodation can be transient and does not require the degree of stability or permanence that a home does.[55] This break will demand a detailed examination of all facts and circumstances of an individual's habitation as suggested in HMRC guidance on record keeping.[56] *Kimber v HMRC*[57] may also illustrate the difference between a place to stay (the home of Mr Kimber's mother) and a 'home' (the property rented near where his children would go to school).

Thirdly, the individual must spend fewer than 16 days in the UK from the day on which he ceases to have a home in the UK.[58]

Fourthly, within six months from the day on which he ceases to have a home in the UK, the individual must have a 'sufficient link' with a country overseas.[59] A 'sufficient link' exists with a country overseas if he is a resident for tax purposes in accordance with the domestic laws of that country, has been present in that country at the end of each day of the six-month period or the individual's only home is in that country or, if he has more than one home, they are all in that country.[60]

The overseas part of the split year is the part from the deemed departure day to the end of the tax year.

3.08 Case 4: Starting to have a home in the UK only

Two cases permit split-year treatment in the year when an individual starts to have a home in the UK. Case 4 deals with individuals starting to have a home in the UK only, while Case 8 deals with individuals starting to have a home in the UK.

An individual may qualify for split-year treatment under Case 4 if they, firstly, were not resident in the UK for the previous tax year for any reason,

53 Sch 45 para 46(2) and (5).
54 Sch 45 para 46(3).
55 RFIG22160.
56 RFIG21920.
57 *Kimber v HMRC* [2012] UKFTT 107 (TC). See **3.06**.
58 Sch 45 para 46(4).
59 Sch 45 para 46(6) and (7).
60 Sch 45 para 53(4).

and, secondly, did not have their only home in the UK (or if the individual had more than one home, one of them is outside the UK) at the start of the relevant year but on a day in that year the individual's only home is in the UK (or if the individual had more than one home, all of them are in the UK) (the 'only home test') and that remains the case for the rest of that year.[61]

Thirdly, for the part of the year before the day the only home test is met, the individual must not have sufficient UK ties under the sufficient ties test, modified to take into account that the period will be less than a full year. The permitted limit for days spent in the UK during that period is reduced by the proportion of the year from the day the only home test is met to the end of the year. This proportion is determined by reference to the number of whole months in the year from the day the only home test is met. The existence of a family tie must, however, be determined by reference to the whole year.[62]

The overseas part of the split year is the part before the day the only home test is met.[63]

3.09 Case 5: Starting full-time work in the UK

Split-year treatment is available in the year in which an individual starts working full time in the UK.[64] In order to qualify for split-year treatment in a year when the individual starts full-time work overseas, they must, firstly, have been non-resident for the previous tax year for any reason.[65]

The second requirement is that there is at least one period of 365 days which starts on the day in the year the individual does more than three hours' work in the UK and during which at least 75% of the total number of days in the period on which the individual works for more than three hours are days on which the individual works in the UK for more than three hours. Thirdly, the individual must meet the requirements for full-time work in the UK. This means working sufficient hours in the UK assessed over that period. Fourthly, there must be no significant breaks from UK work.[66]

Fifthly, for the part of the year before the day full-time work in the UK starts, the individual must not have sufficient UK ties under the sufficient ties test, modified to take into account that the period will be less than a full year.[67] The permitted limit for days spent in the UK during that period is reduced by the proportion of the year from the day full-time work in the UK starts. This proportion is determined by reference to the number of whole months in the

61 Sch 45 para 47(2)–(5).
62 Sch 45 para 47(6) and (7).
63 Sch 45 para 53(5).
64 Sch 45 para 48.
65 Sch 45 para 48(2).
66 Sch 45 para 48(3).
67 Sch 45 para 48(3)(c) and (5).

year from the day full-time work in the UK starts. The existence of a family tie must, however, be determined by reference to the whole year.[68]

HMRC have produced the following table[69] to show the permitted limits for Case 4:

Date	**For 15 substitute**	**For 45 substitute**	**For 90 substitute**	**For 120 substitute**
6–30 Apr	1	4	7	10
1–31 May	2	7	15	20
1–30 Jun	4	11	22	30
1–31 Jul	5	15	30	40
1–31 Aug	6	19	37	50
1–30 Sep	7	22	45	60
1–31 Oct	9	26	52	70
1–30 Nov	10	30	60	80
1–31 Dec	11	34	67	90
1–31 Jan	12	37	75	100
1–29 Feb	14	41	82	110
1 Mar–5 Apr	15	45	90	120

The overseas part of a split year is the period before full-time work in the UK starts. If there is more than one period of full-time work in the UK (without significant breaks), the overseas part starts at the beginning of the first of those periods.[70]

3.10 Case 6: Ceasing full-time work overseas

Split-year treatment may be available in the year in which an individual ceases working full time overseas.[71] In order to qualify the individual must firstly have been non-resident for the previous tax year by reason of working full time overseas (the third automatic overseas test). Secondly, the individual had been resident for one or more of the four tax years immediately preceding that year. Thirdly, the individual is resident in the UK for the next tax year (whether or not it is a split year).[72]

68 Sch 45 para 48(7).
69 RFIG21170. Case 5: Starting full-time work in the UK.
70 Sch 45 para 53(6).
71 Sch 45 para 49.
72 Sch 45 para 49(2) and (4).

The third requirement is that there is at least one period in the year which starts on the first day of the year and ends on another day in the tax year when the individual does more than three hours' work overseas, during which the individual meets the requirements for full-time work overseas. This means working sufficient hours overseas assessed over that period without any significant breaks from overseas work and not exceeding the permitted limit for days on which more than three hours' work is done in the UK. In addition, the individual must also not work in the UK more than three hours per day or spend more time in the UK in that year beyond the permitted limit from the time he starts to work full-time overseas.[73]

Whether sufficient hours are worked overseas is determined in the same way as for the third automatic overseas test by reference to the number of days from the beginning of the year to the date on which overseas work ends.[74] The normal permitted limit for work in the UK (30 days a year under the third automatic overseas test) reduced by the proportion of the year before starting full-time work overseas. Similarly, the permitted limit for days spent in the UK is 90 days a year under the third automatic overseas test is reduced by the same proportion. This proportion is determined by reference to the number of whole months in the year before the day full-time work overseas starts.[75]

HMRC have produced the following table[76] to show the permitted limits for Case 6:

Date	Permitted limit on days where you can work more than 3 hours in overseas part of the year or maximum number of days which may be subtracted from the reference period on account of gaps between employments	Permitted limit on days spent in the UK in overseas part of year
6–30 Apr	2	7
1–31 May	5	15
1–30 Jun	7	22
1–31 Jul	10	30
1–31 Aug	12	37
1–30 Sep	15	45
1–31 Oct	17	52
1–30 Nov	20	60
1–31 Dec	22	67
1–31 Jan	25	75

73 Sch 45 para 49(3).
74 Sch 45 para 49(5) and (7).
75 Sch 45 para 49(8) and (9).
76 RFIG21220. Case 6: Calculating whether individual has worked full-time overseas in the relevant period.

Date	Permitted limit on days where you can work more than 3 hours in overseas part of the year or maximum number of days which may be subtracted from the reference period on account of gaps between employments	Permitted limit on days spent in the UK in overseas part of year
1–29 Feb	27	82
1 Mar–5 Apr	30	90

The overseas part of a split year for Case 6 is the period from the start of the year to the day when full-time work overseas ends. If there is more than one period of full-time work overseas (without significant breaks), the overseas part ends on the last day of the longest of those periods.[77]

3.11 Case 7: The partner of someone ceasing full-time work overseas

A spouse or civil partner of an individual who qualifies for split-year treatment under Case 6 (ceasing full-time work overseas) by accompanying the working spouse or civil partner overseas may also qualify for split-year treatment.[78]

The requirements to qualify are that the individual, firstly, was not UK resident for the previous tax year for any reason, secondly, is UK resident for the next tax year (whether or not it is a split year) and thirdly, has a spouse or civil partner who qualifies for split-year treatment for the relevant year or the previous year. Fourthly, the individual must move to the UK to continue to live together with their spouse or civil partner on their return or relocation to the UK.[79]

Fifthly, the individual must either have no home in the UK at any time, or spend the greater part of the time living in the overseas home where the individual has homes in both the UK and overseas during the period from the beginning of the relevant year to the 'deemed arrival day'.[80] Sixthly, the individual may spend no more days in the UK than the permitted limit during the period from the beginning of the relevant year to the 'deemed arrival day'.[81] The permitted limit for days spent in the UK is 90 days a year reduced by the proportion of the year after the deemed arrival day. This proportion is determined by reference to the number of whole months in the year after the deemed arrival day.[82]

77 Sch 45 para 53(7).
78 Sch 45 para 50.
79 Sch 45 para 50(2)–(4) and (6).
80 Sch 45 para 50(5)(a).
81 Sch 45 para 50(5)(b).
82 Sch 45 para 50(9) and (10).

The 'deemed arrival day' depends on whether the working spouse or civil partner qualifies for split-year treatment under Case 6 for the year of arrival, or the previous tax year of the accompanying spouse or civil partner. If it is in the year of arrival, the 'deemed arrival day' is the later of the day the individual moves to the UK and the first day of the UK part of the relevant year for the working spouse or civil partner under Case 6. If it is the previous tax year, the 'deemed arrival day' is the day the individual moves to the UK.[83]

The overseas part of the split year is the part before the deemed arrival day.[84]

3.12 Case 8: Starting to have a home in the UK

An individual will qualify for split-year treatment if they were, firstly, not resident in the UK for the previous tax year and secondly, are resident in the UK for the tax year after the relevant year and that is not a split year.[85] Thirdly, the individual had no home in the UK at the start of the relevant year but they start to have a home in the UK for the first time in that year, and continued to have a home in the UK for the rest of that year and for the whole of the next tax year.[86] Fourthly, the individual must not have sufficient UK ties for the part of the relevant year before the day starts to have a home in the UK for the first time.[87] The sufficient ties test is modified to take into account that the period will be less than a full year.[88] The permitted limit for days spent in the UK during that period is reduced by the proportion of the year from the day the only home test is met to the end of the year. This proportion is determined by reference to the number of whole months in the year from the day the only home test is met.[89] The existence of a family tie must, however, be determined by reference to the whole year.[90]

The overseas part of the split year is the part before the day the individual starts to have a home in the UK.[91]

Special kinds of resident

3.13 Temporary non-residents

Parliament has extended the jurisdiction to tax on a worldwide basis over individuals who succeed in breaking the residential ties but who become UK

83 Sch 45 para 50(7).
84 Sch 45 para 53(8).
85 Sch 45 para 51(2) and (5).
86 Sch 45 para 51(3).
87 Sch 45 para 51(4).
88 Sch 45 para 51(6).
89 Sch 45 para 51(6) and (7).
90 Sch 45 para 51(8).
91 Sch 45 para 53(9).

resident again within five years of ceasing to be so. Temporary non-residents – that is individuals who have been tax resident in the UK and become not resident for a period of less than five tax years – will be liable to tax in respect to several items of income and capital gains tax on certain gains realised after departure from the UK in the year they resume UK residence.[92] Remittance basis taxpayers who are temporary non-residents are similarly liable to tax in the year of return on remittances made in the intervening years.[93] The tax regime for temporary non-residents is set out in Part 4 of Schedule 43 to the Finance Act 2013.

Part 4 of Schedule 43 is headed 'anti-avoidance'. The consultative document asserts that the statutory residence test:

> '... will therefore need to counteract the risk of individuals creating artificial short periods of non-residence, during which they receive a large amount of income (which accrued during periods of UK residence) free of UK tax and then bring the income back into the UK tax free.'[94]

The notion of 'artificial non-residence' is surprising given the entirely factual nature of residence both under the statutory residence test. The statutory residence test in many respects specifies a particular period or set of conditions quite precisely. HMRC guidance on the General Anti-Abuse Rule in FA 2013, Part 5, says that in such cases, 'taxpayers are entitled to assume that they are on the right side of the line if they have satisfied the statutory condition and there is no contrivance about what they have done.'[95] The provisions existing prior to FA 2013 relating to temporary non-residents demonstrate the fallacy of a link between more certain rules introduced in the SRT and the behaviour the regime for temporary non-residents is aimed at. The temporary non-residents rules apply in any event equally to tax sinners and saints alike. No distinction is made between a short period of non-residence that is motivated by tax considerations, a spell of overseas employment, or a gap year.

The temporary non-residence rules depart from other aspects of the statutory residence regime in that, an individual, who is resident in the UK under domestic law, is only resident for the purpose of these rules, if they are also not resident in another country for the purposes of a tax treaty at any time in the tax year. This status is labelled 'sole UK residence'. The same principle applies to split years. The UK part of a split year is only a period of residence for these rules if the individual is also not resident in another country for the

---

92 These items are identified in Sch 45 paras 116–144 by amendments throughout the tax legislation and in the Temporary Non-Residence (Miscellaneous Amendments) Regulations 2013 (SI 2013/1810) in force from 12 August 2013.

93 Sch 45 para 118.

94 Consultative Document, para 3.50.

95 This principle is articulated in HMRC'S GAAR GUIDANCE (Approved by the Advisory Panel with effect from 15 April 2013) PART D – Examples D2.4.1.

purposes of a tax treaty at any time in the UK part of the tax year.[96] Thus, in applying these rules, a period of UK residence requires both residence in the UK as a matter of domestic law and, where relevant, under any applicable tax treaty. The corollary is that an individual may be UK resident as a matter of domestic law but have a period of temporary non-residence under these rules if they are treaty resident in another country at any time in the tax year or UK part of a split year.

Individuals who cease to be resident may be treated as temporarily non-resident. This will potentially be applicable to an individual who has been a sole UK resident for four out of the seven years immediately preceding the year of departure.[97] Any year in which the individual has split-year treatment is included as a year of residence for this purpose. An individual departs either by ceasing to be resident or becomes treaty non-resident.[98] An individual returns when they are resident and not a treaty non-resident.[99]

An individual is 'temporarily non-resident' if their temporary period of non-residence is five years or less.[100] The temporary residence period is measured from the end of a period of sole UK residence to the start of the next period of sole UK residence (called the 'period of return'). For this purpose, a 'residence period' is either a full tax year, or in the case of an individual with a split year, the overseas part or the UK part of that split year. The five-year period is therefore by reference to time elapsed and not to tax years, as was the case previously.

3.14 Qualifying new residents

Finance Act 2025 introduced a short-term relief from income tax and capital gains tax for certain individuals moving to the UK as an exception to the basic rule that from 6 April 2025, all UK residents are liable to worldwide taxation of both income and capital gains. The 'FIG regime' will permit 'qualifying new residents' to claim exemption from tax on most foreign income and gains.[101]

The FIG regime lasts for four years and the definition of a qualifying new resident is divided into two parts. The first part deals with the year in which an individual initially comes, or returns to, the UK: An individual who is UK resident for the tax year and was not UK resident for each of the 10 tax years before that tax year, is a new resident.[102]

The second part deals with the three years subsequent to the initial year of arrival: An individual who is UK resident for the tax year, and that tax year is

96 Sch 45 para 112.
97 Sch 45 para 110(1)(c).
98 Sch 45 paras 110(1)(d).
99 Sch 45 para 114 and 115.
100 Sch 45 para 110(1)(d).
101 See Chapter 1.
102 ITTOIA s 845B(1)(a) and (c).

one of the next three tax years after the first tax year in which the individual qualified as a new resident, is also a new resident for those three tax years.[103]

In both cases an individual who is a member of the House of Commons or of the House of Lords for any part of that tax year is excluded from qualifying for new resident status.[104]

A transitional measure enables individuals to qualify as new residents from 6 April 2025. Thus the 2022/23, 2023/24 or 2024/25 tax years may also qualify if the individual would have been a qualifying new resident for those years if these provisions had applied in those years.[105] Thus, an individual can be a qualifying new resident for any of those tax years only for the purposes of qualifying for tax years from 2025/26 onwards. In deciding whether 2022/23 had been an initial year when an individual had not been UK resident in the preceding 10 years, 2012/13 was a year before the statutory residence test applied.[106] The previous edition of this work should be consulted for the residence rules applicable for that year.

The definition of qualifying new resident is narrowly drawn so that residence in the 10-year period before arrival in the UK is by reference to residence 'for' those tax years. Thus, an individual who comes to or leaves the UK part way through one of those years will be UK resident for this purpose, regardless of whether they qualify for split year treatment[107] or not. Short periods of actual presence in the UK may therefore disqualify an individual. This does not, however, preclude the application of split-year treatment in those years.

By the same token, the fact that an individual was also resident in another state in any of those preceding 10 years will not have any effect for these purposes. Similarly, since, in the case of individuals, residence in another state for the purposes of a double tax treaty[108] is only for those purposes and will not itself determine residence for this purpose.

Former UK residents will not be precluded from qualifying as new residents for the FIG regime as long as they have been non-resident for the 10 tax years prior to return. Similarly, ceasing to be UK resident in any of the four years when the regime may apply will not disqualify the years of residence during that period. However, such non-residence will not extend or refresh the four-year period.

Long-term UK residents

3.15 Domicile as a key determinant of the territorial scope of liability to inheritance tax is abolished from 6 April 2025.[109] It is replaced with a new

103 ITTOIA s 845B(2)(a) and (c).
104 ITTOIA s 845B(1)(b) and (2)(b) (c) with s 845B(4).
105 ITTOIA s 845B(3).
106 RFIG44000.
107 RFIG44000 Treaty non-residence and split year treatment.
108 See Chapter 2, **2.45**.
109 Finance Act 2025 s 44(4). See also Finance Act 2025 Sch 13 Pt 2 on commencement.

connecting factor: long-term residence. Thus, persons who are not long-term UK residents will not be liable to inheritance tax on 'excluded property. The most important category is property situated outside the UK'.[110] Domicile continues as a connecting factor in tax treaties that deal with the elimination of double taxation on estate and gift taxes.[111]

The meaning of 'Long-term UK resident' individual is complex. The basic test is a combination of an aggregate number of years and consecutive years of UK residence. Firstly, an individual is a 'long-term UK resident' in a tax year if they were UK resident for at least 10 of the previous 20 tax years.[112] Secondly, an individual meeting the first requirement will not be a UK resident if they were non-resident for either of any 10 consecutive tax years during the 19 tax years before the current tax year, or for at least the 'required number' of consecutive tax years ending with the tax year before the current tax year.[113] The 'required number' of years is measured over the 20 tax years ending with the last tax year for which the individual was UK resident. The number of years of UK residence must then be matched with the required number of consecutive years of residence set out in a table as follows:[114]

Number of resident years	Required number of consecutive years of non-residence
13 or less	3
14	4
15	5
16	6
17	7
18	8
19	9
20	10

Special rules apply to individuals who were under the age of 20 immediately before the current tax year ('young persons').[115] In the case of young persons, the number of years that the individual was alive replaces the 20-year period over which residence is measured, and the number of years of UK residence is half the number of years the individual was alive (rounded up, if not a whole number, to the next whole number).[116] A child under the age of 1, or not yet

110 IHTA 1984 s 6(1) and (1A) as Inserted by Finance Act 2025 s 44(2). See also amendments to the meaning of settled property In IHTA 1984 s 48 made by Finance Act 2025 s 45.
111 See Chapter 9, **9.19**.
112 IHTA 1984 s 6A(1). Confusingly, the requirement for consecutive years of residence is expressed in negative terms in the legislation.
113 IHTA 1984 s 6A(2).
114 IHTA 1984 s 6A(3).
115 IHTA 1984 s 6B(2).
116 IHTA 1984 s 6B(1).

born, immediately before the tax year is not a long-term UK resident in a tax year.[117]

Split-year treatment does not apply to the long-term UK resident rules. Residence for this purpose is residence for the whole tax year in question. Certain individuals who were not UK domiciled and who left the UK before the long-term UK resident regime commenced may qualify as not long-term UK resident. This transitional measure excludes an individual who would otherwise be a long-term UK resident from that status if they were not UK domiciled under common law on 30 October 2024,[118] were not UK resident for the tax year from 2025/26 up to and including the tax year in which they would otherwise be a long-term UK resident, and if either they were not resident in the UK in any of the three tax years immediately before that year or were UK resident for fewer than 15 of the 20 tax years immediately preceding that tax year.[119]

Amendments to inheritance tax that flow from the replacement of domicile with long-term residence are set out in Finance Act 2025, Schedule 13.

3.16 Bodies corporate as long-term UK residents

Insofar as domicile of legal persons is relevant to inheritance tax, the concept is replaced with long-term UK residence from 6 April 2025. A body corporate is long-term UK resident if it is incorporated in the UK[120] or otherwise within the charge to tax as a resident company in the previous tax year where it came into existence before the beginning of that tax year.[121] This aligns the inheritance tax status as a long-term UK resident with the corporation tax meaning of corporate residence.122

117 IHTA 1984 s 6B(3). This is a minor relaxation compared to the of the application of the previous domicile rule.

118 The date of publication of the HMRC Policy paper: Reforming the taxation of non-UK domiciled individuals. See Chapter 9 on common law domicile.

119 Finance Act 2025 Sch 13 para.46.

120 This appears to be the common law position: *Gasque v IRC* (1940) 23 TC 210.

121 IHTA 1984 s 6C.

122 See Chapter 6 on the residence of companies.

CHAPTER 4

Ordinary residence

'Sark.'
'Yes, sir,' said the man in the little quayside hut. 'A return fare. Six shillings.'
'A single, my friend,' said Mr Harold Pye.
Mervyn Peake *Mr Pye* Ch 1

4.01 Introduction

The concept of ordinary residence was almost entirely eliminated for tax purposes from 6 April 2013[1] as a major simplification of the tax system. Transitional rules are discussed in **4.13** below. Certain specific statutory regimes replace ordinary residence with tests for eligibility by reference to years of residence. Transitional rules permitted individuals who were ordinarily resident at the end of the 2012/13 year to remain within those regimes for a limited period.

Ordinary residence remains relevant for:

- eligibility for blind person's allowance which is linked to ordinary residence in Scotland or Northern Ireland rather than in the UK under ITA 2007 section 38;
- exemption condition under ITTOIA 2005 section 693 for income from Ulster Savings Certificates which is linked to ordinary residence in Northern Ireland.
- the residence of settlements made before 6 April 2013.[2]

Ordinary residence remains a connecting factor for National Insurance Contributions.

It has been noted at **1.10** above that residence *simpliciter* as interpreted by the courts as a determinant of chargeability may be seen as that same principle carried one stage further. However, ordinary residence is 'a more

1 FA 2013 Sch 46.
2 See Chapter 5, **5.04.**

elusive concept than simple residence. On one Revenue view, it can also be more adhesive, in that a person can remain ordinarily resident even though physically absent from the country throughout the year (and, accordingly, not resident)'.[3] Ordinary residence is, in fact,

> '… a point on a scale which ranges from mere presence in this country through "resident" … to "domicile" which is widely used to specify the nature and quality of the association between person and place which brings the person within the scope of that particular enactment.'[4]

In the context of the Taxes Acts, the term 'ordinarily resident', like the term 'resident', had 'no … technical or special meaning'[5] and has, therefore, been given its natural and ordinary meaning. The courts, however, found some difficulty in deciding not only what that natural meaning might be but also how ordinary residence differs from residence *simpliciter* – though the fact that there is a difference between the two terms was evident from the legislation itself.

While residence is the central determinant of liability, ordinary residence was a determinant of liability only in certain special cases. In some circumstances it limited liability to UK taxation for those whose connection with the UK is more tenuous. Thus, Part 8 of ITTOIA 2005 charged the 'relevant foreign income' of individuals who were resident but not ordinarily resident. Employment earnings of such individuals from duties performed outside the UK were likewise chargeable on the remittance basis.[6] A further graduation was found in the case of employees who are both resident and ordinarily resident but not domiciled in the UK. The 'overseas earnings' of such individuals were taxable on the remittance basis.[7] The parallel limited application of ITEPA 2003 Part 7 (Employment Related Securities) to such individuals was modified by Finance Act 2008.[8]

On the other hand, the higher degree of connection with the UK was required before certain anti-avoidance legislation is applicable. ITA 2007 Part 13 (Tax Avoidance), Chapter 2 (Transfer of Assets Abroad) was only applicable to individuals ordinarily resident in the UK at the material time.

Ordinary residence was also perhaps used in an attempt to extend taxing jurisdiction. It is apparent that ordinary residence is a more enduring personal attribute than residence *simpliciter*, and TCGA 1992 section 2(1) prior to

3 Inland Revenue explanatory note relating to a proposed amendment to Finance Bill 1974, cl 18. HM Treasury and HM Revenue & Customs *Statutory definition of tax residence: a consultation* (June 2011), para 6.6.

4 *R v Barnet London Borough, ex p Shah* [1980] 3 All ER 679 at 681, per Ormrod J.

5 *Levene v IRC* (1928) 13 TC 486 at 507, per Lord Warrington of Clyffe.

6 ITEPA 2003 s 26 (before 6 April 2013).

7 ITEPA 2003 ss 21–24 (before 6 April 2013).

8 Finance Act 2008 Sch 7 para 22.

6 April 2013 may suggest that Parliament had sought to rely on it to impose a charge on a wider range of person:

> 'Subject to any exceptions provided by this Act, a person shall be chargeable to capital gains tax in respect of chargeable gains accruing to him in a year of assessment during any part of which he is resident in the United Kingdom, or during which he is ordinarily resident in the United Kingdom.'

In other words, on this approach a person who succeeds in divesting themselves of the quality of residence *simpliciter* (by, perhaps, absence from the UK for an entire tax year) would, if they remain ordinarily resident here, remain within the charge to capital gains tax on any disposals made during that year.[9]

'Ordinary residence' is a term which is undefined by statute, the question whether or not a person possesses the attributes which that term signify is a question not of law but of fact. The discussion at **3.03** above concerning the determination of questions of fact is, therefore, of equal relevance whether residence *simpliciter* or ordinary residence is the attribute in question.

4.02 The meaning of ordinary residence

Although the question of whether a person is 'ordinarily residing in the UK' is a question of fact, the meaning of those words is a matter of statutory interpretation and thus a matter of law. As such, the words were given careful consideration by the Court of Session in 1926 and by the House of Lords in two leading tax cases decided in 1928. In each case the court made it clear that it was construing the words as bearing their natural and ordinary meaning.

In the case of *Reid v IRC*[10] Lord Clyde LP firmly rejected Miss Reid's argument that, even if she was resident in the UK by reason of her visits and the various ties which bound her to this country, she could not be ordinarily resident since she had always spent the greater part of each year abroad:

> 'The argument was that the meaning of the word "ordinarily" is governed – wholly or mainly – by the test of time or duration. I think it is a test, and an important one; but I think it is only one among many. From the point of view of time, "ordinarily" would stand in contrast to "casually". But [Miss Reid] is not a "casual" visitor to her home country; on the contrary she regularly returns to it, and "resides" in it for a part – albeit the smaller part – of every year. I hesitate to give the word "ordinarily" any more precise interpretation than "in the customary course of events", and anyhow I cannot think that the element of time so predominates in its meaning that, unless [Miss Reid] "resided" in the United Kingdom for at least six months and a day, she could not be said "ordinarily" to reside there in the year in question.'[11]

9 But see further **4.04** below.
10 (1926) 10 TC 673.
11 (1926) 10 TC 673 at 680.

This point was taken up in the case of *Levene v IRC*[12] by Rowlatt J who said:

> '"Ordinarily" may mean either preponderatingly in point of time or time plus importance, or it may mean habitually as a matter of course, as one might say: in the ordinary course of a man's life, although in time it might be insignificant … I think that "ordinary" does not mean preponderatingly, I think it means ordinary in the sense that it is habitual in the ordinary course of a man's life, and I think a man is ordinarily resident in the United Kingdom when the ordinary course of his life is such that it discloses a residence in the United Kingdom …'[13]

In the House of Lords, Lord Warrington of Clyffe affirmed this view, saying of ordinary residence that it is:

> '… impossible to restrict its connotation to its duration. A member of this House may well be said to be ordinarily resident in London during the Parliamentary session and in the country during the recess. If it has any definite meaning I should say it means according to the way in which a man's life is usually ordered.'[14]

In that same case, the Lord Chancellor, Viscount Cave, said:

> 'The expression "ordinary residence" … is contrasted with … occasional or temporary residence; and I think it connotes residence in a place with some degree of continuity and apart from accidental or temporary absences. So understood, the expression differs little in meaning from the word "residence" …'[15]

In *Lysaght v IRC*[16] Viscount Sumner said:

> 'I think the converse to "ordinarily" is "extraordinarily", and that part of the regular order of a man's life, adopted voluntarily and for settled purposes, is not "extraordinary".'[17]

In 1981, the words 'ordinarily resident' again fell to be construed by the courts and, in *R v Barnet London Borough, ex p Shah*,[18] Lord Denning MR said:

> 'The words "ordinarily resident" mean that the person must be habitually and normally resident here, apart from temporary or occasional absences of long or short duration.'[19]

---

12 (1928) 13 TC 486.
13 (1928) 13 TC 486 at 493.
14 (1928) 13 TC 486 at 509.
15 (1928) 13 TC 486 at 507.
16 (1928) 13 TC 511.
17 (1928) 13 TC 511 at 528.
18 [1982] 1 All ER 698.
19 [1982] 1 All ER 698 at 704.

4.03 The Genovese/Arthur syntheses

The conclusions of the House of Lords in *Shah* were summarised by Special Commissioner Clark in *Genovese v Revenue & Customs*[20] as follows:

> 'In *Shah*, the House of Lords considered the natural and ordinary meaning of the words "ordinarily resident". Lord Scarman, with whose speech the other Lords all concurred, expressed the following conclusions:
>
> (1) Following *Levene* and *Lysaght*, the words are to be construed in their natural and ordinary meaning as words of common usage in the English language (341H);
> (2) The words are not to be interpreted as comparable with domicile (343C);
> (3) They do not imply an intention to live in a place permanently or indefinitely (343E–F);
> (4) Unless the statutory framework or legal context requires a different meaning, the words refer to a person's abode in a particular country which he or she has adopted voluntarily as part of the regular order of his or her life for the time being, whether of short or long duration (343G);
> (5) The mind of the individual is relevant in two (and only two) particular respects. The residence must be voluntarily adopted, and there must be a degree of settled purpose, having sufficient continuity to be described as settled (344B–C);
> (6) The purpose, while settled, may be for a limited period, and common reasons for a choice of regular abode include education, business or profession, employment, health, family, or merely love of the place (344C);
> (7) The "real home" test is wholly inconsistent with the natural and ordinary meaning of the words as construed in *Levene* and *Lysaght* (345D);
> (8) The test requires objective examination of immediately past events, and not intention or expectation for the future (345F–H).'[21]

Lord Justice Newey, in the Court of Appeal also summarised the points derived from the cases in *Arthur v Revenue & Customs*[22] as follows;

> 'Guidance on the meaning of "ordinarily resident" can be found in three decisions of the House of Lords: *Levene v Inland Revenue Commissioners* [1928] AC 217, *Inland Revenue Commissioners v Lysaght* [1928] AC 234 and *R (Shah) v Barnet LBC* [1983] 2 AC 309. Those cases provide authority for the following propositions:
>
> (i) The expression "ordinary residence" "connotes residence in a place with some degree of continuity and apart from accidental or temporary absences" (*Levene*, at 225, per Viscount Cave LC);

20 *Genovese v Revenue & Customs* [2009] UKSPC 741.

21 *Genovese v Revenue & Customs* [2009] UKSPC 741 at para 35. The case must be approached with some caution since the appellant was unrepresented. See also the summary in *Grace v Revenue & Customs Commissioners* [2008] EWHC 2708 (Ch) at para 39(vii) to (x).

22 [2017] EWCA Civ 1756 at para 16. See **4.06** below for the facts of the case.

(ii) "[T]he converse to 'ordinarily' is 'extraordinarily' and … part of the regular order of a man's life, adopted voluntarily and for settled purposes, is not 'extraordinary'" (*Lysaght*, at 243, per Viscount Sumner). Consistently with this, "ordinarily resident" "refers to a man's abode in a particular place or country which he has adopted voluntarily and for settled purposes as part of the regular order of his life for the time being, whether of short or long duration" (*Shah*, at 343, per Lord Scarman);

(iii) "Ordinary residence" differs little from "residence" (*Levene*, at 222, per Viscount Cave LC). "Ordinarily resident" means "no more than that the residence is not casual and uncertain but that the person held to reside does so in the ordinary course of his life" (*Lysaght*, at 248, per Lord Buckmaster);

(iv) A person can be resident in a place even though "from time to time he leaves it for the purpose of business or pleasure" and, conversely, "a person who has his home abroad and visits the United Kingdom from time to time for temporary purposes without setting up an establishment in this country is not considered to be resident here" (*Levene*, at 222-223, per Viscount Cave LC);

(v) A person can also be resident in a place even though he would prefer to be elsewhere. In *Lysaght*, Lord Buckmaster said (at 248):
"A man might well be compelled to reside here completely against his will; the exigencies of business often forbid the choice of residence, and though a man may make his home elsewhere and stay in this country only because business compels him, yet none the less, if the periods for which and the conditions under which he stays are such that they may be regarded as constituting residence, as in my opinion they were in this case, it is open to the Commissioners to find that in fact he does so reside";

(vi) A person may reside in more than one place (*Levene*, at 223, per Viscount Cave LC);

(vii) "Ordinary residence" is not synonymous with "domicile" or "permanent home" (*Shah*, at 342-343 and 345, per Lord Scarman);

(viii) "Immigration status" "may or may not be a guide to a person's intention in establishing a residence in this country" (*Shah*, 348, per Lord Scarman); and

(ix) "There are two, and no more than two, respects in which the mind of the 'propositus' is important in determining ordinary residence": "[t]he residence must be voluntarily adopted" and "there must be a degree of settled purpose", which could potentially be "a specific limited purpose" (Shah, at 344 and 348, per Lord Scarman). Lord Scarman explained in Shah (at 344):
"The purpose may be one; or there may be several. It may be specific or general. All that the law requires is that there is a settled purpose. This is not to say that the 'propositus' intends to stay where he is indefinitely; indeed his purpose, while settled, may be for a limited period. Education, business or profession, employment, health, family, or merely love of the place spring to mind as common reasons for a choice of regular abode. and there may well be many others. All that is necessary is that the purpose of living where one does has a sufficient degree of continuity to be properly described as settled."'

4.04 The relation of residence to ordinary residence

Lord Denning's interpretation of the words 'ordinarily resident'[23] expands Viscount Cave's phrase 'with some degree of continuity' into 'habitually and normally' and takes ordinary residence to be residence *simpliciter* which is customary, usual and confirmed by habit. Thus, Miss Reid was ordinarily resident because the residence status she attracted to herself by reason of the regularity of her visits to the UK[24] and her various links with this country[25] was confirmed by habit as being residence of a customary and usual kind rather than residence which was exceptional, unusual or accidental.

Although Miss Reid undoubtedly had engaged in a great deal of wandering – one month in France, next month in Spain, the month after in Austria, the month after that in Portugal – the Commissioners decided no: Miss Reid every year, without fail (though only for some three and a half months) returned to the UK and it was this factor which added the quality of ordinariness to her residence *simpliciter*.

It should be noted, however, that had the regularity of Miss Reid's visits to the UK and her links with this country not, in the opinion of the Commissioners, been sufficient to imbue her with the quality of UK residence *simpliciter*, she could not, within either Viscount Sumner's, Viscount Cave's or Lord Denning's understanding of the term, have been attributed with the quality of being ordinarily resident during the years in question. In law, ordinary residence springs from residence *simpliciter*, and if residence *simpliciter* is never acquired then ordinary residence cannot be acquired either. Viscount Cave said:

> 'I find it difficult to imagine a case in which a man while not resident here is yet ordinarily resident here.'[26]

The link between ordinary residence and residence *simpliciter* in the manner described is again highlighted in the *Miesegaes* case,[27] where the Special Commissioners considered that they had:

> '… first [to] decide whether [Mr Miesegaes] was resident in the United Kingdom in each of the years in question, and, second, if he was so resident, whether his residence had the quality of ordinary residence,'[28]

and Morris LJ commented:

23 See **4.02** above.
24 See **4.02** above.
25 See **4.02** above.
26 *Levene v IRC* (1928) 13 TC 486 at 507.
27 *Miesegaes v IRC* (1957) 37 TC 493.
28 *Miesegaes v IRC* (1957) 37 TC 493 at 495.

> 'It seems to me that the Special Commissioners were correct in their approach when they decided that first they should consider whether [Mr Miesegaes] was resident in the United Kingdom in each of the years in question and, in the second place, whether his residence had the quality of ordinary residence.'[29]

TCGA 1992 s 2(1) was originally drafted on the assumption that a person may be ordinarily resident in the UK without being resident *simpliciter* here, which provides that, subject to certain exceptions:

> '... a person shall be chargeable to capital gains tax in respect of chargeable gains accruing to him in a year of assessment during any part of which he is resident in the UK, or during which he is ordinarily resident in the UK.'

The contrary is the basis for the income tax legislation discussed in **4.01** above. In *Gaines-Cooper,* it was the appellant's case that it was not possible to be ordinarily resident in the UK for any year in which one was not resident and that as the appellant was not resident in the UK for the years in question he was not ordinarily resident in those years either. The conclusions of Special Commissioners Brice and Hellier were:

> '[T]hat the Appellant was resident in the United Kingdom in the years of assessment under appeal and that his residence here was continuous in the sense that it continued from year to year. It was ordinary and part of his everyday life bearing in mind that his everyday life was far from ordinary. We are also of the view that the Appellant would still be ordinarily resident in the United Kingdom even if there were an occasional year when he was not resident here.'[30]

Little reasoning is provided in support of this proposition other than that the concept of 'ordinary residence' requires more than mere residence but connotes residence in a place with some degree of continuity and 'ordinary' means normal and part of everyday life. In *Grace*, Special Commissioner Brice decided that:

> '[If] an individual is not resident in the United Kingdom, then it is difficult to find that he is ordinarily resident here. I have concluded that the Appellant was not resident in the United Kingdom and also conclude that he was not ordinarily resident here.'[31]

On appeal, the parties agreed that the questions of residence and ordinary residence stand or fall together.[32] In *Genovese*, an unrepresented taxpayer, who was apparently resident throughout the period in question, tried unsuccessfully to argue that he was not ordinarily resident. In concluding that Mr Genovese was ordinarily resident, Special Commissioner Clark found that:

29 *Miesegaes v IRC* (1957) 37 TC 493 at 502.
30 *Gaines-Cooper v HMRC* [2006] UKSPC SPC568 at para 190.
31 *Grace v Revenue & Customs* [2008] UKSPC SPC 663 at para 49.
32 *Grace v Revenue & Customs Commissioners* [2008] EWHC 2708 (Ch) at para 1.

> '[T]he taxpayer's primary reason for his presence in the UK was employment. Mr Genovese had chosen to come to work in London, and the consequence was that he had to remain here while working for UBS until he or UBS decided that he should take up duties elsewhere. His presence in the UK for this purpose, coupled with the presence of his family and the taking up of accommodation in the London flat, did amount to voluntarily adopting an abode in the UK.'[33]

In *Tuczka v HMRC*[34] the Upper Tribunal rejected a submission that for a person to be ordinarily resident in the UK, he must have the intention of staying here permanently or at least for an indefinite period. It was argued that, if an individual intends to remain only for a limited period, his stay would be temporary which precluded a finding of ordinary residence.[35] The Upper Tribunal likewise rejected an alternative submission, that an intention to reside here for only two and a half years, or 33 months, was too short to constitute a 'settled purpose'.[36] The distinction between residence *simpliciter* and ordinary residence is not as wide or as basic as was suggested on behalf of Dr Tuczka. 'That,' said Mr Justice Roth, 'may explain why the researches of counsel found no reported tax case where residence was not in issue and the only question was whether the taxpayer was also ordinarily resident.'[37]

While these cases illustrate that as a matter of fact, residence *simpliciter* and ordinary residence will normally coincide, in the author's view they must coincide as a matter of statutory construction. The addition of the word 'ordinary' merely qualifies an existing residence *simpliciter* by the addition of certain elements. It is not a separate legal notion of residence. The First-tier Tribunal in *Carey v HMRC*[38] came to the opposite conclusion where both parties agreed that the taxpayer had ceased to be resident and only ordinary residence was in issue. The Tribunal accepted that such cases were rare but relied on the fact that TCGA 1992 sections 2 and 16 are expressed to apply to a person who is either resident or ordinarily resident. The issue arose in relation to a claim for a capital loss of £145,827 on the disposal of shares acquired by the exercise of an option over shares in his employer, to be set off against the corresponding employment income of £145,827 arising in that year from the exercise of the option. Such relief was only available under ITA 2007 section 131 if he was ordinarily resident. On 4 January 2011 Mr Carey informally left his UK employment to embark on what he described as sabbatical leave without pay and then left the UK on 15 January 2011 to take up a post in Rwanda to work in impoverished areas of the developing world. He did so until

33 *Genovese v Revenue & Customs* [2009] UKSPC 741 at para 42.

34 *Tuczka v Revenue & Customs* [2011] UKUT 113 (TCC). The converse may be true however. In *Megwa v Revenue & Customs* [2010] UKFTT 543 (TC), the taxpayer intended to make the UK his home and became ordinarily resident (and resident) on the day he moved there with his family.

35 At para 16.

36 At para 17.

37 At para 18.

38 *Carey v HMRC* [2015] UKFTT 0466 (TC).

10 April 2012 after which he set up his own business in East Africa. He did not return to the UK at all in the 2011/12 tax year but said that he intended to do so for social reasons. Formal employment with his UK employer terminated on 11 December 2011. There was no evidence that he ever returned to the UK. The decision is wrong both in principle and on the facts. The assumption on which TCGA 1992 section 2(1) is drafted is erroneous. Although a person cannot be ordinarily resident in the UK unless they are also resident *simpliciter* here, a person may, in certain circumstances be resident *simpliciter* in the UK, year after year, without being ordinarily resident here. Those circumstances will subsist where a person's residence *simpliciter* lacks one or more of the elements emphasised by Lord Scarman when he said:

> 'I unhesitatingly subscribe to the view that 'ordinarily resident' refers to a man's abode in a particular place or country which he has adopted voluntarily and for settled purposes as part of the regular order of his life for the time being, whether of short or long duration.'[39]

It is to these three key features of voluntary adoption, settled purpose and the regular order of life – none of which is essential to the acquisition of residence *simpliciter* status but all of which are essential to the acquisition of ordinary residence status – that we must now turn our attention.

4.05 A voluntarily adopted place of abode

It is clear from the facts of the case in which Viscount Sumner gave his interpretation of the words 'ordinarily residing' that he cannot have used the words 'adopted voluntarily' in the sense of 'free of any kind of external constraint' for Mr Lysaght was in Great Britain only because his business commitments compelled him to be here. He would, no doubt, have preferred to be at home in Ireland rather than in the Spa Hotel in Bath, but in choosing to be a director of John Lysaght Ltd he had accepted that he would have to spend one week or so of each month in the UK. The phrase 'adopted voluntarily' must, therefore, have been understood by Viscount Sumner as being not inconsistent with submission to such constraints as a person's chosen order of life imposed upon him.

On the face of it, however, the first case which came before the courts following the *Lysaght* case and which centred on the phrase 'adopted voluntarily' took the meaning of those words some way beyond that. It concerned Miss Mackenzie, an Australian, who, at the age of 28, came on a visit to England with her mother. There was no evidence as to how long the visit was intended to last but, in the event, Miss Mackenzie, having stayed here four months, remained here until her death at the age of 82 because, after spending

39 *Shah v Barnet London Borough Council* [1983] 1 All ER 226 at 235.

those four months here, she was, in 1885, certified as insane and detained, first in Holloway Mental Hospital until 1893, then in the Coppice Lunatic Hospital at Nottingham until her death. The case was an estate duty case which arose because of a disagreement over the meaning of the words 'ordinarily resident' in F(No 2)A 1915 section 47(1), and counsel for the administrator of Miss Mackenzie's estate submitted that:

> 'Miss Mackenzie could not be said to be ordinarily resident in September, 1885, when she was certified as of unsound mind, and that during the whole of the rest of her life she was under constraint and unable to exercise any will of her own, and that that period, the last 54 years of her life, cannot be taken into account at all as making her ordinarily resident in this country … [T]he words of Viscount Sumner "adopted voluntarily" indicate that no residence can be treated as ordinary residence unless it is the result of a voluntary act on the part of the person residing there.'[40]

Morton J could not agree:

> 'The matter does not wholly depend on choice … I do not understand Viscount Sumner … as saying that a period of residence in this country which is involuntary must be wholly disregarded for the purpose of ascertaining whether or not a person is ordinarily resident, and it must not be left out of account that Miss Mackenzie came to this country, one presumes, voluntarily at the age of 28, and, as a result of the circumstances … described, never left it.'[41]

Morton J then went on to comment on some hypothetical case submitted by counsel for the administrator of Miss Mackenzie's estate:

> 'They put the case of a prisoner of war who has come to this country and been detained here, it might be, for a year. They say that he would not be ordinarily resident, because the element of constraint is present. They take again the case of a foreigner with a home abroad, who comes to this country on a visit and commits some crime or offence against the laws of this country, and is imprisoned for a considerable time, and ultimately dies in this country. There, they say, he would not be held to be ordinarily resident … [S]uch cases must be dealt with on their particular facts, if and when they arise, but I can well imagine, in the case of a prisoner of war, that, if a man had a permanent residence in Germany and came over here in an aeroplane to attack this country, and was captured and kept here for a considerable period, it might well be held that his ordinary residence was his home in Germany.[42]

Comparing Morton J's judgment as regards Miss Mackenzie and his views on the hypothetical case of the German prisoner of war, it is clear that it was in Miss Mackenzie's initial voluntary entry to the UK for an indefinite period

40 *Re Mackenzie* (1940) 19 ATC 399 at 402 and 403.

41 *Re Mackenzie* (1940) 19 ATC 399 at 403 and 404.

42 *Re Mackenzie* (1940) 19 ATC 399 at 403 and 404.

that he found a justification for holding her to have been ordinarily resident here throughout all the years which followed. What he seems to have been saying is that the words are 'voluntarily adopted' not 'voluntarily continued and pursued'. If the beginning is a voluntary matter it is of no consequence that the continuance is enforced. Thus, the hypothetical German could not be ordinarily resident in the UK since his initial entry to this country would not be a matter of free will but of military orders emanating from those in command over him. Indeed, during the 1939–45 war, members of the allied forces who became resident in the UK were generally treated by the Inland Revenue as not ordinarily resident and so, too, were refugees and displaced persons.

This understanding of Viscount Sumner's words seems perfectly reasonable and the implicit rephrasing of 'adopted voluntarily' as 'adopted (but not necessarily continued) voluntarily' does them no violence.

It has been suggested, however, that in *Shah v Barnet London Borough Council*[43] Lord Scarman rejected this approach and, despite his explicit acceptance of the authority of Viscount Sumner's dictum,[44] so qualified Viscount Sumner's words as to rob them of any meaning. What Lord Scarman said was this:

> 'The residence must be voluntarily adopted. Enforced presence by reason of kidnapping or imprisonment, or a Robinson Crusoe existence on a desert island with no opportunity of escape, may be so overwhelming a factor as to negative the will to be where one is.'[45]

The relation of the second sentence to the first in this quotation is by no means clear, but if, as one writer has suggested,[46] it is to be taken as meaning that:

> '… to be ordinarily resident an individual must have adopted his residence voluntarily, except for extreme cases such as imprisonment or a desert island existence with no opportunity to escape where the imposed circumstances will override the individual's intention,'

then 'adopted (but not necessarily continued) voluntarily' has become 'adopted voluntarily or involuntarily', which is a quite different matter. It is suggested that the correct approach to Lord Scarman's second sentence must be to take it as a list of circumstances in which a place of abode will be involuntarily adopted and in which, accordingly, the attribution of ordinary residence will *not* ensue. This alternative way of reading Lord Scarman's remarks implies the insertion of a perfectly logical additional sentence between the two quoted so that the passage reads as follows:

---

43 [1983] 1 All ER 226.

44 See **4.04** above.

45 *Shah v Barnet London Borough Council* [1983] 1 All ER 226 at 235.

46 J L Wosner, 'Ordinary Residence, the Law and Practice' [1983] *British Tax Review* 347 at 348.

> 'The residence must be voluntarily adopted. [Only if a person is where he is because at some point he has chosen to be there can the kind of residence known as ordinary residence ensue; but being where one is is not always a matter of choice.] Enforced presence by reason of kidnapping or imprisonment, or a Robinson Crusoe existence on a desert island with no opportunity of escape, may be so overwhelming a factor as to negative the will to be where one is.'

The *Mackenzie* case discussed above is not the only case where, on the face of it, the court appeared to set aside Viscount Sumner's requirement that residence must be voluntarily adopted before it can become ordinary residence. *Miesegaes v IRC*[47] concerned the residence status of Stanley Miesegaes who, during the years 1947/48 to 1951/52, had been a schoolboy boarding at Harrow. Counsel for Mr Miesegaes argued that even if Mr Miesegaes had been resident *simpliciter* in the UK during those years, such residence could not have constituted ordinary residence because it had not been voluntary residence; it had been institutional. Pearce LJ could not accept that argument. Referring to Viscount Sumner's interpretation of the words 'ordinarily resident' which he later quoted, he said:

> 'Education is too extensive and universal a phase to justify such descriptions as "unusual" and "extraordinary" ... The argument based on the institutional or compulsory nature of a boy's life at school is misleading. The compulsion is merely the will of his parents who voluntarily send him to that school. It would be hazardous, and in my opinion irrelevant, to investigate whether adolescents are residing voluntarily where their lot is cast and how far they approve of their parents' choice of a home or school.'[48]

Far from constituting a rejection of Viscount Sumner's test, however, those words are a strong affirmation of it. Pearce LJ is saying not that one can set aside Viscount Sumner's words but that, in order to give them due weight in circumstances where the person concerned is not a person of full capacity, one must have regard to the will of the person's parents, trustees or guardians in determining whether or not his place of abode has been adopted voluntarily. That is because, in law, an *incapax* has no will but the will of those who are legally responsible for him.[49] Accordingly, during the years 1947/48 to 1951/52, Stanley Miesegaes was ordinarily resident in Harrow because he was resident *simpliciter* in Harrow for each of those years for the settled purpose of being educated and cared for there and Harrow had been voluntarily adopted *by his father* (who, until his death on 10 July 1948, had custody and control of Stanley at all material times) as Stanley's place of abode.

---

47 (1957) 37 TC 493.

48 (1957) 37 TC 493 at 501.

49 Had this principle been invoked in the *Mackenzie* case, Miss Mackenzie's ordinary residence status could have been established on grounds far more convincing than those on which it was established.

These two principles concerning the ordinary residence status of a person who, in law, has no will of his own were brought together in the case of *R v Waltham Forest London Borough Council, ex p Vale*.[50] Judith Vale, a severely mentally handicapped child born in London in 1956, was, in 1961, moved by her parents to Dublin where, because of her handicap, she was, until May 1984, boarded at various rural community homes. The last of these was Camp Hill at Wexford. In 1978, her parents returned to England and took up residence in the London Borough of Waltham Forest, visiting Judith two or three times a year. In 1984, Judith became so severely disturbed that, on 6 May, her parents brought her from Ireland to live with them until such time as she could be accommodated at Stoke Place, a residential home in Buckinghamshire. In the event, Judith was placed there just one month later on 6 June 1984. Judith's parents sought the funding of this placement from the London borough in which they lived but this was refused on the ground that Judith was not ordinarily resident within the borough at the time of her placement in the home in Buckinghamshire and that, under the National Assistance Act 1948 section 24(1), this relieved the borough of responsibility. Judith's parents sought a judicial review of that decision and Taylor J held that:

> 'Where the propositus … is so mentally handicapped as to be totally dependent upon a parent or guardian, the concept of her having an independent ordinary residence of her own which she has adopted voluntarily and for which she has a settled purpose does not arise. She is in the same position as a small child. Her ordinary residence is that of her parents because that is her "base" … It may well be that if the parents delegate their guardianship of her to a school or home for greater or shorter periods she will acquire a second ordinary residence at that establishment … It may well be therefore that in the present case Judith, although ordinarily resident with her parents throughout, had a second ordinary residence at Camp Hill for the duration of her stay there, and again acquired a second ordinary residence when she went to Stoke Place. For the period May to June 1984, however, she had only one ordinary residence: at home.'[51]

It would seem to be established, therefore, that an infant or incapacitated person will be ordinarily resident wherever his parents, trustees or guardians are ordinarily resident and, if the person resides elsewhere in accordance with the will of those having legal responsibility for him and as part of the settled order of his life, in that other place also. In cases where there is no incapacity, however, a person's residence must be voluntarily adopted by the person himself before it can acquire the character of ordinary residence.

---

50 11 February 1985, QB. Unreported except in (1985) *The Times*, 25 February.
51 (1985) *The Times*, 25 February, QB.

4.06 Settled purposes

In *Shah v Barnet London Borough Council*,[52] Lord Scarman said that ordinary residence was dependent not only on a person's voluntary adoption of an abode in some place or country, but also on:

> '... a degree of settled purpose. The purpose may be one or there may be several. It may be specific or general. All the law requires is that there is a settled purpose. This is not to say that the propositus intends to stay where he is indefinitely; indeed his purpose, while settled, may be for a limited period. Education, business or profession, employment, health, family or mere love of the place spring to mind as common reasons for a choice of regular abode. And there may well be many others. All that is necessary is that the purpose of living where one does has a sufficient degree of continuity to be properly described as settled.[53]

In *Reid v IRC*,[54] the settled purpose of Miss Reid in spending some three and a half months in the UK each year was chiefly, it seems, to visit her homeland and her sister.

In *Lysaght v IRC*,[55] the settled purpose of Mr Lysaght's three months' residence in the UK each year was business. He came here to attend directors' meetings of John Lysaght Ltd and to deal with business matters arising in connection with that company.

In *Levene v IRC*,[56] the settled purposes of Mr Levene's regular periods of residence in the UK were to obtain medical advice, to visit relatives, to take part in Jewish religious observances, to visit the graves of his parents and to deal with his tax affairs.

In *Reed v Clark*,[57] the settled purpose of Dave Clark in going to Los Angeles and staying there throughout the tax year 1978/79 was to work there and to avoid a UK tax liability on income of $450,000. In his judgment of the case, Nicholls J said:

> 'Artificial tax avoidance schemes do not find much favour with the courts today. In this case the position, as I see it, is that when deciding issues of residence, ordinary residence and occasional residence all the reasons (including any desire to avoid a liability to UK income tax) underlying a person's being in a particular place are part of the overall picture. They are part of the material to be looked at and considered when deciding those issues. The presence of a tax avoidance intention may help to show, for instance, why a person went abroad at all, or at the particular time he did, how long he intended to remain away, or where his home in fact was in the year of assessment. But residence abroad for a carefully chosen limited period of work there

52 [1983] 1 All ER 226.
53 [1983] 1 All ER 226 at 235.
54 (1926) 10 TC 673.
55 (1928) 13 TC 511.
56 (1928) 13 TC 486.
57 [1985] STC 323.

> … is no less residence abroad for that period just because the major reason for it was the avoidance of tax. Likewise with ordinary residence.'[58]

Although the cases cited above provide examples of settled purposes, they provide no detailed explanation of the term itself. Thus, the question what is meant by 'settled purpose' remained unanswered until it came to the fore in the case of *Shah v Barnet London Borough Council*.[59] That case concerned the eligibility of students for local authority grants in connection with their education. Such eligibility depends on whether or not a student is 'ordinarily resident' in the UK; but, in the Education Act 1962, as in the Taxes Acts, the term 'ordinarily resident' is undefined. Several of the education authorities involved tried to suggest that education could not be a settled purpose for the purposes of establishing ordinary residence and that, to establish a settled purpose:

> '… there must be shown an intention to live here on a permanent basis as part of the general community; if a person's presence here was for a 'specific or limited purpose only', eg to pursue a course of study, he would not be ordinarily resident.'[60]

Lord Scarman, however, firmly rebutted that suggestion:

> 'A man's settled purpose will be different at different ages. Education in adolescence or early adulthood can be as settled a purpose as a profession or business in later years … study can be as settled a purpose as business or pleasure. And the notion of permanent or indefinitely enduring purpose as an element in ordinary residence derives not from the natural and ordinary meaning of the words "ordinarily resident" but from a confusion of it with domicile.'[61]

Earlier,[62] Lord Scarman had said, 'all that is necessary is that the purpose of living where one does has a sufficient degree of continuity to be properly described as settled'. A settled purpose is, therefore, a purpose which, though it need not provide a person with a motivation for becoming permanently or indefinitely present in a particular place, will provide him with the motivation to be more than transitorily or fleetingly present there. The purpose must, in other words, have a certain intrinsic durability. The difference between the two kinds of purpose may be illustrated by contrasting the motivation of the man who takes a holiday in the Cotswolds with that of the man who makes being in the Cotswolds part of his life; or the motivation of the woman who pays a visit to her invalid mother with that of the woman who makes caring for her invalid mother part of her life. In the first of both cases, the purpose is

58 [1985] STC 323 at 346.
59 [1983] 1 All ER 226.
60 [1983] 1 All ER 226 at 237.
61 [1983] 1 All ER 226 at 236, 238 and 239.
62 [1983] 1 All ER 226 at 235.

essentially transitory and results in a deviation from the person's normal mode of life; but in the second of both cases the purpose has an inbuilt element of continuity which results in the normal mode of life itself being modified so as to accommodate the presence of the person in the place in question. In either case the purpose which possesses an intrinsic element of continuity may, of course, be terminated very shortly after the mode of life has been altered to accommodate that purpose: the man may discover a preferred alternative to the Cotswolds and may further modify his mode of life so as to exclude presence in the Cotswolds and allow for presence in Tenerife; and the woman's mother may die. But in neither case can the early termination of the purpose change the settled nature it once possessed or retrospectively divest the person of the ordinary residence status to which it will have given rise.

How small a degree of continuity of purpose is needed for a purpose to be settled is well illustrated in *University College London v Newman*.[63] Edward Newman was a New Zealand citizen who, in 1977, left New Zealand and, after travelling extensively, arrived in the European Community in August 1978 whereupon, using France as his base, he became,

> '... a rather aimless drifter who has spent his time in what is inelegantly but descriptively called colloquially "bumming" around Europe.'[64]

In October 1983, however, he embarked upon a degree course at University College London and claimed to be eligible for lower rate fees on the grounds of having been ordinarily resident within the European Community during the course of the three years ended 1 September 1983 within the terms of the Education (Fees and Awards) Regulations 1983 Sch 2(2). In the Westminster County Court, McDonnell J held that he had not been ordinarily resident as claimed, but, in the Court of Appeal, his judgment was reversed. Croom-Johnson LJ said that Mr Newman,

> '... had been living in the EC for the necessary three years. But was he "ordinarily resident"? He has put down roots nowhere. He used France "as my base for travelling". He went from country to country, in short spells, returning again and again. His work record is spasmodic, and was described by the judge as "the token effort required to ensure that he receives social security payments".'[65]

Nevertheless, Croom-Johnson LJ concluded that if McDonnell J had asked himself 'Has Mr Newman been shown to have been ordinarily resident in the EEC for the three qualifying years'? and had he applied Lord Scarman's test (ie had Mr Newman's purpose of living where he did a sufficient degree of continuity to be properly described as settled?), the answer would have

63 CA, 19 December 1985. Unreported except in (1986) *The Times*, 8 January.

64 (1986) *The Times*, 8 January, CA.

65 (1986) *The Times*, 8 January, CA.

to be 'yes … Mr Newman was ordinarily resident, after his casual fashion, somewhere in the EC for the whole of the qualifying three years'.[66]

It was accepted in the Court of Appeal that Mr Newman had not been ordinarily resident in any particular European Community Member State during the three-year period, but that is not relevant to the point being made. On the basis of the court's judgment, Mr Newman would have been ordinarily resident in the UK had he confined himself to merely 'bumming around' England, Scotland, Wales and Northern Ireland. 'Bumming around' may be a settled purpose.

In *Turberville v HMRC*[67] the appellant, born in Aberdeen, was a successful senior executive in the oil industry whose career had taken him from New Zealand in 1979 through Saudi Arabia, Malaysia, Nigeria, the US and the UK among others. He was sent to the UK by Shell in February 1997 and worked for them there until October 1998. He left them for a Dallas-based group but after a short break he was based in the UK for them until the beginning of July 2001 when he went to Dallas. He lost his job in Dallas at the end of October 2002 that would contractually have continued until June 2004. A consulting agreement required him to help in the UK until 31 January 2003, which in practice ended in November 2002. He had rented an apartment in Monaco from 1 December 2002, acquiring a *carte de sejour* there. He travelled between the UK and Monaco on five occasions between 27 November 2002 and 4 January 2003, finally driving to Monaco on 9 January 2003. Although he was ordinarily resident in the UK by July 2001, he was found to have lost that status when he left on 1 July 2001 (although this was only effective for the tax year 2002/03 since the 2001/02 year could not be split). The time he spent in the UK after October 2002 cannot be treated as part of a pattern starting from his residence in the UK before going to Dallas. It was held to be physical presence that was no more than a stop-gap measure.

Voluntarily adopted residence in the UK is itself insufficient to constitute ordinary residence. The individual must also have a settled purpose. In *Ward v HMRC*,[68] the taxpayer was an Australian citizen, seconded to London to work for a UK company within an Australian banking group until March 2009. For personal reasons, he asked to extend his secondment to June 2009. His employer agreed, but he was required to vacate his company-provided accommodation. His work permit was extended for six months. Then his intention was to move back to Australia at the end of the extended secondment and his furniture and other personal effects, including his car, were sent to Australia in anticipation of his return. Due to illness in his girlfriend's family, and his girlfriend becoming pregnant, he requested and was granted a further extension to April 2010 on the basis that he would both revert to working for an Australian group company and transfer back to the Australian payroll, from July 2009. He applied for an

66 (1986) *The Times*, 8 January, CA.
67 *Turberville v HMRC* [2010] UKFTT 69 (TC).
68 *Ward v HMRC* [2016] UKFTT 0114 (TC).

extension of his work permit to October 2010. He married in September 2010, and returned to Australia in January 2011. The First-tier Tribunal ruled that although he remained voluntarily in the UK during the tax years 2009/10 and 2010/11, he did not have a sufficient settled purpose to be part of the ordinary pattern of his life. Thus Mr Ward was resident but not ordinarily resident for those years.

In contrast, another peripatetic Australian who came to work in the UK, where he lived with his family during the three years in which his status was disputed, was found to be ordinarily resident. In *Mackay v HMRC*,[69] Mr Mackay had voluntarily, but reluctantly, come to the UK to work. His work required a substantial amount of travel. His engagement involved a series of short-term projects, could be summarily terminated and two prospective sales of the business made his work precarious. He also decided, before coming to the UK, that he would, in any event, leave the UK within three years, even if this meant resigning. The First-tier Tribunal found that the UK was his base both for work and domestically.[70] He had a settled purpose of fulfilling the duties of his employment which was sufficient to make him ordinarily resident. The Tribunal accepted that the purpose for which an individual is in the UK can change and that different purposes should not necessarily be looked at together over a period.[71] Employment here was a single purpose. A temporary purpose in the context of employment was described as 'something intended, planned or expected to be much shorter than 18 months, not something which merely might be shorter.'[72] After reviewing various time periods in several decisions, Judge Hellier held that the period for which Mr Mackay intended or expected to be in the UK from the beginning of 2005 was sufficient to be settled, with the result that he was ordinarily resident in all three years.[73]

4.07 Regular order of life

Given that a person voluntarily adopts the UK as a place of abode and comes here in pursuit of one or more settled purposes, over what period must they be present here in pursuit of those purposes before their presence becomes part of the 'regular order' of their life and before they can thus be attributed with ordinary residence status? The body of case law preceding the *Shah* case[74] had suggested that the answer is three or more years – not because any of the judges hearing the cases concerned had declared that that was the required period but because, in every instance, the appellants had, in fact, visited the UK in three or more consecutive years before the Revenue chose to assert that the

69 *Mackay v HMRC* [2017] UKFTT 0441 (TC).
70 *Mackay v HMRC* [2017] UKFTT 0441 (TC), at para 126.
71 *Mackay v HMRC* [2017] UKFTT 0441 (TC), at para 116.
72 *Mackay v HMRC* [2017] UKFTT 0441 (TC), at para 134.
73 *Mackay v HMRC* [2017] UKFTT 0441 (TC), at paras 137 and 138.
74 *Shah v Barnet London Borough Council* [1983] 1 All ER 226 at 236.

status of ordinary residence had been acquired and before the Commissioners (subsequently supported by the courts) upheld its assertion that that was so. The point was crisply made by First-tier Tribunal Judge Clark in *Tuczka v HMRC*[75] that:

> '[T]he suggestion … that a longer period of time would be necessary to establish that a pattern of residence had become "habitual" is not consistent with the authorities. …We feel that the examination of the "three-year practice" in paragraph 3.9 of HMRC's booklet IR20 and the search for some form of linkage between that and the background law led to an over-emphasis on the question of the length of … stay in the UK. It is clear that Lord Scarman's reference in *Shah* (at 342) to Lord Denning's use of the expression "habitually and normally resident here" was intended to emphasise two features mentioned by Viscount Sumner in *Lysaght*, namely residence adopted voluntarily and for settled purposes; the word "habitually" did not imply a period of time, but related to the quality of the manner of residence in the UK.'

Where the settled purpose involves not merely visits to the UK but continuous presence here, a person's presence in the UK will necessarily have become part of the regular order of his life after only a few days have elapsed, and – just as early termination or fulfilment of the purpose will not retrospectively rob that purpose of any settled nature it possessed[76] – early termination or fulfilment of the purpose will not prevent the person's presence here from being presence as part of the regular order of his life. In the *Shah* case, Lord Scarman had said:

> 'If there be proved a regular, habitual mode of life in a particular place, the continuity of which has persisted despite temporary absences, ordinary residence is established provided only it is adopted voluntarily and for a settled purpose.'[77]

Likewise, in *Reed v Clark*,[78] Nicholls J was satisfied that a period of just over a year abroad was not too short a period for a person to have established an ordinary residence overseas.

The test which Nicholls J would (following Lord Scarman) seem to have been applying, however, was: did the period of residence in question, however long or short, represent an intrusion into or a deviation from the person's regular and habitual mode of life, or was it, in fact, a component part of the person's regular and habitual mode of life for the time being? If it was intrusive or deviatory it could not be ordinary residence, but if it was a component part of the normal pattern it could not be other than ordinary residence.

This would seem to bring the matter round full circle. In the *Levene* case, Lord Hanworth had said:

---

75 *Tuczka v HMRC* [2010] UKFTT 53 (TC) at para 55. Upheld by the Upper Tribunal [2011] UKUT 113 (TCC) at para 14.

76 See **4.06** above.

77 *Shah v Barnet London Borough Council* [1983] 1 All ER 226 at 236.

78 [1985] STC 323.

> 'I find it difficult to attach any distinction of meaning to the word "ordinarily" as affecting the term "resident", unless it be to prevent facts which would amount to residence being so estimated on the ground that they arose from some fortuitous cause, such as illness of the so-called resident or of some other person, which demanded his continuance at a place for a special purpose otherwise than in accordance with his own usual arrangements and shaping of his movements ...'[79]

In other words, residence always will be ordinary residence unless it either lacks settled purpose or is enforced. That was the stance of the courts in 1928 and that, despite Revenue insistence (not always to the taxpayer's detriment) during the intervening years that ordinary residence necessitates the establishment of an annually recurrent pattern of residence *simpliciter*, has now been affirmed by the courts as being their stance today.

One further point must be made. Viscount Cave,[80] Lord Denning[81] and Lord Scarman[82] all made reference to the irrelevance of temporary absences in the context of the 'regular order of life' which is under discussion here. What each was saying is that once a person has, by reason of his voluntary presence in the UK in pursuit of one or more settled purposes, made his presence here part of the regular order of his life for the time being and thus attracted to himself the status of ordinary residence, his absence from the UK will not affect that status provided that the absences are temporary, occasional or accidental. It is worth observing that this principle of disregarding temporary absences provides additional support for the proposition that a person who makes voluntary regular visits to the UK in pursuit of settled purposes is ordinarily resident here. If the periods between visits are treated as temporary absences from the UK and are disregarded, the visitor's periodic presence in the UK is, effectively, transformed into a continuous presence. In *Karim v HMRC*[83] the taxpayer, who had moved to Portugal, could not substantiate first, that she was in the UK because of her mother's illness or, secondly, that she was here to wind up her affairs and thus her visits were not transient or to supply passing needs.

Ordinary residence is not in contrast to 'occasional' residence. It is enough that the residence 'is not casual and uncertain but that the person held to reside does so in the ordinary course of his life'. In *Arthur v Revenue And Customs*,[84] Mr and Mrs Arthur married in Ghana in 2008. At the time, Mrs Arthur was living in the UK and her husband in Ghana. He visited his UK resident wife and children intermittently and worked for a period and claimed the Jobseekers Allowance while living with his wife in the UK. He had obtained indefinite leave to remain in the UK and was registered to vote. This was sufficient to

79 *Levene v IRC* (1928) 13 TC 486 at 496.
80 *Levene v IRC* (1928) 13 TC 486 at 507.
81 *R v Barnet London Borough, ex p Shah* [1982] 1 All ER 698 at 704.
82 *Shah v Barnet London Borough Council* [1983] 1 All ER 226 at 236.
83 *Karim v HMRC* [2009] UKFTT 368 (TC) at para 40.
84 *Arthur v Revenue & Customs* [2017] EWCA Civ 1756.

conclude that Mr Arthur was 'ordinarily resident' at the relevant time since a 'settled purpose' can be 'a specific limited purpose', for 'a limited period' and adopted 'for the time being, whether of short or long duration.' This was the case even if visits to the UK were for special occasions (the birth of his daughter, helping his wife to move house, the birth of his son), and to help take care of their children.[85]

4.08 Unlawful residence

It has already been explained that residence is a question of fact not of law[86] so that, unless an Act contains specific provision to the contrary, residence does not need to be lawful for it to be residence which is voluntarily adopted and for a settled purpose as part of the regular order of a person's life. Thus although a deserting seaman who is living in the UK in breach of the immigration laws could not be ordinarily resident here for the purposes of the Commonwealth Immigration Acts since those Acts make specific provision to that effect,[87] he may be ordinarily resident here for tax purposes since the Taxes Acts contain no such prohibiting provision. The principle underlying these rules is that a person who would appear to be ordinarily resident to anyone observing the way in which he is living but who is not entitled lawfully so to live cannot be allowed to benefit from his apparent status but 'for the purposes of taxation he will not be allowed to deny his apparent status'.[88] This, according to Oliver LJ in *R v Secretary of State for Home Department, ex p Margueritte*[89] made 'good common sense'.

4.09 Dual or no ordinary residence

An individual may be ordinarily resident in two places at one and the same time was established in bankruptcy law in *Re Norris, ex p Reynolds*[90] and has been admitted in tax law also:

> 'I am not sure there is anything impossible in a person "ordinarily residing" in two places.'[91]

85 *Arthur v Revenue & Customs* [2017] EWCA Civ 1756 at paras 31 and 32.
86 See **4.02** above.
87 *Re Abdul Manan* [1971] 2 All ER 1016.
88 *R v Barnet London Borough Council, ex p Shah* [1982] 1 All ER 698 at 706, per Eveleigh LJ.
89 [1982] 3 All ER 909.
90 *Re Norris, ex p Reynolds* (1888) 4 TLR 452.
91 *Reid v IRC* (1926) 10 TC 673 at 680, per Lord Clyde LP.

> 'I think … that a man can have two ordinary residences not because he commonly is to be found at those places, but because the ordinary course of his life is such that he acquires the attribute of residence at those two places.'[92]

That a person may be ordinarily resident in two countries at the same time was confirmed by the House of Lords in *Shah*.[93]

That a person may be ordinarily resident nowhere was affirmed in *University College London v Newman*.[94] Croom-Johnston LJ said:

> 'I agree that it is possible for someone to be ordinarily resident nowhere. People who spend their lives sailing about the world are such. So are the well-known class of tax-evaders who move on from country to country, always one move ahead of the tax man.'[95]

4.10 HMRC practice

HMRC provides limited comment on the meaning of ordinary residence in their National Insurance Manual, preferring to refer to the ordinary meaning of the term as discussed by the courts in relation to income tax.[96] They emphasise that whether an individual person is 'ordinarily resident' is a question of fact and will depend on the particular facts of the case. They also observe that an individual may be ordinarily resident in two places at the same.[97] They offer the following non-exhaustive list of factors in the case of a person leaving or coming to the UK:

- Will the person be returning to Great Britain or Northern Ireland during the period of employment abroad?
- Will the person's family – spouse/partner and/or children – be staying in the UK?
- Will the person retain a home in Great Britain or Northern Ireland during their period abroad?
- If the person retains a home, will it be available for their use when they return?
- Will the person be returning to Great Britain or Northern Ireland at the end of the period abroad?

---

92 *Levene v IRC* (1928) 13 TC 486 at 494, per Rowlatt J.

93 *R v Barnet LBC, ex parte Shah* [1983] 2 AC 309 at p 342.

94 CA, 19 December 1985. Unreported except in (1986) *The Times*, 8 January.

95 (1986) *The Times*, 8 January, CA. See also *Turberville v HMRC* [2010] UKFTT 69 (TC) at para 9, which involved a peripatetic executive rather than a tax-evader.

96 NIM33555.

97 NIM33560. See **4.09**.

Answering yes to any, or all, of the above questions, they say, is an indicator the individual remains 'ordinarily resident'. Answers of no would indicate it is less likely that the person will remain ordinarily resident.

They may also consider;

- How long has the person lived in Great Britain or Northern Ireland prior to going abroad?
- What will be the purpose(s) of any return visit(s)?98

98 NIM33560.

CHAPTER 5

Residence of trusts and estates

Introduction

5.01 A trust is, in law, a relationship rather than a person. It is the equitable obligation which is created when one person (the settlor) transfers assets (the trust property) to another person (the trustee) who is to hold, control and deal with those assets for the benefit of third parties (the beneficiaries) of whom the trustee himself may be one and any one of whom may enforce the obligation. If the trust is created by the settlor *inter vivos* it is usually referred to as a settlement and the trust property is known as settled property.

Residence, on the other hand, is a personal attribute – a quality that a person attracts to himself by virtue of the strength of his association with a particular place or country. The liability to tax in relation to trusts is by reference to the persons concerned as a result. In the case of the trustees, their personal residence will thus determine their fiscal affiliation as the representative owners of the trust property.

Prior to Finance Act 2006 the position was unsystematic and problematic where there were resident and non-resident trustees. Different rules applied for income tax and capital gains tax. In relation to income tax, in *Dawson v IRC*[1] the House of Lords ruled that, where the general administration of the trust was ordinarily carried on outside the UK and a majority of the trustees were non-resident, a UK-resident trustee was not assessable under Schedule D in respect of income derived from sources outside the UK. It was held that the trust income did not accrue to an individual trustee in his personal capacity and that the trustee had no right of control over it except, in conjunction with the co-trustees, to see that it was applied in accordance with the terms of the trust.[2]

1 [1989] STC 473.
2 [1989] STC 473 at 479, per Lord Keith.

Finance Act 2006[3] aimed at a structured and systematic treatment of the subject. For the first time it made the tests to be applied to determine the residence status of the trustees of a settlement identical for income tax and capital gains tax. The present rules in ITA 2007 sections 474–476 for income tax are effective from 5 April 2007 and follow the latest efforts of the Tax Law Rewrite Project, replacing the wording in FA 2006. The capital gains tax equivalent provisions are TCGA 1992 section 69(1) and (2).

The Finance Act 2006 also provided that the trustees of a settlement are to be treated as a single person for the purposes of the Taxes Act unless the context requires otherwise. Also, the meaning of 'settled property' and, for most purposes, of 'settlement' and 'settlor' are now identical for the two taxes.

Trusts

5.02 Residence

The new rules start by bestowing a collective legal personality on the trustees. Thus, the trustees of a settlement are to be treated as a single 'deemed person' for the purposes of the Taxes Act unless the context requires otherwise.[4] If different parts of the settled property in relation to a settlement are vested in different bodies of trustees, the residence rules still apply in relation to the different bodies as if they were all one body.[5] As part of the process of rationalisation and simplification, the meaning of 'settled property' and, for most purposes, of 'settlement' and 'settlor', are also identical for the two taxes.

5.03 Single residence trustees

Where all the trustees are resident in the UK, the position is straightforward. The trustees (ie the 'deemed person') is treated for income tax and capital gains tax purposes as resident and ordinarily resident in the UK. Where all the trustees are not resident in the UK, then conversely the trustees are neither resident nor ordinarily resident in the UK.

5.04 Mixed residence trustees

Where there are trustees who are resident and trustees who are non-resident in the UK, then the residence of the persons who comprise the deemed person

3 Sch 13 (income tax) and Pt 1 of Sch 12 (capital gains tax).
4 ITA 2007 s 474(1).
5 ITA 2007 s 474(2).

does not determine the residence of that deemed person. The focus of attention shifts to the settlor. This is the case where at least one trustee is resident in the UK and at least one is not. If there is at least one of each, then it does not matter how many more trustees may be resident or non-resident. Thus, a majority of non-resident trustees does not make the deemed person non-resident, and neither does a majority of resident trustees make for a resident trust.

Instead, the residence of the deemed person is decided by whether the settlor was resident or (prior to 6 April 2025) domiciled in the UK at the 'relevant time'.[6] From that date the test is by reference only to the residence of the settlor at the relevant time.[7] Ordinary residence is also a factor for settlements made before the 2013/14 year.[8] If, at a time when the settlor made the settlement (or is treated for income tax or capital gains tax purposes as making the settlement) the settlor was UK resident (or prior to 6 April 2025 domiciled in the UK), then the trustees are resident in the UK from the time the settlement is made.[9]

A transfer of property between settlements can affect the residence of the trustees. Thus, if there is a transfer of property between settlements, and a settlor is treated as a settlor in relation to the transferee settlement[10] as a result, and immediately before the transfer, that settlor meets the residence condition (or prior to 6 April 2025 the domicile condition) as a settlor in relation to the transferring settlement then they also meet that condition as a settlor in relation to the transferee settlement from the time they become such a settlor until they cease to be such a settlor.[11]

Trusts taking effect on death require a determination of the settlor's status at that time. If the settlement arose on the settlor's death, whether by will or intestacy or in any other way, and immediately before the settlor's death, they were UK resident (or prior to 6 April 2025 domiciled) in the UK, then the trustees are resident in the UK from the date of death of the settlor.[12]

The trustees will not be neither resident in the UK in cases where the settlor is not UK resident (or prior to 6 April 2025 domiciled) in the UK at the relevant time. Furthermore, where the settlor has met these conditions at the relevant time, the trustees will cease to be resident when the settlor ceases to be treated as a settlor in relation to the settlement.

It will be apparent that these statutory provisions, in effect, also abolished the possibility of a distinction between residence and ordinary residence for trustees at the same time as ordinary residence for individuals was abolished by Finance Act 2013.

6 'Condition C' see ITA 2007 s 476.
7 Finance Act 2025 s 40 and Sch 9, para 11.
8 Finance Act 2013, s 219 and Sch 46, para 57(3).
9 ITA 2007 s 476(3). TCGA 1992 s 69 (2CA).
10 Under ITA 2007 s 470.
11 ITA 2007 s 476(4).
12 ITA 2007 s 476(2).

5.05 Non-resident trustees with a UK permanent establishment

As has been seen, the residence of the single deemed person constituting the trustees is in part determined by examining the residence of the trustees who make up that deemed person. The residence of each trustee is determined by reference to the rules applicable in the case of individual trustees in Chapters 2 and 3 and in the case of corporate trustees in Chapter 7. An exception is made in the case of non-resident trustees operating in the UK. ITA 2007 section 475(6) reads:

> '475(6) If at a time a person ("T") who is a trustee of the settlement acts as trustee in the course of a business which T carries on in the United Kingdom through a branch, agency or permanent establishment there, then for the purposes of subsections (4) and (5) assume that T is UK resident at that time.'

The expression 'branch or agency' is now used only in relation to income tax to determine the extent of any UK representative's liability in respect of a trade carried on in the UK by a non-resident individual,[13] as well as the limit on liability to income tax of non-UK residents[14] and capital gains tax.[15]

Permanent establishment is the equivalent expression in relation to non-resident companies carrying on a trade in the UK[16] in Corporation Tax Act 2010 section 1141. In general:

> '1141(1) For the purposes of the Tax Acts a company has a permanent establishment in a territory if, and only if–
>
> (a) it has a fixed place of business there through which the business of the company is wholly or partly carried on, or
>
> (b) an agent acting on behalf of the company has and habitually exercises there authority to do business on behalf of the company.'

The consequence of a non-resident trustee acting as such in the course of a business is that such trustee is treated as resident in the UK for the purpose of determining the residence and ordinary residence of the single deemed person.

HMRC accept that for trustees the 'branch' and 'agency' tests apply to non-corporate trustees and the 'permanent establishment' test to corporate trustees.[17] Although in most cases the analysis will be similar, features particular to the permanent establishment concept are applicable to corporate trustees only.[18] In their view, the first step is to ask whether the trustee is carrying on a business

13 FA 1995 s 126(8).
14 ITA 2007 s 811.
15 TCGA 1992 s 9.
16 ICTA 1988 s 11(1).
17 HMRC Guidance Note, 3 August 2009: Trustee Residence Guidance, Version 1 July 2009, paragraph 5. HMRC Trusts Settlements and Estates Manual TSEM10020: trust residence for Income Tax and Capital Gains Tax purposes – periods from 6 April 2007.
18 Paragraph 7.

in the UK, and, if so, is it carrying on that business through a branch, agent, or permanent establishment in the UK? In each case, the business in question is that of providing professional trustee services for a fee. This question does not relate to the business of a particular trust that might be conducted by the trustee. It is only if both questions are answered in the positive that the examination then turns to the activity of being a trustee of a particular trust whose residence is tested.[19]

A trustee is 'carrying on the function of being a trustee' in the context activities of being a trustee of a particular trust when it performs the core activities of a trustee and not those activities which are auxiliary or preparatory. This applies equally to non-corporate trustees.[20] A trustee is the person who has a legal duty to manage the assets of that trust in the best interests of the beneficiary or beneficiaries. The trustee manages, employs and disposes of the trust assets in accordance with both the terms of the trust and the duties and responsibilities which the law places upon trustees. The core activities of a trustee are regarded by HMRC as including:

1 the general administration of the trusts;
2 the over-arching investment strategy;
3 monitoring the performance of those investments; and
4 decisions on how trust income will be dealt with and whether distributions should be made.[21]

Preparatory or auxiliary activities can include information gathering meetings, including meetings with independent agents or with beneficiaries but, as mentioned below, each case will have to be considered individually.[22] However, rather more contentiously, HMRC also take the view that the frequency as well as the nature or significance of the individual activities and meetings go to whether the non-UK resident corporate trustee was acting as a trustee through that permanent establishment. This they say arises where, in relation to a particular trust, there is considerable administrative work – such as meetings with investment managers or beneficiaries – being carried on in the UK through a permanent establishment, so that such meetings have become a major element of the trustee's activities in relation to that trust, and no longer preparatory or auxiliary.[23]

The activity of providing services to a non-UK resident trustee, whether by a connected person or not, does not of itself create a dependent agency permanent establishment under Finance Act 2003 s 148(1)(b). In the view of HMRC it is necessary to consider the capacity in which the person provides the services to the trust on behalf of the non-UK resident trustee. Where the

19 Paragraph 8.
20 Paragraph 9.
21 Paragraph10.
22 Paragraph 11.
23 Paragraph 12.

services are only those that the person is contractually obliged to provide under their agreement with the non-UK resident trustee and are remunerated at arm's length, then they regard this as unlikely to create a dependent agency permanent establishment.[24] HMRC views on the application on the existence or otherwise of a permanent establishment of a non-resident trustee and whether the trustee acts as such in the course of a business carried on through a permanent establishment in the UK in specified circumstances are set out in a Guidance note agreed by HMRC with certain professional bodies.[25]

5.06 Individual trustees with split-year treatment

Individuals who become or cease to be UK resident part way through a tax year may be accorded split-year treatment.[26] They are, however, deemed to be resident throughout the year.[27] Thus the residence of the settlement during the overseas part of a split year of a trustee is determined on the basis that the trustee is resident even during that overseas part. A narrow exception applies to an individual who becomes or ceases to be a trustee of a settlement during a tax year. If the individual is a trustee of the settlement only during the overseas part of the year, then the individual is treated as if they had been non-UK resident for the year and consequently for the part of the year when they were a trustee of the settlement.[28]

This exception does not apply to a trustee who acts as such in the course of a business which they carry on in the UK through a branch, agency or permanent establishment there. Such trustees are always UK resident.[29]

5.07 Residence for tax treaties

As is the case with any other person, the trustees may be treated as resident in the UK under its laws but at the same time treated as a resident in another country for the purposes of its tax laws. Qualification as a person and a resident will normally bring with it access to treaty benefits under treaties patterned on the OECD Model:

---

24 Paragraph 3.2.

25 Trustee Residence Taxguide 06/15 agreed by HMRC, reissued August 2015 by the Tax Faculty of the Institute of Chartered Accountants in England and Wales, the Chartered Institute of Taxation and the Society of Trust and Estate Practitioners. TSEM10055: professional trustees not resident in the UK – branch, agency or permanent establishment.

26 See **2.30.**

27 See **2.31**.

28 ITA 2007 s 475(7) and (8) for income tax and TCGA 1992 s 69 (2DA) for capital gains tax. Inserted by FA 2013 Sch 45, paras 102 and 103 respectively.

29 ITA 2007 s 475(9) for income tax and TCGA 1992 s 69 (2DB) for capital gains tax. Inserted by FA 2013 Sch 45, paras 102 and 103 respectively.

> '4(1) For the purposes of this Convention, the term "resident of a Contracting State" means any person who, under the laws of that State, is liable to tax therein by reason of his domicile, residence, place of management or any other criterion of a similar nature, and also includes that State and any political subdivision or local authority thereof. This term, however, does not include any person who is liable to tax in that State in respect only of income from sources in that State or capital situated therein.'

Where a tax treaty is in place, such dual residence may be resolved for the purposes of the treaty by the following mechanism:

> '4(3) Where by reason of the provisions of paragraph 1 a person other than an individual is a resident of both Contracting States, then it shall be deemed to be a resident only of the State in which its place of effective management is situated.'

The commentary to the OECD Model does not directly consider the position of trusts. However, the Special Commissioners have considered the meaning of the expression 'place of effective management' in two decisions. In *Trustees of Wensleydale's Settlement v IR Commrs*[30] the success or failure of a capital gains tax avoidance scheme turned entirely upon whether the trustees of a settlement were deemed to be a resident of the Republic of Ireland for purposes of the Ireland- UK double tax treaty. As 'a person other than an individual' and a resident of both the Republic of Ireland and of the UK, this was determined by whether 'its place of effective management was situated' in Ireland. In the absence of much guidance the Special Commissioner considered that 'effective' implies realistic, positive management. On the evidence he found that the Irish trustee was a trustee in name rather than in reality, signing all the documents placed before her. On this basis it was held that the place of effective management of the trust was not in the Republic of Ireland.

A similar conclusion was reached in *Trevor Smallwood Trust v R & C Commrs*[31] which also concerned a not dissimilar tax avoidance scheme where a trust moved from the UK to Mauritius. The Special Commissioners believed 'effective' should be understood in the sense of the French *effective* (*siège de direction effective*) which connotes real, French being the other official version of the OECD Model. Having regard to the ordinary meaning of the words in their context and in the light of their object and purpose, the place of effective management depended on where the real top-level management (or the realistic, positive management) of the trustee, as trustee, was to be found. They accepted that the administration of the trust moved to Mauritius, but in

30 (1996) Sp C 73.

31 *Trevor Smallwood & Mary Caroline Smallwood Trustees of the Trevor Smallwood Trust v R & C Commrs; Trevor Smallwood Settlor of the Trevor Smallwood Trust v R & C Commrs* [2008] UKSPC 669. In the High Court ([2009] EWHC 777 (Ch)), Mann J ruled that the question of dual residence did not arise and consequently Art 4(3) of the treaty was not engaged.

their view the 'key' decisions were made in the UK and consequently, the trust's 'place of effective management' was in the UK.

The Court of Appeal,[32] however, divided on where the place of effective management was and how it was to be determined. Patten LJ, with whom Ward LJ agreed, was of the view that although the Mauritius trustees were appointed as part of a pre-existing scheme and they accepted the trusteeship on the basis that the shares would be sold as part of that exercise and that the shares were indeed sold in accordance with the scheme, they retained their right and duties as trustees to consider the matter at the time of alienation and did not agree merely to act on the instructions which they received from the accountants who advised on the scheme. Thus it was not open to say that effective management was exercised by anyone other than the trustees in Mauritius. Hughes LJ, dissenting, considered that because first, the trustees are treated as a single and continuing body of persons, the place of effective management of the trust is that of the trustees as a continuing body; and secondly, the scheme was devised and orchestrated throughout from the UK, which included that the trust should be exported to Mauritius for a brief temporary period and then returned, within the fiscal year, to the UK, there was a scheme of management which went above and beyond the day-to-day management exercised by the trustees for the time being, and the control of it was in the UK. The majority view of the court is to be preferred. The dissent of Hughes LJ seems to be unduly influenced by the existence of a tax avoidance scheme to articulate any principle of general application and appears to rely on blending both past and present trustees together.

Dual resident trusts and estates will be affected by OECD proposals made pursuant to the OECD/G20 Base Erosion and Profit Shifting Project to change the treaty rule for resolving dual residence cases aimed at corporate tax avoidance, discussed at **7.6**.

Estates

5.08 Residence of estates

Unlike the residence of trustees, the residence of personal representatives of deceased estates was not comprehensively reformed by the Finance Act 2006. Legislation only addresses the case of mixed personal representatives. HMRC have taken the position that the personal representatives are deemed to have the same residence and domicile status as the deceased had at the date of death.[33]

32 *HMRC v Smallwood & Anor* [2010] EWCA Civ 778. See generally Jonathan Schwarz, *Schwarz on Tax Treaties* (Wolters Kluwer CCH, 2025) Ch 6 on treaty residence.

33 HMRC Capital Gains Manual CG30650.

The statutory treatment of personal representatives of a deceased person is somewhat similar in the case of mixed residence personal representatives to that of trustees. For income tax purposes, if the personal representatives of a deceased person include one or more persons who are UK resident and one or more persons who are non-UK resident, then if the deceased died resident or domiciled in the UK, the UK-resident persons are treated, in their capacity as personal representatives, as UK resident. In contrast, prior to 6 April 2025, if the deceased died not resident or domiciled in the UK, the UK-resident persons were treated, in their capacity as personal representatives, as not UK resident.[34] From 6 April 2025, personal representatives are treated as resident if the deceased died on or after that date while a UK resident or a long-term UK resident.[35] For capital gains tax purposes, 'resident' has the same meaning in TCGA 1992 as in the Income Tax Acts.[36] No mitigation is available to personal representatives who come to or leave the UK and qualify for split-year treatment. They are resident even during the overseas part of a split year.

34 ITA 2007 s 834.
35 ITA 2007 s 834(3) as amended by Finance Act 2025 s 40 and Sch 9, para. 9(2).
36 TCGA 1992 s 9(1).

CHAPTER 6

Residence of companies

A Company Limited? What may that be?
The term, I rather think, is new to me.

Sir W S Gilbert, *Utopia Limited* (Finale)

6.01 Introduction

A corporation is a legal entity. It is, under the law, an artificial person, separate and distinct from its members and endowed with an existence independent of their existence.[1]

Although a corporation's personality is artificial, it is not fictitious. Since 1889 the word 'person' in any Act of Parliament has included 'a body of persons corporate' unless the contrary intention appears,[2] and a corporation may, accordingly, be fined for contempt of court,[3] be convicted of an offence involving a fraudulent intent,[4] and be a 'respectable and responsible person' to whom to assign a lease.[5] This chapter examines the residence of companies. Corporation tax has undergone the rewrite process and its fruits are to be found in the Corporation Tax Act 2009 which generally has effect for accounting periods ending on or after 1 April 2009 and the Corporation Tax Act 2010 which generally has effect for accounting periods ending on or after 1 April 2010.The term 'company' is not, of course, descriptive only of a limited company but, under CTA 2010 section 1121, must be taken to mean, in this context, 'any body corporate or unincorporated association' excluding 'a partnership, a local authority or a local authority association'. More to the point, it may possess the status of residence:

1 *Salomon v Salomon & Co* [1897] AC 22.
2 Interpretation Act 1978 s 5 and Sch 1.
3 *R v J G Hammond & Co* [1914] 2 KB 866.
4 *R v ICR Haulage Ltd* [1944] KB 551.
5 *Ideal Film Renting Co v Nielson* [1921] 1 Ch 575.

> 'Now the definition of the word "residence" is founded upon the habits and relations of the natural man and is therefore inapplicable to the artificial and legal person whom we call a corporation. But for the purpose of giving effect to the words of the Legislature an artificial residence must be assigned to this artificial person, and one formed on the analogy of natural persons.'[6]

The territorial basis of taxation applies to companies who are chargeable to corporation tax on their profits.[7] Profits for this purpose means income and chargeable gains.[8] A UK-resident company is chargeable to corporation tax on all its profits wherever arising,[9] but a company not resident in the UK is not within the charge to corporation tax unless it carries on a trade in the UK through a permanent establishment there, carries on a trade anywhere of dealing in or developing UK land, carries on a trade of dealing in or developing UK land or has other UK property income.[10] Where it does so, it is chargeable to corporation tax only on profits attributable to those sources including profits arising from loan relationships or derivative contracts relating to those sources of profit or income.[11] A company that is not resident in the UK may also be liable to income tax on certain income from sources within the UK not attributable to a permanent establishment.[12]

Until 1988 there was no statutory definition of residence for companies. The statutory definitions are now conveniently gathered in CTA 2009 Part 2 Chapter 3. In terms, these statutory provisions apply for the purposes of the Corporation Tax Acts.[13] The predecessor legislation applied these statutory provisions for the purposes of the Taxes Acts.[14] The rewrite approached this extension by incorporating CTA 2009 Part 2 Chapter 3 by reference into specific enactments.[15]

Although HMRC has long-standing published practice in this area (principally Statement of Practice SP 1/90 and the more thoughtful International Tax Handbook, Chapter 3)[16], the application of this practice did not given rise to the same interpretative difficulties faced in the pre-2013 individual residence area. Updated guidance in the International Manual INTM120000 and following now includes helpful examples of when HMRC will question the residence

6 *Calcutta Jute Mills Co Ltd v Nicholson* (1876) 1 TC 83 at 103, per Huddleston B.
7 CTA 2009 s 5.
8 CTA 2009 s 2(2).
9 CTA 2009 s 5(1).
10 CTA 2009 s 5(2).
11 CTA 2009 ss 5(2A) to 5(3B).
12 ITA 2007 s 815.
13 See ICTA 1988 s 831(1)(a): 'the Corporation Tax Acts' means the enactments relating to the taxation of the income and chargeable gains of companies and of company distributions (including provisions relating also to income tax).
14 Effectively extending the provisions to income tax and capital gains tax. See TMA 1970 s 118(1), 'Taxes Acts' and related provisions.
15 See TMA 1970 s 109A; TCGA 1992 s 286A; ITA 2007 s 835A.
16 INTM120210 Company residence: guidance originally published in the International Tax Handbook.

of companies and those circumstances in which they will normally not review residence.[17] As will be explained,[18] the courts have been required to interpret the expression and a substantial body of case law has resulted.

Finance Act 2025 introduced the concept of 'long-term UK residence' for bodies corporate applicable to inheritance tax only.[19]

6.02 UK incorporated companies

The residence of companies is now addressed in CTA 2009 Part 2 Chapter 3. Any company incorporated in the UK is deemed to be resident in the UK for the purposes of the Corporation Tax Acts.[20] Any other rule determining residence is excluded.[21] The case law which determined the test of residence on the basis of the location of a company's central control and management is of no relevance to any company which is incorporated in the UK. Although the term residence continues to be applied to such companies, the ordinary meaning of the term has been suspended in favour of a formal test. Thus, the tax liability of companies incorporated in the UK is determined by the place of incorporation and not any factual enquiry as to where or how it conducts its business.

There are two limited exceptions to the incorporation rule by way of transitional relief from the time of adoption of the rule in 1988.[22] The first operates if the company was non-resident before 14 March 1988 and had become so before then, pursuant to a general or a specific Treasury consent[23] obtained under what was ICTA 1988 section 765 or its predecessors.[24]

If the consent was a specific consent, and if the company does not cease to carry on business, the company can remain non-resident regardless of where it is based, and it only becomes UK resident if it in fact becomes resident under the central management and control test.[25]

If the consent was a general consent, a further condition has to be satisfied, namely that the company was taxable in a foreign territory.[26] By 'taxable' is meant being liable to tax on income by reason of domicile, residence or place of management.[27] The second application of the exception is for companies which commenced business before 15 March 1988 and become non-resident

---

17 INTM120120 Company residence: when to question residence.
18 **6.03** and following.
19 See Chapter 3, **3.16.**
20 CTA 2009 s 14(1). See **6.03** below.
21 CTA 2009 s 14(2).
22 CTA 2009 Sch 2 Pt 5.
23 CTA 2009 Sch 2 Pt 5 para 13(1). It must also have remained non-resident to 1 April 2009.
24 See CTA 2009 Sch 2 Pt 5 para 15(2). ICTA 1988 s 765 was repealed by FA 2009.
25 CTA 2009 Sch 2 Pt 5 para 13(2).
26 CTA 2009 Sch 2 Pt 5 para 13(2)(c).
27 CTA 2009 Sch 2 Pt 5 para 15(1).

on or after 15 March 1988 but before 1 April 2009, pursuant to a specific consent applied for before 15 March 1988.[28] If it ceases to carry on business, or becomes resident under the central management and control test, the exception will cease to apply.[29]

6.03 Residence under case law

Wisely, the Tax Law Rewrite Committee refrained from attempting to put the case law test of residence into statutory form. The test of central control and management is now only in most cases applicable to foreign incorporated companies. Thus, a foreign incorporated company will be resident in the UK if the central management and control of the company is exercised in the UK.

The phrase 'central management and control' was coined not by Parliament but by Lord Loreburn in one of the earliest of all the cases concerning company residence, *De Beers Consolidated Mines v Howe,*[30] at the beginning of the twentieth century. The company was incorporated in South Africa (then the Cape Colony) and its head office was formally at Kimberley where the general meetings were held there. Profits were made out of diamonds raised in South Africa and sold under annual contracts for delivery in South Africa. Further, some of the directors and Life Governors lived in South Africa, and there were directors' meetings at Kimberley as well as in London. But the majority of directors and Life Governors lived in England. The directors' meetings in London were the meetings where the real control was always exercised in practically all the important business of the company, except the mining operations. London always controlled the negotiation of the contracts with the syndicates to whom the diamonds were sold, determined policy in the disposal of diamonds and other assets, the working and development of mines, the application of profits, and the appointment of directors. London also always controlled matters that required to be determined by the majority of all the directors, which included all questions of expenditure except wages, materials, and such like at the mines, and a limited sum which might be spent by the directors at Kimberley. The House of Lords rejected incorporation as the determinant of residence. In finding the company resident in the UK, Lord Loreburn formulated the principle as:

> 'A company resides, for the purposes of Income Tax, where its real business is carried on … I regard that as the true rule; and the real business is carried on where the central management and control actually abides'.

---

28 CTA 2009 Sch 2 Pt 5 para 14(1).

29 CTA 2009 Sch 2 Pt 5 para 14(2).

30 *De Beers Consolidated Mines Ltd v Howe* (1906) 5 TC 198 at 213.

In *Bullock v Unit Construction Co Ltd*,[31] Lord Radcliffe summarised the position as it existed in 1959 as:[32]

> '… the necessity of establishing some common standard for the treatment of different taxpayers meant that the Courts of Law were bound in course of time to produce and apply some general principle of their own to form an acceptable test of residence … [T]he principle was adopted that a company is resident where its central management and control abide: words which, according to the decision of the House of Lords that finally propounded the test, *De Beers Consolidated Mines Ltd v Howe*,[33] are equivalent to saying that a company's residence is where its "real business" is carried on … .
>
> … as precise and unequivocal as a positive statutory injunction … I do not know of any other test which has either been substituted for that of central management and control, or has been defined with sufficient precision to be regarded as an acceptable alternative to it. To me … it seems impossible to read Lord Loreburn's words without seeing that he regarded the formula he was propounding as constituting the test of residence.'

6.04 The Untelrab/Development Securities syntheses

From a practical perspective, a brief statement of principles is most desirable. In *Untelrab Ltd & Ors v McGregor* (HMIT),[34] the first published decision of the Special Commissioners dealing with company residence, an attempt was made to synthesise the principles developed in a large number of cases over more than a century as follows:

> 'From these authorities we have identified the following principles:
>
> - that the residence of a company is where the directors meet and transact their business and exercise the powers conferred upon them;
> - that if the directors meet in two places then the company's residence is where its real business is carried on and the real business is carried on where the central management and control actually abides;
> - that a determination as to whether a case falls within that rule is a pure question of fact to be determined by a scrutiny of the course of business and trading;
> - that the actual place of management, and not the place where a company ought to be managed, fixes the place of residence of a company;
> - that it is an exceptional case for a parent company to usurp control from its subsidiaries; a parent company usually operates through the boards of its subsidiaries;

---

31 (1959) 38 TC 712.
32 (1959) 38 TC 712, per Lord Radcliffe at 738.
33 (1906) 5 TC 198.
34 (1995) SpC 55.

- that although a board might do what it was told to do it did not follow that the control and management of the company lay with another, so long as the board exercised their discretion when coming to their decisions and would have refused to carry out an improper or unwise transaction; and
- that when deciding the issue of residence one should stand back from the detail and make up one's mind from the picture which the whole of the evidence presents.'[35]

The case is one that represents two modern circumstances where arguments between companies and the Revenue have been most acute. The first, as in *Untelrab*, is where a company forms part of an international group of companies and the operations of group members are affected to a greater or lesser extent by group policies led from the parent company. The second is in relation to privately owned companies where it claimed that the power of a dominant shareholder prevails. Very often these are special purpose vehicles set up to perform a specific function within a corporate group or in organising an individual's affairs.

Untelrab concerned subsidiaries of a UK-resident public company incorporated in the Channel Islands and Bermuda. Their directors were lawyers and accountants, resident in those territories. Board meetings were held there and the day-to-day management of the companies undertaken there. Although managed overseas, in certain respects, they adopted group policy as formulated by the parent company. The Special Commissioners found that the board of Untelrab met in Bermuda and transacted the company's business there. At board meetings proposals were discussed and decisions were made by the directors in the best interests of the company. They would have refused to carry out any proposal which was improper or unreasonable. The UK-resident parent company did not control the board in the exercise of their powers. It could have taken steps to remove the directors but could not control them in their conduct of Untelrab's business.[36] The decision was not appealed. It was, however, endorsed by Park J in the High Court in *Wood v Holden.*[37]

Lord Justice Newey, in the Court of Appeal also summarised the points derived from the cases in *HMRC v Development Securities Plc & Ors*[38] as follows:

- The overarching principle is that a company resides for tax purposes where its real business is carried on, and that is where central management and control actually abides;
- The principle applies in relation to subsidiaries, including special purpose vehicles;

35 *Untelrab Ltd & Ors v McGregor* (HMIT) (1995) SpC 55 at para 74.

36 *Untelrab Ltd & Ors v McGregor* (HMIT) (1995) SpC 55 at para 73.

37 [2005] EWHC 547 (Ch) at para 26.

38 *Revenue and Customs v Development Securities Plc & Ors* [2020] EWCA Civ 1705, [2021] STC 84, [2021] BTC 1.

- It is the actual place of management, not that in which it ought to be managed, which fixes the residence of a company;
- A company may be resident in a jurisdiction other than that of its incorporation not only where a constitutional organ exercises management and control elsewhere, but if the functions of the company's constitutional organs are usurped, in the sense that management and control is exercised independently of, or without regard to, its constitutional organs, or if an outsider dictates decisions (as opposed to merely proposing, advising and influencing decisions);
- On the other hand, central management and control of a subsidiary will not be taken to be in a jurisdiction other than that of its incorporation just because it is following a tax planning scheme propounded by its parent. Nor need it matter that a company's board takes decisions without full information or even in breach of the directors' duties;
- Events before or after the particular date in question may be relevant as casting light on the position on that date; and
- Where a company is resident is essentially a question of fact.

The case involved the establishment of Jersey subsidiaries of the UK group to undertake one-off transactions in order to achieve an increase in the amount of loss relief within the group.[39] While these judgments provide a convenient summary of elements of the central management and control rule, they should not be regarded as a comprehensive statement of the law applicable to all circumstances.

6.05 A question of fact

In relation to the application of the central management and control test, Lord Loreburn, having formulated the rule,[40] continued in *De Beers*:

> 'It remains to be considered whether the present case falls within that rule. This is a pure question of fact, to be determined, not according to the construction of this or that regulation or byelaw, but upon a scrutiny of the course of business and trading.'[41]

Although the enquiry into exercise of central management and control is a factual enquiry, special considerations apply in the context of a legal person. Early case law proceeded by analogy with individuals. Thus, in the seminal decision in *De Beers*, Lord Loreburn said:

39 *Revenue and Customs v Development Securities Plc & Ors* [2020] EWCA Civ 1705, [2021] STC 84, [2021] BTC 1 at para 14.

40 See **6.03**.

41 *De Beers Consolidated Mines v Howe* (1906) 5 TC 198 at 213.

> 'In applying the conception of residence to a Company, we ought, I think, to proceed as nearly as we can upon the analogy of an individual. A Company cannot eat or sleep, but it can keep house and do business. We ought, therefore, to see whether it really keeps house and does business. An individual may be of foreign nationality, and yet reside in the United Kingdom. So may a Company.'[42]

While the habits and lifestyle of an individual form the obvious fact base, in the case of companies, the question as to which facts ought to be examined is less obvious and has been controversial. Case law and administrative practice has focused on identifying, what is meant by 'central management and control', who exercises it and where that exercise takes place. These elements are interrelated but may be considered individually for ease of analysis.

Because the residence of a company is to be determined by the location of its central management and control, and because that location is a question of fact, a finding by the Commissioners that a company is resident in this place or that will be unassailable provided the Commissioners have before them evidence from which their finding can be made and providing they do not misdirect themselves in law.[43] The court's approach is well-illustrated by Lord Loreburn's conclusion in the *De Beers* case:[44]

> 'The Commissioners, after sifting the evidence, arrived at the two following conclusions, viz: … (2) That the head and seat and directing power of the affairs of the Appellant Company were at the office in London, from whence the chief operations of the Company, both in the United Kingdom and elsewhere, were, in fact, controlled, managed and directed. That conclusion of fact cannot be impugned, and it follows that this Company was resident within the United Kingdom for the purposes of Income Tax.'[45]

6.06 Who exercises central management and control?

Bullock v Unit Construction Co Ltd[46] has for many years formed the basis of a very broad approach to the factual enquiry by the Revenue. There, Unit Construction Company Ltd, a UK-resident subsidiary of Alfred Booth & Co Ltd, a UK-resident parent company, made subvention payments to three of its fellow subsidiary companies in Kenya and claimed that those payments were, under FA 1953 section 20, permissible deductions in arriving at its profits for tax purposes. This would have been so only if the three Kenyan subsidiaries also were resident in the UK, but the Inland Revenue contended that they were not. The three subsidiaries had been incorporated in Kenya and their articles of association expressly placed their management and control in the hands of

42 *De Beers Consolidated Mines v Howe* (1906) 5 TC 198 at 212.
43 See **3.03** above.
44 *De Beers Consolidated Mines v Howe* (1906) 5 TC 198.
45 *De Beers Consolidated Mines v Howe* (1906) 5 TC 198 at 213–214.
46 (1959) 38 TC 712.

their directors and required directors' meetings to be held outside the UK. That being so, the three Kenyan subsidiaries must, said the Revenue, be resident outside the UK. The Commissioners found as a *fact*, however, that, due to trading difficulties which the subsidiaries had encountered,

> '... at the material times ... the boards of directors of the African subsidiaries ... were standing aside in all matters of real importance and in many matters of minor importance affecting the central management and control, and ... the real control and management was being exercised by the board of directors of Alfred Booth & Co Ltd in London.'[47]

Accordingly, the Commissioners found that each of the African subsidiaries was resident in the UK, and their finding was ultimately upheld in the House of Lords. Referring to the reversals the decision had suffered at the hands of the High Court and the Court of Appeal, Viscount Simonds said:

> '... the contention of learned Counsel for the Crown which has so far found favour with the courts is no less than this, that if by the constitution of the company, that is, by its memorandum and articles of association interpreted in the light of the relevant law, that is, in this case the law of Kenya, the management of the company's business is contemplated as being exercised, and ought therefore to be exercised, in Kenya or at any rate outside the United Kingdom, then for the purpose of British Income Tax law the facts are to be disregarded and the control and management which as a fact are found to abide in the United Kingdom are to be regarded as abiding outside it. There is no doubt, I think, that the management of the African subsidiaries, which were incorporated in Kenya under the Kenya Companies Ordinance and registered in Nairobi, was placed in the hands of their directors and that their articles of association expressly provided that directors' meetings might be held anywhere outside the United Kingdom. Nor can there be any doubt – for this is the unchallengeable finding of the Commissioners – that the management of the business of the companies was not exercised in the manner contemplated. Whence it follows that the business was conducted in a manner irregular, unauthorised and perhaps unlawful ...
>
> My Lords, I should certainly be prepared to admit that the many Judges who in the past have pronounced upon this question had not in mind such a case as this. But, with great respect to those who take a different view, the present case does not seem to lie outside the principle underlying their judgment. Nothing can be more factual and concrete than the acts of management which enable a Court to find as a fact that central management and control is exercised in one country or another. It does not in any way alter their character that in greater or less degree they are irregular or unauthorised or unlawful. The business is not the less managed in London because it ought to be managed in Kenya. Its residence is determined by the solid facts, not by the terms of its constitution, however imperative. If indeed I must disregard the facts as they are, because they are irregular, I find a company without any central management at all. For, though I may disregard existing facts, I cannot invent facts

47 (1959) 38 TC 712 at 721–722.

> which do not exist and say that the company's business is managed in Kenya. Yet it is the place of central management which, however much or little weight ought to be given to other factors, essentially determines its residence. I come, therefore, to the conclusion … that it is the actual place of management, not the place in which it ought to be managed, which fixes the residence of a company.'[48]

The broad approach is highlighted in the HMRC Statement of Practice on company residence:

> 'In some cases … central management and control is exercised by a single individual. This may happen when a chairman or managing director exercises powers formally conferred by the company's Articles and the other board members are little more than cyphers, or by reason of a dominant shareholding or for some other reason. In those cases the residence of the company is where the controlling individual exercises his powers.[49]
>
> Generally, however, where doubts arise about a particular company's residence status, the Inland Revenue adopt the following approach:
>
> (i) They first try to ascertain whether the directors of the company in fact exercise central management and control.
> (ii) If so, they seek to determine where the directors exercise this central management and control (which is not necessarily where they meet).
> (iii) In cases where the directors apparently do not exercise central management and control of the company, the Revenue then look to establish where and by whom it is exercised.'[50]

The full extent to which this approach is considered to apply is illustrated in *Wood v Holden (Inspector of Taxes)*[51] where the Court of Appeal affirmed the decision of the High Court judge who had overruled the conclusion of Special Commissioners Wallace and Brice that a Netherlands company was resident in the UK.

The case arose from a scheme to avoid capital gains tax on the sale of trading companies by two UK-resident individuals. The scheme had been designed by a firm of accountants who also attended to its implementation. The shares in the trading companies came to be held by a Netherlands-incorporated company itself owned by a British Virgin Islands company which was in turn owned by trustees of offshore family trusts. The sole director of the Netherlands company was a Dutch trust company. HMRC argued that the company registered in the Netherlands (but surprisingly, not the BVI company) was nevertheless resident in the UK. The HMRC case was that the Dutch corporate director did not in fact take the decisions but did what it was told to do by Mr Wood or by the firm of UK-based chartered accountants acting on his behalf. This contention was

48 (1959) 38 TC 712 at 735–736.
49 SP 1/90, para 13. HMRC International Manual INTM120200: Statement of Practice 1/90.
50 SP 1/90 para 15.
51 2006 STC 443.

upheld by the Special Commissioners[52] but not by the High Court or the Court of Appeal. The House of Lords refused leave to appeal. In the Court of Appeal Chadwick LJ said at para 27:

> 'In my view the judge was correct in his analysis of the law. In seeking to determine where "central management and control" of a company incorporated outside the United Kingdom lies, it is essential to recognise the distinction between cases where management and control of the company is exercised through its own constitutional organs (the board of directors or the general meeting) and cases where the functions of those constitutional organs are "usurped" – in the sense that management and control is exercised independently of, or without regard to, those constitutional organs. And, in cases which fall within the former class, it is essential to recognise the distinction (in concept, at least) between the role of an "outsider" in proposing, advising and influencing the decisions which the constitutional organs take in fulfilling their functions and the role of an outsider who dictates the decisions which are to be taken. In that context an "outsider" is a person who is not, himself, a participant in the formal process (a board meeting or a general meeting) through which the relevant constitutional organ fulfils its function.'

The Netherlands company's directors had not been bypassed and they had not stood aside. They had also decided to accept the agreement proposed by the accountants and had made the decision to sign and execute the documents. Theirs was an effective decision by a constitutional organ, exercising management and control.

This reveals two categories of management pattern to consider. The first category is where management and control of the company is exercised by its own constitutional organs. The second category concerns where the functions of those constitutional organs are 'usurped'. Where it is determined that management and control is exercised by the company's constitutional organs, it is necessary to examine what those organs do and where they are. Where management and control is usurped, the place and nature of the usurper's action must be the focus of attention.

Constitutional organs cannot be comprised of 'fake' directors. In *Bywater Investments Limited & Ors v Commissioner of Taxation*,[53] the Australian High Court ruled that, where it was intended from the outset that an Australian resident, who had disguised his ownership and control of non-Australian companies, would make all the decisions for those companies, and that a husband and wife resident in Switzerland appointed as directors, whose only role would be to implement the Australian's decisions, the Australian resident exercised central management and control. The Swiss directors' role was a

---

52 *Sub nom R & Anor v Holden (HM Inspector of Taxes)* [2004] UK SPC422.

53 *Bywater Investments Limited & Ors v Commissioner of Taxation* [2016] HCA 45. See endorsement of the decision by the Court of Appeal in *Revenue and Customs v Development Securities Plc & Ors* [2020] EWCA Civ 1705, [2021] STC 84, [2021] BTC 1 at para 13.

'fake'. In that case, the constitutional organs of the company did not, and were not intended to, exercise central management and control of the companies.[54]

6.07 Delegated management and control

Delegated management and control and *central* management and control are mutually exclusive concepts. Indeed, delegation is itself an exercise of management and control.

In *Calcutta Jute Mills v Nicholson*,[55] Huddleston B held that the central management and control of the Calcutta Jute Mills, though ostensibly exercised by a director in India, was actually exercised from the company's office in London where the board of directors met:

> 'From that office would issue all the orders to the managing director in Calcutta. No doubt, until he received orders to the contrary, he would have full power and discretion to do what he liked in Calcutta; but at any moment, from this head office, they might have revoked his authority, or altered any arrangement which he had made connected with the working of the company.'[56]

The director in Calcutta was, for all his powers, a mere delegate and one had, therefore, to look beyond him to the delegators from whom his powers had been derived and by whom they were being sustained.

In *American Thread Company v Joyce*[57] the delegation of powers to the American Thread Co Ltd was ostensibly managed and controlled by an executive committee of directors in New York. The Master of the Rolls was, however, quite clear that central management and control lay in Manchester, England:

> 'Now the current business the daily purchasing and selling of raw materials and making them into thread is, no doubt, carried out by the executive committee in New York, the executive committee of three. Who appoint them? The English board. It must be done by the English board where the majority of the directors, four out of seven, reside. They are appointed by them, their salary is fixed by them, in fact the whole control of the machine, so to say, is kept and carefully kept at Manchester.'[58]

In *News Datacom Ltd & News Data Security Products Ltd v Revenue & Customs*,[59] an executive committee of the board of directors existed as permitted by the articles of association. It was concerned with day-to-day operational

54 *Bywater Investments Limited & Ors v Commissioner of Taxation* [2016] HCA 45 at paras 75 to 77.
55 (1876) 1 TC 83.
56 (1876) 1 TC 83 at 107.
57 (1913) 6 TC 163.
58 (1913) 6 TC 163.
59 [2006] UKSPC SPC561.

matters and seven of its nine meetings were in the UK. HMRC argued that it, rather than the board, exercised central management and control. The Special Commissioners found that the executive committee exercised no part in the 'controlling brain' of the company.

What all these cases illustrate, therefore, is that, in determining the location of a company's central management and control, it is necessary to ask of those who appear to be exercising such control, 'To whom do you look over your shoulder? From whom do you derive your powers and who is able to modify or withdraw them?' If the answer is, 'No one. We derive our powers from the shareholders who appointed us and, short of the shareholders removing us from office, no-one can interfere with our powers', identification of those who exercise central management and control will have been made.[60] If the answer is otherwise it will provide a pointer either to those who truly exercise central management and control or to a person or persons who are one step nearer to the centre than those to whom the question was addressed.

6.08 Shareholder control

It must be stressed that the test of corporate residence involves the identification of the place of central management *and* (not *or*) control. In other words, the control in question is that which relates to the highest level of management of a company's business and must not, therefore, be confused with the control which vests in a company's shareholders per se. The distinction was stressed by Moulton LJ in *Stanley v Gramophone and Typewriter Ltd*[61] when he said:

> '... the individual corporator does not carry on the business of the corporation; he is only entitled to the profits of that business to a certain extent, fixed and ascertained in a certain way, depending upon the constitution of the corporation and his holding in it. This legal proposition ... is not weakened by the fact that the extent of his interest in it entitles him to exercise a greater or lesser amount of control over the manner in which the business is carried on. Such control is inseparable from his position as a corporator, and is a wholly different thing both in fact and in law from carrying on the business himself. The Directors and employees of the corporation are not his agents, and he has no power of giving directions to them which they must obey. It has been decided by this court in the *Automatic Self-cleaning Filter Syndicate Co Ltd v Cunninghame*[62] that in an English Company by whose Articles of Association certain powers were placed in the hands of the Directors the shareholders could not interfere with the exercise of those powers by the Directors even by a majority in General Meeting. Their course is to obtain the requisite majority to remove the Directors and put persons in their place who agree to their policy. This shows that the control of individual corporators is something wholly different from the

60 The distinction between shareholder control and central management and control is discussed at **6.08** below.

61 (1908) 5 TC 358.

62 [1906] 2 Ch 34.

> management of the business itself. Nor is this principle less true when the holding of the individual corporator is so large that he is able to override the wishes of the other corporators in matters relating to the control of the business of the Company. The extent but not the nature of his power is changed by the magnitude of his holding.'[63]

It follows, therefore, that a company whose business is, in fact, managed and controlled by a board of directors in, say, London, will none the less be resident in England even if, say, 98% of its shares are owned by an individual resident in France. This proposition was specifically approved by the Court of Appeal in *Bullock v Unit Construction Co Ltd*[64] and still stands. The Court of Appeal also assented to the proposition, however, that:

> '... a shareholder who holds sufficient in a company can *de facto* control its affairs by his ability to remove directors who disagree with his policy and to vote others into their places.'[65]

The significance of a shareholder's power was given detailed consideration in *American Thread Co v Joyce*.[66] There, the Crown contended that the operations of the American company were controlled from Manchester not merely because a majority of directors met there but also because the English parent company owned the entire share capital of the American company.

In the Court of Appeal, Buckley LJ went to some lengths to emphasise that it was not shareholder control on which the finding that the American company was resident in the UK rested:

> 'The shareholders can, no doubt, by virtue of their votes control the corporation; they can compel directors ... to do their will, but it does not follow that the corporators are managing the corporation. The contrary is the truth; they are not. It is the directors who are managing the affairs of the corporation ... [T]he executive committee in New York were in fact controlled ... on this side in extraordinary sessions of the Board which were held once a fortnight, and the real control, the head and seat and directing power of the affairs of the Company were here. It was in that sense that the control was here ... .'[67]

Before leaving the question of shareholder control, attention must – for the sake of completeness – be drawn to *Apthorpe v Peter Schoenhoffen Brewing Co Ltd*[68] which concerned the wholly owned American brewing subsidiary of an English company. The directors of the English company had full power of management and control of the affairs of the American company but they

63 (1908) 5 TC 358 at 376.
64 (1959) 38 TC 712 at 729–730, per Romer LJ.
65 (1959) 38 TC 712 at 730.
66 (1913) 6 TC 163.
67 (1913) 6 TC 163.
68 (1899) 4 TC 41.

delegated these powers to a committee of management in Chicago. The Commissioners found that:

> '... the head and seat and directing power of the [English] Company were at the [English] Company's registered office in the City of London, and that if the business at Chicago and the profits made thereby were technically the business and profits of the American company the American company was for such purpose the agent of the [English] Company.'[69]

In its statement of practice, the Revenue declares its position on wholly owned subsidiaries to be as follows:

> 'It is particularly difficult to apply the "central management and control" test in the situation where a subsidiary company and its parent operate in different territories. In this situation, the parent will normally influence, to a greater or lesser extent, the actions of the subsidiary. Where that influence is exerted by the parent exercising the powers which a sole or majority shareholder has in general meetings of the subsidiary, for example to appoint or dismiss members of the board of the subsidiary and to initiate or approve alterations to its financial structure, the Revenue would not seek to argue that central control and management of the subsidiary is located where the parent company is resident. However, in cases where the parent usurps the functions of the board of the subsidiary (such as *Unit Construction* itself) or where that board merely rubber stamps the parent company's decisions without giving them any independent consideration of its own, the Revenue draw the conclusion that the subsidiary has the same residence for tax purposes as its parent.[70]

This may reflect the case law described in this chapter if it is read as going no further than *Untelrab* and *Wood v Holden*. However, the statement then goes on to say that:

> 'The Revenue recognise that there may be many cases where a company is a member of a group having its ultimate holding company in another country which will not fall readily into either of the categories referred to above. In considering whether the board of such a subsidiary company exercises central management and control of the subsidiary's business, they have regard to the degree of autonomy which those directors have in conducting the company's business. Matters (among others) that may be taken into account are the extent to which the directors of the subsidiary take decisions on their own authority as to investment, production, marketing and procurement without reference to the parent.'[71]

This is plainly at odds with the current state of the law but remains unamended. Nonetheless, the application of the law to particular circumstances, especially where tax planned schemes are implemented by foreign subsidiaries, may be challenging, given the intensely factual nature of the enquiry.

---

69 (1899) 4 TC 41 at 46.
70 SP 1/90, para 16.
71 SP 1/90, para 17.

Development Securities (No 9) Ltd & Ors v Revenue and Customs,[72] also involved the residence of non-UK incorporated companies for a limited and specific purpose. As was the case in *Untelrab Ltd v McGregor*,[73] subsidiaries were formed in Jersey in order to undertake specific transactions as part of a tax planning arrangement. The directors of the subsidiaries were Jersey resident directors provided by a Jersey law firm and the company secretary of the UK resident parent company, who was a UK resident. In the First-tier Tribunal, Judge Harriet Morgan noted that it does not necessarily follow that central management and control of an overseas group company, which has been formed for a specific purpose is UK resident simply because it follows the parent company's plan and does what is expected, if proper consideration is given to the proposal and the directors are in fact exercising their discretion.[74] She considered that the case was unusual because the Jersey companies were set up only to acquire assets for an amount substantially in excess of their market value. This single transaction that they were to undertake was inherently uncommercial from their perspective. Consequently, the transaction could only be valid as a matter of corporate law if the UK parent company specifically approved the transaction and the Jersey companies were adequately funded such that there was no prejudice to creditors. In addition, the directors resigned after making their decisions as companies were to become UK tax resident six weeks after acquiring the assets.[75]

Although the directors were serious in their concern to check the legality of the proposed actions and regarded it as their responsibility to ensure that the Jersey companies and they themselves were not acting unlawfully, she regarded checking that there were no legal impediments as insufficient to constitute taking the decision about the proposed action. Judge Morgan concluded that the strategic decision, that is, whether it was a good plan for the Jersey companies to acquire the assets at a price in excess of their value, was not made by the board of directors in Jersey.[76]

These circumstances were distinguished from *Wood v Holden*, where the board considered a proposal and, having taken appropriate advice, decided that it was in the best interests of the companies to enter into the transaction. Since the transaction was not in the interests of the Jersey companies and could only take place with parent company approval, 'the inescapable conclusion is that the board was simply doing what the parent… in effect instructed it to do. In the circumstances, the line was crossed from the parent influencing and giving strategic or policy direction to the parent giving an instruction.'[77]

72 *Development Securities (No 9) Ltd & Ors v Revenue and Customs* [2017] UKFTT 565 (TC).
73 *Untelrab Ltd v McGregor* [1996] STC (SCD) [see **6.4**].
74 *Development Securities (No 9) Ltd & Ors v Revenue and Customs* [2017] UKFTT 565 (TC), at para 401.
75 [2017] UKFTT 565 (TC), at para 402.
76 [2017] UKFTT 565 (TC), at paras 416 and 417.
77 [2017] UKFTT 565 (TC), at para 426.

The First-tier Tribunal decision is not easy to square with *Wood v Holden* because the company's directors did not stand aside but decided, as a constitutional organ, to accept the proposal of the parent company in accordance with the company's corporate requirements. It does however indicate the difficulty in drawing the dividing line between on the one hand, directors who sign documents 'mindlessly, without even thinking what the documents are', and an effective decision of a constitutional organ on the other. The finding in *Development Securities* that the directors simply agreed to take the formal actions required as the final part of what they were engaged to do from the outset, sits on the boundary. Discrepancies and lack of credibility in the taxpayer's evidence will also play a part.

On appeal,[78] the Upper Tribunal unanimously overturned the decision. Mr Justice Marcus Smith and Judge Guy Brannan first considered that the mere fact that the directors had a specific task entrusted to them by their parent, after which they were to resign, did not say anything about where central management and control vested. Second, the First-tier Tribunal's conclusion that the transaction was uncommercial was based on a misunderstanding of the nature of the transactions and of the Jersey directors' duties in relation to those transactions. They did not consider the transactions as uncommercial simply because they paid more than the value of properties since the funding was not provided by them but by the parent company even if they could be described as artificial. The directors' duty was to act in the interests of the shareholders and the scheme was in the interests of the parent which they properly discharged by making decisions at meetings in Jersey.[79]

The Court of Appeal,[80] however restored the First-tier decision that the companies were UK resident. Each of the judges gave separate reasons. Lord Justices Newey and David Richards both considered that the Jersey directors had, in effect been instructed and carried out the instruction after checking the legality of the plan. Lord Justice Nugee decided on the basis of technical issues, in the way the taxpayer dealt with the appeal from the Upper Tribunal but had "very considerable reservations about the FTT's reasoning" which he declined to endorse.[81] He however, acknowledged that central management and control is not confined to 'actively engaging' with the decision in the sense of considering for themselves the merits and demerits of a proposal. The question they said 'is not why the directors made the decision they did, or how much thought they gave to it, or what they did or did not take, or should or should not have taken, into account. The question is a much simpler one, namely: did they

78 *Development Securities PLC & Ors v Revenue and Customs* [2019] UKUT 169 (TCC), [2019] BTC 518, [2019] STC 1424.

79 [2019] UKUT 169 (TCC), at paras 39 to 54.

80 *Revenue and Customs v Development Securities Plc & Ors* [2020] EWCA Civ 1705, [2021] STC 84, [2021] BTC 1.

81 The failure of the respondent taxpayer to file a respondent's notice setting out an alternative to the appellant's grounds of appeal [2020] EWCA Civ 1705, at para 94.

make the decision?'[82] Differing views of six judges in three courts indicate the difficulty of distinguishing influence from instructions, even on detailed evidence.

6.09 Elements of central management and control

In the two cases in which the test was first established,[83] all business activities of the companies concerned were carried out, and largely controlled, overseas. Calcutta Jute Mills Co manufactured and sold jute in India and the Cesena Sulphur Co manufactured and sold sulphur in Italy. All Calcutta's property was situated in India – indeed the directors of Calcutta did not have even an office in the UK but met in that belonging to one of their number! – and Cesena's main books, accounts and banking accounts were maintained in Italy. Yet, on the basis of the 'real business' test, the court held that both companies were resident in the UK. Clearly, therefore, it cannot have been the day-to-day management and control of the business activities of those companies which Kelly CB and Huddleston B had in mind when they decided that the 'real business' of those companies was carried on, not overseas, but in the UK.

The clue as to what they did have in mind is provided by Kelly CB who said that:

> '… the answer to the question, Where does a joint stock company reside? is, … where its governing body is to be met with and found, and where its governing body exercises the powers conferred upon it by the Act of Parliament, and by the Articles of Association, where it meets and is in bodily and personal presence for the purposes of the concern.'[84]

The 'real business' of Calcutta Jute Mills Ltd and of Cesena Sulphur Co Ltd was, in other words, carried on, not in India or Italy, but in the place from which the decision to carry out operations in India or Italy had emanated. As Huddleston B said of the Cesena Sulphur Co Ltd's business:

> 'No doubt the manufacturing part may be done and was done in Italy; so supposing that in another part of the world they found sulphur and carried on their business there, the manufacturing part of the business would be carried on there, no doubt; but the administrative part of the business would be carried on at the place from which all the orders came, from which all the directions flowed, and where the appointments were made, where the appointments of the officers were revoked, where the agents were nominated, where their powers were recalled, where the money was received (whatever may have been sent), where the dividends were

82 [2020] EWCA Civ 1705, at para 103.

83 *Calcutta Jute Mills Co Ltd v Nicholson* (1876) 1 TC 83 and *Cesena Sulphur Co Ltd v Nicholson* (1876) 1 TC 88.

84 (1876) 1 TC 83 at 95.

> payable, and where the dividends were declared. We find that all these Acts are performed in London. I cannot help thinking that the main place of business of the Company is in England … .'[85]

The place of central management and control is, then, not necessarily the place in which a company's manufacturing or trading activities take place but the place in which the parameters governing those activities are set and the place in which the fundamental policies to be implemented in the UK or elsewhere are adopted.

The activities that make up management and control of a closely held, entrepreneurially run company were examined in *Laerstate BV v HMRC*.[86] Laerstate BV a Netherlands incorporated company was the vehicle for taking control of Lonrho Plc, a UK-based multinational company quoted on the London Stock Exchange by a German entrepreneur Mr Dieter Bock. On 9 December 1992, Mr Bock became the sole shareholder of Laerstate and was appointed a director in addition to the existing director Mr Edward Trapman, a business associate of Mr Bock. On 9 December 1992, the Laerstate participation in Lonrho was secured by subscription for new shares, a purchase of existing shares and associated put and call options over further shares from a company ultimately owned by Mr Tiny Rowland, who then controlled Lonrho, and financed by a loan from a German bank. Mr Bock became joint managing director and CEO of Lonrho in London on 10 February 1993. Although he remained a German resident, Mr Bock spent significant periods of time in the UK including staying in a family flat from April 1994 and thus became UK resident. During 1996 the sale of the shares in Lonrho were negotiated. Mr Bock resigned as a director on 30 August 1996 and the sale took place in November of that year. The complexity of the arrangements for the purchase, ownership and sale of the Lonrho shares were such that more or less continuous management activity was required.

Laerstate argued that acts of central management and control can be identified as board resolutions where this precedes the signing of a document, or the signing of the document itself where there is no resolution which in each case were outside the UK. First-tier Tribunal Judges Avery Jones and Berner considered that:

> '[the] test does not confine itself to a consideration of particular actions of the company, such as the signing of documents or the making of certain board resolutions outside the UK if, in a given case, a more general overview of the course of business and trading demonstrates that as a matter of fact central management and control abides in the UK.'[87]

In their view:

---

85 (1876) 1 TC 88 at 107.

86 *Laerstate BV v HMRC* [2009] UKFTT 209 (TC).

87 At para 28.

> 'In relation to the actions taken by the Appellant and the Appellant's board, it is clear that the mere physical acts of signing resolutions or documents do not suffice for actual management.'[88]

The Tribunal found that in the period Mr Bock was a director, under the constitution of the company independently authorised to represent the appellant at law and otherwise. Both at the times when board meetings were held and during the period when there were no such meetings, Mr Bock himself conducted the business of Laerstate. They accepted that on occasion he did so with the assistance, cooperation and concurrence of Mr Trapman and that acts of management took place in various locations, including in the Netherlands and Germany, but throughout the period during which Mr Bock was a director they found that he carried out activities of a strategic and policy nature and managed the business of Laerstate, and that he did so to a substantial extent in the UK. Although Mr Trapman was a director, the evidence shows that his involvement was very much secondary to that of Mr Bock, who was responsible for all the negotiation and strategic decisions on matters at these times. For a considerable time there were no board meetings even though there were significant management activities taking place. Those management activities were undertaken by Mr Bock, substantially in the UK.[89] They suspected that he had concluded that he should not be a director at the time of disposal of the shares in Lonrho[90] and found that the company had been run in the same way as when Mr Bock was a director.

In contrast, the UK resident director of a Jersey incorporated company who was also secretary of the UK resident parent company in *Development Securities (No 9) Ltd & Ors v Revenue and Customs*[91] did not himself make strategic and management decisions. His function was mostly administrative as a communicator, co-ordinator and facilitator.

6.10 Finance as a key element

If, as has been demonstrated at **6.09** above, policy-making is the primary expression of central management and control, the raising and allocation of the funds without which a company's policies could not be implemented must be an almost equally important manifestation of such management and control.

In *American Thread Co v Joyce*,[92] for instance, the Master of the Rolls noted that the business of the New York company was one in which seasonable purchases of cotton had to be made, and commented:

88 At para 33.
89 At para 16.
90 At para 18.
91 *Development Securities (No 9) Ltd & Ors v Revenue and Customs* [2017] UKFTT 565 (TC) at paras 431 and 432. [See **6.8**].
92 (1913) 6 TC 163.

'Those purchases of cotton necessarily involve considerable financing. The whole policy depends really upon aye or no, shall we finance to the extent of, I think in one case it appears, £300,000. The New York people cannot do that at all. The whole purse-strings in the sense of money coming in by borrowing are kept most zealously at Manchester, and by means of those purse strings they are able to control and do control the policy of the Company and the mode in which they carry on their business of buying and selling.'[93]

Similarly, in *De Beers Consolidated Mines Ltd v Howe*,[94] the Lord Chancellor took as evidence that the company was resident in the UK the fact that:

'London has … always controlled … all questions of expenditure except wages, materials, and such like at the mines, and a limited sum which may be spent by the Directors at Kimberley.'[95]

A further factor to be considered – though one which alone is not, it seems, determinative of central management and control[96] – is the declaration of dividends. In *Calcutta Jute Mills Co Ltd v Nicholson*,[97] it was asserted (in support of the proposition that the company was resident in India) that the activities of the company in England were minimal, consisting of little more than the dividing between the English shareholders of the amount, less expenses, remitted to this country from India. Huddleston B refuted such a contention by pointing out that:

'The operation of the Company in London was, not to divide the amount sent among the shareholders, but it was to "declare" the amount; and I apprehend that, within the meaning of that clause, the directors in London, who had full power, might say, "Well, we do not approve of this system upon which the division has been made, and we shall require a different dividend for the future", or something of that kind, – showing plainly that they exercise the authority, and that they are the persons who are the principal body … .'[98]

Similarly, in the *American Thread Company* case,[99] one of the factors which led Hamilton J to uphold the finding of the Commissioners that the central management and control of the American company rested with the English directors was that:

93 (1913) 6 TC 163.
94 (1906) 5 TC 198.
95 (1906) 5 TC 198 at 213.
96 In *Egyptian Hotels Ltd v Mitchell* (1914) 6 TC 542 at 552 Lord Sumner said that 'The mere declaration and payment of a dividend here out of profits earned in a business otherwise wholly carried on abroad, does not prevent the business in which the profits have already been earned from having been wholly carried on abroad. To say that part of a Company's business is to pay dividends, if it has earned them, seems to me to be a play upon words.'
97 (1876) 1 TC 83.
98 (1876) 1 TC 83 at 107.
99 (1913) 6 TC 163.

'In each year the directors, sitting in extraordinary session in England, recommend what the dividend on the common stock should be … But in the year 1904, when the dividend was 16 per cent, though the Board by resolution recommended that rate, the gentleman who sent the cablegram to the American directors said that the Board had decided that the dividend should be 16 per cent, and went on to say: "Arrange for usual formal resolutions as regards dividends on preferred shares and common stock without delay". Accordingly, the 16 per cent was announced … .'[100]

These words of Hamilton J make it clear that, so far as dividends are concerned, the person or group of persons who actually decides upon the quantum of the dividend, that is the directors and not the persons who formally resolve to pay it or give their formal approval to its declaration, that is, the shareholders.

6.11 Degree of activity

The degree of activity does not form part of the test and must be put in context. In *Wood v Holden (Inspector of Taxes)*[101] in the Court of Appeal Chadwick LJ[102] adopted the analysis of Park J in the High Court as compelling where he said:

'[64] … The making of the board resolutions and the signing and execution of documents which the Commissioners say were the only acts of management and control of Eulalia all took place in the Netherlands. A company is resident where its central management and control are situated. How, therefore, can Eulalia have been resident in the United Kingdom? How can it have been resident anywhere other than the Netherlands?

[65] … What [the Commissioners] seem really to be saying is that, although the only acts of control and management took place outside the United Kingdom, there was not much involved in them. But the test of a company's residence is still the central control and management test: it is not the law that that test is superseded by some different test if the business of a company is such that not a great deal is required for central control and management of its business to be carried out.

[66] … If directors of an overseas company sign documents mindlessly, without even thinking what the documents are, I accept that it would be difficult to say that the national jurisdiction in which the directors do that is the jurisdiction of residence of the company. But if they apply their minds to whether or not to sign the documents, the authorities … indicate that it is a very different matter … .'

Park J also rejected the notion that 'effective decisions … require some minimum level of information' with the implication that decisions taken by a director that were not informed somehow did not count.

100 (1913) 6 TC 163.
101 [2006] EWCA Civ 26.
102 At paras 35 and 36.

Engaging with the substantive decision as opposed to understanding and considering the lawfulness of the directors' actions was regarded as an important factor by Newey, LJ in *HMRC v Development Securities PLC*.[103] Nugee, LJ considered that even where the directors feel they are instructed and that is why they decided to enter into the transactions, did not mean that they did not decide to do so at all.[104]

6.12 Administrative functions

The undertaking of activities to comply with company law such as those of a company secretary are not indications of residence.[105] More recently in *News Datacom*,[106] the Special Commissioners concluded that a single meeting in the UK was concerned only with ministerial matters and matters of good housekeeping. The meeting was not concerned with policy, strategic, or management matters relating to the conduct of the business of the company. It did not reflect a manifestation of the controlling brain or where the business of the company was really carried on. It was not an exercise of central management and control. It was the tidying up operation, conducted by alternate directors. The circumstances are unusual and the extent to which any principle is established is questionable.

6.13 Influence compared with management and control

Influencing of company policy by persons who are not authorised to make decisions as part of the constitutional organs of the company is not an exercise of central management and control, at least in cases where the functions of those organs have not been 'usurped'. As Chadwick LJ said at para 27 in *Wood v Holden*:

> '[I]t is essential to recognise the distinction (in concept, at least) between the role of an "outsider" in proposing, advising and influencing the decisions which the constitutional organs take in fulfilling their functions and the role of an outsider who dictates the decisions which are to be taken. In that context an "outsider" is a person who is not, himself, a participant in the formal process (a board meeting or a general meeting) through which the relevant constitutional organ fulfils its function.'

---

103 *Revenue and Customs v Development Securities Plc & Ors* [2020] EWCA Civ 1705, [2021] STC 84, [2021] BTC 1, at para 84.

104 *Revenue and Customs v Development Securities Plc & Ors* [2020] EWCA Civ 1705, [2021] STC 84, [2021] BTC 1, at para 104

105 *Todd v Egyptian Delta Land and Investment Co Ltd* (1929) 14 TC 119, contrary to *Swedish Central Railway Co Ltd v Thompson* (1925) 9 TC 342.

106 *News Datacom Ltd & News Data Security Products Ltd v Revenue & Customs* [2006] UKSPC SPC561.

Thus the design and superintending of the transaction by the accountants on behalf of their client did not constitute an exercise of central management and control.[107]

6.14 Location of central management and control

Identification of the person or group of persons who exercise *de facto* central management and control of a company does not, of course, conclude the question of a company's residence. There remains the final step of identifying the place from which they exercise that central management and control.

Where, as will usually be the case, full powers of management and control are vested in the directors of a company and those powers are exercised by the directors or delegated to others under their control,[108] the place where the directors habitually meet to make their decisions on policy, finance and related matters will be the place of central management and control. This is stressed in case after case.

In *Calcutta Jute Mills Co v Nicholson*,[109] for example, Kelly CB says that a company resides

> '… where its governing body is to be met with and found, and where its governing body exercises the powers conferred upon it … where it meets and is in bodily and personal presence for the purposes of the concern … at the office or place of dwelling … where the directors meet.'[110]

Similarly, in *De Beers Consolidated Mines Ltd v Howe*,[111] the Lord Chancellor said:

> '… it is clearly established … that the Directors' Meetings in London are the meetings where the real control is exercised in practically all the important business of the Company… .'[112]

This recurrent emphasis on the place of directors' meetings must not, however, lead one to suppose that the location of directors' meetings is *the* test of company residence. As Lord Radcliffe pointed out in *Bullock v Unit Construction Co Ltd*:[113]

107 See **6.08** and **6.12** on the difficulty in distinguishing influence from instruction in cases where subsidiaries are involved.
108 See **6.07** above.
109 (1876) 1 TC 83.
110 (1876) 1 TC 83 at 95–96.
111 (1906) 5 TC 198.
112 (1906) 5 TC 198 at 213.
113 (1959) 38 TC 712.

'... the necessity of establishing some common standard for the treatment of different tax payers meant that the Courts of Law were bound in course of time to produce and apply some general principles of their own to form an acceptable test of residence. No doubt it might have taken a variety of forms ... the site of meetings of the directors' board [was a] possible candidate ... for selection as the criterion. In fact, as we know, the principle was adopted that a company is resident where its central control and management abide ... .'[114]

Even if central management and control is in the hands of the directors because their role has not been usurped, their place of meeting may not determine the company's place of residence if their meetings there are merely a matter of form. The Revenue Statement of Practice[115] puts it as follows:

'In general the place of directors' meetings is significant only in so far as those meetings constitute the medium through which central management and control is exercised. If, for example, the directors of a company were engaged together actively in the United Kingdom in the complete running of a business which was wholly in the United Kingdom, the company would not be regarded as resident outside the United Kingdom merely because the directors held formal board meetings outside the United Kingdom.'[116]

This statement is now mostly limited to those extreme cases where the directors as a matter of proper exercise of their functions have already made the decisions that constitute central management and control in the UK but hold meetings pretending that the decisions are made elsewhere. In *Wood v Holden*, Park J said,[117] 'that the principle almost always followed is that a company is resident in the jurisdiction where its board of directors meets. In the previous sentence I have said "almost always" because it is possible for a company to be resident in one territory even if it does not hold directors' meetings there' (where the board's function is usurped).[118]

Such judicial statements have not deterred HMRC from pressing the point. The HMRC position was argued in *News Datacorp* thus:

'129. Mr Brennan QC submitted that the test of corporate residence is the *De Beers* test. This required the questions to be asked where is the real business of the company carried on and where does central management and control actually abide?

114 (1959) 38 TC 712 at 738.
115 SP 1/90.
116 SP 1/90 para 14.
117 SP 1/90 para 21.
118 HMRC have indicated a sympathetic and flexible approach to this in relation to COVID-19 pandemic. They state that 'we do not consider that a company will necessarily become resident in the UK because a few board meetings are held here, or because some decisions are taken in the UK over a short period of time. The existing HMRC guidance makes it clear that we will take a holistic view of the facts and circumstances of each case.' (HMRC International Manual INTM120185 – HMRC Approach to Company Residence in response to the Covid-19 Pandemic (April 2020)).

> 130. These questions were to be answered in all cases by reference to the course of business and trading.
>
> 131. The test of central management and control is not to be treated as a test which depends solely on the location where the directors meet. The search is for the principal seat of business – it is there where the central management and control actually abides (see the *Calcutta Jute* case at page 96). This carries with it connotations of continuity because of the use of phrases such as "actually abides", "carries on business", "keeping house". It is not sufficient, therefore, to look simply at the period during July 1992 when the relevant transactions were carried out: instead it is necessary to consider the overall pattern of conduct established over a period of time – residence does not change on every occasion where there is short-term change in the location of board meetings.
>
> 132. The location of directors' meetings could have been but was not chosen as the test for corporate residence (see Lord Radcliffe in *Unit Construction* [1960] AC 351 at 365).'

The correct approach now in the case of legal persons is to pay attention to the legal framework and constitution that gives them life. There have thus far been no cases concerning companies where the board does not function through meetings but via written resolutions or where meetings are held by telephone or video conference.

The residence of a company is where the directors perform the functions that constitute central management and control, not where they reside. In *John Hood & Co Ltd v Magee*,[119] for instance, Mr Hood was the sole director of a company incorporated in Belfast and registered in New York. The Commissioners found that, although the company traded in both Ireland and America, it kept house and did its real business in Belfast where Mr Hood held the majority of his board 'meetings'. Kenny J said: 'It is a mere accident that Mr Hood resides in New York.'[120]

Gibson, J put it thus:

> 'The residence of the company cannot be determined by Mr Hood's choice of his own residence. No doubt, wherever he went, he carried his functions with him ... All the same, he was not the company, it owned his brain and capacity as well as the business. The tap-root of the fruit-bearing tree was at Belfast.'[121]

Clearly, the residence of individual directors may be of some significance from an evidentiary perspective.

119 (1918) 7 TC 327.
120 (1918) 7 TC 327 at 358.
121 (1918) 7 TC 327 at 350.

6.15 Dual or multiple residence

In this chapter the quest hitherto has been that, no matter how complex the affairs of a company or how dispersed over the face of the earth its activities might be, it may be possible to find the place of central management and control exercised in the UK. Exceptionally, that place may not be the UK exclusively. As Lord Radcliffe says in *Bullock v Unit Construction Co Ltd*:[122]

> '... the facts of individual cases have not always so arranged themselves as to make it possible to identify any one country as the seat of central management and control at all. Though such instances must be rare, the management and control may be divided or even, at any rate in theory, peripatetic. Situations of this kind do not arise just to tease the minds of Judges: they are the product of some peculiar necessity, political or otherwise.'[123]

Such a division of management and control will necessitate a finding of dual residence, and, although the first such finding was not made until 1925, the possibility of such a finding had been admitted earlier.

In 1915, *Mitchell v Egyptian Hotels Ltd*[124] came before the court and, in an oblique way, the matter was moved forward a stage. Egyptian Hotels Ltd had admitted to being resident in the UK and its residence status was, therefore, not in question. It was held, however, that the company was managed and controlled in Egypt so as to be liable to tax on its profits under Schedule D, Case V. Viscount Cave saw this decision as being a tacit acceptance of the principle of dual residence:

> '... the facts ... were sufficient ... to establish residence in Egypt, so that, if a company can have but one residence – namely, the place where its control and management abides, it must have been held that the company being resident in Egypt was not resident here, and accordingly was not taxable at all; but no such suggestion was made either by counsel or by any member of the tribunals by which the decision was given and upheld. This being so, while the case does not expressly decide that a company may have two residences for income tax purposes, the decision appears to be inconsistent with any other view.'[125]

This opinion was expressed by Viscount Cave LC in the context of his judgment in *Swedish Central Rly Co Ltd v Thompson*,[126] the first case in which an actual finding of dual residence was made and upheld. The decision in that case was, however, later described as 'unfortunate ... having regard to the course of authority both before and after its date',[127] and the facts reveal why.

122 (1959) 38 TC 712.
123 (1959) 38 TC 712 at 739.
124 (1915) 6 TC 542.
125 (1925) 9 TC 342 at 374.
126 (1925) 9 TC 342 at 374.
127 *Bullock v Unit Construction Co Ltd* (1959) 38 TC 712 at 740, per Lord Radcliffe.

The company concerned had been incorporated in England for the purpose of constructing, maintaining and leasing a railway between Frovi and Ludvika in Sweden. During the period with which the case was concerned the company had fulfilled all these objectives and was merely drawing an annual rental under a lease granted to a Swedish traffic company. The registered office of the company was maintained in London and there the company seal was kept, formal administrative business was dealt with by a committee of three directors, transfers of shares were made and registered, and the accounts were drawn up and audited. All directors' and shareholders' meetings were, however, held in Stockholm and there the minimal business activity of the company (the receipt of rents) was carried on. It was found as a fact by the Special Commissioners that the central control and management was in Sweden but that the company was also resident in the UK, and their findings were upheld in the House of Lords. In another part of the speech from which the earlier quotation is taken, Viscount Cave LC said that:

> '… when the central management and control of a company abides in a particular place the company is held for the purposes of income tax to have a residence in that place; but it does not follow that it cannot have a residence elsewhere. An individual may clearly have more than one residence (see *Cooper v Cadwalader*[128]); and in principle there appears to be no reason why a company should not be in the same position. The central management and control may be divided and it may "keep house and do business" in more than one place; and if so it may have more than one residence.'[129]

The finding of the Commissioners, however, had been not that central management and control was divided, but that it lay in Sweden. Once upheld by the House of Lords, therefore, the case began to be regarded as an authority for the proposition that, while central management and control was one test of corporate residence, there was another test also: that of the location of administrative control. This was the approach taken by the Crown in *Egyptian Delta Land and Investment Co Ltd v Todd*,[130] but, there, in the House of Lords, Viscount Sumner went to great lengths to stamp out the idea and to forestall any endorsement of it by his brethren:

> 'All that was decided in the *Swedish Central Railway* case was that the company could have two residences, one in England as well as one in Sweden. Your Lordships were not asked to decide more. It is true that by admission the controlling power over the business was in Sweden, but other business was done in London the character and importance of which, though set out in the Case, was not discussed at the Bar. It was a matter of degree on the facts and your Lordships cannot be deemed to have come to some unexpressed conclusion on that ground merely because you did not for yourselves declare … that there was no evidence of business carried on

128 (1904) 5 TC 101.
129 *Swedish Central Rly Co Ltd v Thompson* (1925) 9 TC 342 at 372.
130 (1929) 14 TC 119.

in England ... Nor is it decisive of the point to say now that the business done in England was only administrative. It was in fact a good deal more, and in the static condition of the company's affairs it was not much less important than the Swedish part. If new questions arose the Swedish directors could settle them, but as things were little had to be done anywhere except "administration" ... and that was fairly divided between the two countries.'[131]

In other words, the question whether the Swedish Central Railway Co Ltd had more than one residence had been a question of fact for the Commissioners to determine, and the House of Lords, having held that there was some evidence on which the Commissioners' finding of dual residence could have been made, had felt itself unable to interfere with that finding. That did not mean, however, that the control of administrative duties (which was the only control the London board appeared to exercise) was an alternative test of residence. It was not, and the Law Lords had never said it was. Central control and management remained the only test and one must reconcile that with the Commissioners' decision by assuming a finding of divided central management and control.

Viscount Sumner's speech was a skilful piece of oratory – verbally shoring-up the meagre facts until they were able (if only just) to carry the weighty conclusion the Commissioners had placed on them – and it was much needed, for the facts in the *Egyptian Delta* case[132] then before the House of Lords, though not, on the face of it, dissimilar from the facts in the *Swedish Railway* case,[133] had led the Commissioners to find that Egyptian Delta Land and Investment Co Ltd was resident in Egypt only!

Viscount Sumner contrived a distinction between the two findings by declaring that such management and control as there was in the *Swedish Railway* case[134] was almost equally divided between London and Stockholm while, in the *Egyptian Delta* case,[135] the whole of the central management and control was situated in Cairo. This method of reconciling the apparently irreconcilable found such favour with Lord Radcliffe that, in *Bullock v Unit Construction Co Ltd*,[136] he declared:

'I am myself of the opinion that the best way of treating the matter is to regard the *Swedish Central Railway Company* and the *Egyptian Delta Land Company* decisions as if they were in effect one decision of the House and the speech of Viscount Sumner in the later case as affording an authoritative commentary on the significance of the earlier. He was party to both of them. If this is done much of the difficulty disappears; for it is clear that Lord Sumner wished it to be understood that the Swedish Central Railway Company's business and administration were of such a nature that what managing and controlling had to be done was in fact done as

131 (1929) 14 TC 119 at 143.
132 (1929) 14 TC 119.
133 (1925) 9 TC 342.
134 (1925) 9 TC 342.
135 (1929) 14 TC 119.
136 (1959) 38 TC 712.

> much on English as on Swedish soil. He regarded the key of the earlier decision as being contained in the words of Lord Cave: "The central management and control of a company may be divided, and it may 'keep house and do business' in more than one place; and if so it may have more than one residence".[137] On this basis the 1925 decision of the House is … a decision on that special class of case[138] … where the facts themselves are genuinely such as to not to admit of a finding that central management and control are exercised in or from any one country.'[139]

The second case in which a finding of dual residence was made was *Union Corpn Ltd v IRC*.[140] The case concerned a company which had been incorporated in South Africa but which carried on its activities partly in London and partly in South Africa. Management and control at the highest level was divided between the directors in the UK and those in South Africa but final and supreme authority lay with the directors in London. On those facts, therefore, the Commissioners found that the company was resident in the UK. That finding was rejected by the Court of Appeal as being wrong in law.

Sir Raymond Evershed MR found himself in difficulties but derived assistance from the Australian case of *Koitaki Para Rubber Estates Ltd v Federal Comr of Taxation*[141] in which Dixon J had said:

> '… a finding that a company is a resident of more than one country ought not to be made unless the control of the general affairs of the company is not centred in one country but is divided or distributed among two or more countries. The matter must always be one of degree and residence may be constituted by a combination of various factors, but one factor to be looked for is the existence in the place claimed as a residence of some part of the superior or directing authority by means of which the affairs of the company are controlled.'[142]

In the light of this judgment, and of the English authorities, Sir Raymond Evershed MR rejected the Special Commissioners' view and arrived at the conclusion that:

> '… there must, in order to constitute residence, be not only some substantial business operations in any given country but also present some part of the superior and directing authority … [T]he question of the extent of the superior or directing authority required (as well as of the business operations being performed) is one of fact to be determined by the Special Commissioners.'[143]

In other words, final and supreme arbitrating authority is not the same thing as central management and control and if the latter is found to be divided

137 *Swedish Central Rly Co Ltd v Thompson* (1925) 9 TC 342 at 372.
138 *Swedish Central Rly Co Ltd v Thompson* (1925) 9 TC 342 at 372.
139 *Bullock v Unit Construction Co Ltd* (1959) 38 TC 712 at 740.
140 (1952) 34 TC 207.
141 (1940) 64 CLR 15.
142 (1952) 34 TC 207 at 241.
143 (1952) 34 TC 207 at 275.

to a significant degree between two or more territories a finding of multiple residence must be made – even if in one of those territories is a person or group of persons with the power of ultimate arbitrament.

It is important to understand that the decision in *Union Corpn Ltd v IRC*[144] has not established a new or modified test of residence but has merely provided a basis for decision where *the* test of residence ('Where does the central control and management of this company abide?') will not admit of the single-territory answer which the word 'central' in the test question demands. Sir Raymond Evershed's solution was to 'fragment' the principle underlying the test of residence and to 'establish a residence for tax purposes wherever the exercise of some portion of controlling power and authority can be identified'.[145] Lord Radcliffe suggested this solution might still be open to question,[146] but the remainder of his dicta in *Bullock v Unit Construction Co Ltd*[147] make it clear that any basis for decision which involved a concept other than central management and control could never be countenanced.

6.16 Residence for tax treaty purposes

The purpose and effect of double taxation treaties has already been described at **2.45** above. In relation to companies, Article 4(1) of the OECD Model provides:

> '4(1) For the purposes of this Convention, the term "resident of a Contracting State" means any person who, under the laws of that State, is liable to tax therein by reason of his domicile, residence, place of management or any other criterion of a similar nature, and also includes that State and any political subdivision or local authority thereof. This term, however, does not include any person who is liable to tax in that State in respect only of income from sources in that State or capital situated therein.'

Prima facie, a company incorporated in the UK or one whose central management and control is exercised there is liable to tax on its world-wide profits. It will be a resident of a contracting state – that is, the UK – for treaty purposes. The meaning and application of this provision to companies was examined by the First-tier Tribunal in *G E Financial Investments Limited v HMRC*.[148] The case concerned a company incorporated in the UK and thus UK resident. The company entered in to a 'stapled stock' arrangement with a company incorporated in the United States which meant that shares could only be owned in both companies simultaneously, United States tax law treated a non-US incorporated company as a US person for tax purposes, thereby

144 (1952) 34 TC 207 at 275.
145 *Bullock v Unit Construction Co Ltd* (1959) 38 TC 712 at 739, per Lord Radcliffe.
146 *Bullock v Unit Construction Co Ltd* (1959) 38 TC 712 at 739, per Lord Radcliffe.
147 (1959) 38 TC 712.
148 *G E Financial Investments v Revenue & Customs* [2021] UKFTT 210 (TC).

subjecting the UK incorporated company to tax on its worldwide income. The company was a resident of the UK within Article 4(1) of the United Kingdom – United States double tax treaty. In issue was whether it was also a resident of the US within Article 4(1). Judge Brooks held that the US tax rule that treated the UK company as a US resident for US domestic law did not make the company a US resident for treaty purposes on the basis that the US stapled entity rule was not a 'criterion of a similar nature' to 'domicile, residence, citizenship, place of management, place of incorporation' in Article 4(1) of the Treaty each of which requires attachment or connection to a contracting state.[149]

On appeal the Upper Tribunal[150] overturned the decision. It considered that the connection between the criteria listed in Article 4(1) is that they are commonly accepted ways in which 'full', or worldwide, taxation is imposed, 'nothing more and nothing less'.[151] On that basis, a stapled company, being subjected to full or worldwide taxation was a US resident within Article 4(1) as 'any other criterion of a similar nature.'

The Court of Appeal[152] restored the First-tier Tribunal decision. Lady Justice Falk said that the words 'of a similar nature' required another factor to be something of a similar nature,… character or quality to the listed criteria.[153] She rejected the proposition that anyone subject to worldwide taxation in a state is a resident within Article 4(1).[154] Thus, speaking for the Court, she held that the US stapled stock rules were not a criterion of a similar nature:

> 'The US connections required by s.269B are limited to a) stapling of more than 50% by value of the foreign corporation's shares to those of a domestic corporation, and b) direct or indirect ownership as to 50% or more by US persons. Both of these requirements relate to the ownership and control of the relevant company. Neither requires any form of link between the company itself and the United States, whether a formal legal one (such as incorporation, the location of its registered office or similar) or a factual one (such as place of management). The facts that the entity to which the company is stapled is itself US incorporated and that both entities are ultimately US owned cannot suffice. In contrast, the criteria specified in Article 4(1) all describe legal or factual connections between the entity itself and the relevant Contracting State of a kind that may justify worldwide taxation.'[155]

Where a tax treaty is in place, such corporate dual residence may be resolved for the purposes of the treaty by the following mechanism:

149 *G E Financial Investments v Revenue & Customs* [2021] UKFTT 210 (TC), at paras 59 to 66.
150 GE Financial Investments v Revenue & Customs [2023] UKUT 146 (TCC).
151 At para 148.
152 *Revenue and Customs v GE Financial Investments* [2024] EWCA Civ 797.
153 At para 67.
154 At para 94.
155 At para 122. In the author's view, the Upper Tribunal's analysis is preferable.

> '4(3) Where by reason of the provisions of paragraph 1 a person other than an individual is a resident of both Contracting States, then it shall be deemed to be a resident only of the State in which its place of effective management is situated.'

Whether the company is also at the same time resident of the other contracting state will depend on the domestic tax law of that state. Thus a finding of dual residence as described at **6.15** above will not itself entail dual residence for treaty purposes.

There has been little consensus internationally on the meaning of 'place of effective management' and recent attempts by the English courts to interpret and apply it to companies have not been entirely satisfactory.

The OECD Commentary on Article 4(3) has itself been controversial. Its latest version found in the 2017 OECD Model Treaty reads:

> '24.1 An entity may have more than one place of management, but it can have only one place of effective management at any one time.
>
> 24.2 The place of effective management is the place where the key management and commercial decisions that are necessary for the conduct of the entity's business are in substance made, *i.e.* the place where the actions to be taken by the entity as a whole are, *in fact*, determined and all. *All the* relevant facts and circumstances must be examined to determine the place of effective management.
>
> 24.3 The place of effective management will ordinarily be the place where the most senior person or group of persons (for example a board of directors) makes its decisions, which normally corresponds to where it meets. There are cases, however, where the key management and commercial decisions necessary for the conduct of the entity's business are in substance made in one place somewhere by a person or group of persons but are formally finalized somewhere else by it or by another person or group of persons. In such cases, it will be necessary to consider other factors. Depending on the circumstances, these other factors could include:
>
> – Where a board of directors formally finalizes key management and commercial decisions necessary for the conduct of the entity's business at meetings held in one State but these decisions are in substance made in another State, the place of effective management will be in the latter State.
> – If there is a person such as a controlling interest holder (e.g. a parent company or associated enterprise) that effectively makes the key management and commercial decisions that are necessary for the conduct of the entity's business, the place of effective management will be where that person makes these key decisions. For that to be the case, however, the key decisions made by that person must go beyond decisions related to the normal management and policy formulation of a group's activities (e.g. the type of decisions that a parent company of a multinational group would be expected to take as regards the direction, co-ordination and supervision of the activities of each part of the group).
> – Where a board of directors routinely approves the commercial and strategic decisions made by the executive officers, the place where the executive officers perform their functions would be important in determining the place of effective management of the entity. In

> distinguishing between a place where a decision is made as opposed to where it is merely approved, one should consider the place where advice on recommendations or options relating to the decisions were considered and where the decisions were ultimately developed.'

Indofood International Finance Ltd v JP Morgan Chase Bank NA[156] involved the Indonesia-Netherlands tax treaty in a commercial dispute governed by English law. The court was asked to deal with what an Indonesian court would have decided was the place of effective management of a hypothetical Dutch company. Two judges in the Court of Appeal declined to decide the case on this point but Sir Andrew Morritt, the Chancellor expressed the following views:

> 'As counsel for the issuer pointed out the test, as elaborated by the OECD commentary, refers to the place where "key" decisions are taken. The provisions of the trust deed and, more particularly, of the note conditions show clearly that they must be taken by the parent guarantor. Whilst I do not doubt that the board of directors of Newco would be permitted to determine what to do with the handling charges and equity capital and would be responsible for complying with the requirements of Dutch law, those are hardly the "key" decisions. Let it be assumed that the issuer and Newco are otherwise resident in Holland and the question arose whether to interpose Newco it is, in my view, plain beyond doubt that such a decision and the terms of any interposition would not be left to the issuer or Newco but would be decided by the board of the parent guarantor. In particular it would not be left to the board of the issuer or of Newco to decide whether to assign or to accept the benefit of the loan agreement between the parent guarantor and the issuer and if so on what terms. Questions in relation to any subsequent migration, substitution or interposition of another company between the parent guarantor and Newco or between Newco and the issuer would be decided by the board of the parent guarantor. In my view it is plain that the place of effective management of the issuer is Indonesia and that the place of effective management of Newco, if interposed between the parent guarantor and the issuer, would be Indonesia too.'[157]

These comments cast little light on the expression as the key decisions referred to are shareholder issues rather than those relating to the management of the hypothetical company.

In *Wood v Holden* the Commissioners accepted the HMRC submission that in the present context there is no difference between central management and control and the place of effective management.[158] Park J said: 'Article 4(3) requires there to be identified a 'place' of effective management, and it has to be a place situated in one of the two States'[159] and 'when it comes to applying the detailed wording of article 4(3) what was the 'place … situated' in the

156 [2006] EWCA Civ 158.
157 At para 57.
158 At para 146.
159 [2005] EWHC 547 (Ch) para 77.

United Kingdom which was Eulalia's 'place of effective management'?'[160] The Court of Appeal[161] did not address the issue.

In *Trevor Smallwood Trust v R & C Comrs*[162] the Special Commissioners reviewed this case and the OECD commentary as it applies to companies but ultimately merely concluded that 'having regard to the ordinary meaning of the words in their context and in the light of their object and purpose, we should approach the issue of POEM as considering in which state the real top level management is found'.[163] When the matter came before the Court of Appeal, it ruled that on the basis of *Wood v Holden*, since the directors of the trust company in Mauritius were in place and exercised their powers as such, the fact that they might agree to act in accordance with the instructions they received from accountants in the UK did not permit a conclusion that the POEM was in the UK.[164]

Where a company incorporated in one contracting state has its central management and control entirely in the other contracting state, then the place of effective management cannot be in the state of incorporation by reason of formal connection there. Similarly, if a director's role in a contracting state is merely a 'fake' or a 'façade', then place of effective management cannot be in that state.[165]

Exceptionally, UK tax treaties may depart from the OECD model in resolving dual residence problems by reference to the place of effective management of the taxpayer. These treaties do not adopt any rule but, instead, require such dual residence and to be resolved by agreement between the competent authorities of the contracting states.[166] Historically, such treaties were rare. They are, however, becoming common in UK tax treaties. The absence of any rule means that taxpayers are unable to determine their tax liabilities, which is left to the discretion of tax administrations. Dissatisfied taxpayers will need to look to administrative law remedies such as judicial review, rather than by way of appeal to the tribunal's and courts.

---

160 At para 78.

161 [2006] EWCA Civ 26.

162 *Trevor Smallwood & Mary Caroline Smallwood Trustees of the Trevor Smallwood Trust v R & C Comrs; Trevor Smallwood Settlor of the Trevor Smallwood Trust v R & C Comrs*, [2008] UKSPC 669.

163 At para 130. On appeal to the High Court ([2009] EWHC 777 (Ch)), Mann J ruled that the question of dual residence did not arise and consequently Art 4(3) of the treaty was not engaged.

164 *HMRC v Smallwood & Anor* [2010] EWCA Civ 778 at para 63. See **6.06** above and generally Jonathan Schwarz, *Schwarz on Tax Treaties* (Wolters Kluwer, 2021) Ch 5 on treaty residence.

165 *Bywater Investments Limited & Ors v Commissioner of Taxation* [2025] HCA 45 per Gordon, J, at paras 171 and 184.

166 See, for example, Convention between the Government of the United Kingdom of Great Britain and Northern Ireland and the Government of Canada for the Avoidance of Double Taxation and the Prevention of Fiscal Evasion with Respect to Taxes on Income and Capital Gains of 8 September 1978 (SI 1980/709) as amended by Protocol of 15 April 1980 (SI 1980/1528), Protocol of 16 October 1985 (SI 1985/1996) and Protocol of 7 May 2003 (SI 2003/2619), Art 4(3).

This approach may become the norm as a result of Actions 2 and 6 of the OECD/G20 Base Erosion and Profit Shifting (BEPS) Project.[167] The final reports have resulted in a change to Article 4(3) of the OECD model, by providing that cases of dual treaty residence of persons other than individuals would be solved on a case-by-case basis by the competent authorities, rather than the current legal rule based on place of effective management. The new version envisages that where a person other than an individual is a resident of both states, the competent authorities of the states must endeavour to determine, by mutual agreement, which state such a person is resident for the purposes of the treaty, having regard to its place of effective management, the place where it is incorporated or otherwise constituted and any other relevant factors. In the absence of such agreement, such a person will not be entitled to any treaty relief or exemption except to the extent and in such manner as may be agreed by the competent authorities. This radical approach plainly overshoots the stated objective to ensure that dual resident entities are not used to obtain the benefits of treaties unduly. This revised approach is included in Article 4(1) of the Multilateral Convention to Implement Tax Treaty Related Measures to Prevent Base Erosion and Profit Shifting which includes all treaty-related BEPS proposals.[168] In ratifying the Convention, the United Kingdom has chosen to apply this rule to all its tax treaties covered by the Convention.[169]

6.17 Transfer of residence abroad

Following the decision of the courts that the place of a company's central management and control was the sole determinant of its place of residence, it became commonplace for companies engaged extensively in overseas activities to amend their articles of association and to transfer their central management and control abroad once the burden of UK taxation became significantly greater than that which would be imposed were they to be resident overseas. Of the companies involved in the cases discussed in this chapter, two, at least, changed their place of residence in this way: The Cesena Sulphur Company became resident in Italy and The American Thread Company became resident in America,[170] and, in 1928, when the validity of The Egyptian Delta Land

167 OECD, *Neutralising the Effects of Hybrid Mismatch Arrangements*, Action 2 – 2015 Final Report; *Preventing the Granting of Treaty Benefits in Inappropriate Circumstances*, Action 6 – 2015 Final Report, OECD/G20 Base Erosion and Profit Shifting Project (OECD Publishing, Paris, 2015).

168 OECD, *Multilateral Convention to Implement Tax Treaty Related Measures to Prevent Base Erosion and Profit Shifting* signed at Paris on 7 June 2017.

169 United Kingdom Reservations and Notifications, Notification of Existing Provisions in Listed Agreements Pursuant to Art 3(6).

170 See paras 3 and 4 of the case stated in *Bradbury v English Sewing Cotton Co Ltd* (1923) 8 TC 481 at 482.

and Investment Co Ltd's change of residence was being challenged, Viscount Sumner was able to affirm that:

> 'Many companies have, at the cost of some trouble and expense, transferred their control and management abroad on the faith of decisions, or if you will, *dicta*, to the effect that by so doing they could legitimately reduce the burden of their taxation.'[171]

A company incorporated outside the UK may cease to be resident there by moving its central management and control outside the territory. A company incorporated in the UK will only cease to be resident if it is able to benefit from tax treaty under which it is treated as resident in the other contracting state by application of the tie-breaker in Article 4(3) or equivalent provisions.

6.18 Treaty non-resident companies

Under CTA 2009 section 18, a company which would otherwise be regarded as resident in the UK and is regarded for the purpose of any double taxation relief arrangements as resident in a territory outside the UK and not resident in the UK is treated as non-resident.

6.19 European Companies

The European Company Regulation[172] came into force on 8 October 2004. The Regulation permitted the formation of a European Company (SE), which would be subject to the tax law of the country within the EU in which it was resident. Under the company laws applicable in the UK, it is not possible for a company incorporated in the UK to transfer its registered office out of the UK and likewise, there is no company law mechanism to accept the transfer into the UK of the registered office of a foreign incorporated company. However, an SE is permitted to transfer its registered office between Member States of the European Union and one which transfers its registered office to the UK, in accordance with Article 8 of the Council Regulation, upon registration there is regarded for the purposes of the Taxes Acts as resident in the UK; the central management and control test is displaced by registration.[173] However, an SE does not cease to be regarded as resident in the UK by reason only of the subsequent transfer from the UK of its registered office.[174] This would suggest that a transfer out of the registration would have had to be accompanied by

171 *Egyptian Delta Land and Investment Co Ltd v Todd* (1929) 14 TC 119 at 156.

172 Council Regulation (EC) 2157/2001 on the Statute for a European Company (Societas Europaea).

173 CTA 2009 s 16(2) and (3).

174 CTA 2009 s 16(4).

the exercise of central management and control outside the UK. The same rules[175] apply to a European Cooperative Society (SCE) under the Statute for a European Cooperative Society.[176]

Following the UK's withdrawal from the EU, any UK registered Societas Europaea converted to a UK Societas from 1 January 2021 the end of the Brexit transition period. They therefore continues in a similar manner to a UK incorporated public limited company. No new UK Societas may be formed, and they may not be transferred outside the UK.[177]

6.20 Residence for special statutory purposes

For most corporation tax purposes, a single question is posed: is the company a resident of the UK or not? If it is not, then the corporation tax system does not care where its residence may be found.[178] This indifference is replaced with specific statutory measures in relation to three elements of the corporation tax system, namely group relief, controlled foreign companies and transfer pricing. Each of these has its own mechanism for identifying the territory of residence of a non-UK resident company. In the case of the controlled foreign companies and transfer pricing rules, the mechanisms include determining which of two or more foreign territories the company in question is resident in for those purposes.

6.21 Group relief

Losses and certain other amounts incurred in one member of a group of UK-resident companies may be set off by way of group relief against profits in other UK-resident companies.[179] If, in the material accounting period of the company which would otherwise be the surrendering company, that company is a 'dual resident investing company', no such losses or other amounts may be surrendered by it.[180] Dual resident company is referred to in CTA 2010 as follows:

> '109(1) This section applies if in the surrender period the surrendering company is UK resident and is also within a charge to non-UK tax under the law of a territory because–

175 CTA 2009 s 17.

176 EC Council Regulation No 1435/2003 on the Statute for a European Cooperative Society (SCE).

177 The European Public Limited-Liability Company (Amendment etc.) (EU Exit) Regulations 2018, SI 2018/1298.

178 *News Datacom Ltd v Atkinson* (HMIT) [2006] UKSPC 561 para 123.

179 CTA 2010 Pt 5, Ch 2.

180 CTA 2010 s 109(2).

(a) it derives its status as a company from that law,
(b) its place of management is in that territory, or
(c) it is for some other reason treated under that law as resident in that territory for the purposes of that tax.'

In the case of dual resident investing companies the inability to surrender group relief occurs if the company is liable to tax in another territory under foreign law. The language of section 109 borrows from Article 4(1) of the OECD Model Treaty in specifying that if the company is within the foreign tax charge by reason of its place of incorporation or place of management, then it is treated as a dual resident. The same is true if the territory applies some other residence test. A place of management in this sense is likely not limited to the UK 'central management and control' test. It is, however, insufficient that the company be regarded as dual resident for UK corporation tax purposes. A company is only dual resident for this purpose if it is also a resident of another territory under the tax laws of that territory. It does not matter for these purposes if the company is resident in more than one foreign territory under more than one foreign law.

6.22 Controlled Foreign Companies

If a company is not resident in the UK, and is controlled by a UK-resident person or persons, then it is a CFC and the Controlled Foreign Companies provisions apply. The CFC charge is imposed in relation to a CFC's accounting period if the CFC has chargeable profits for that period and none of the entity level exemptions set out in TIOPA 2010 Part 9A, Chapters 10 to 14 applies for that period. In such a case, the chargeable profits of that CFC and its creditable tax (if any) for that period are apportioned among its shareholders and taxed in the hands of UK-resident corporate shareholders with at least a 25% interest in that company.[181]

For this purpose, the question whether a company is non-UK resident is determined by reference to the normal rules of company residence described in this chapter. The residence of a CFC in a particular territory will determine whether it qualifies for certain exemptions. TIOPA 2010 section 371TA sets out a hierarchy of tests to determine the particular territory in which a CFC is resident for these purposes.

As is the case with dual resident companies, the prime residence test borrows heavily from Article 4(1) of the OECD Model:

> '371TB (1) The CFC is taken to be resident in the territory under the law of which, at all times during the relevant accounting period, the CFC is liable to tax by reason of domicile, residence or place of management.'

181 See generally: Pt 9A of TIOPA 2010 inserted by Sch 20 FA 2012.

Thus the residence of a CFC is determined in the first instance by local tax law of the territory in question. Resolution of the foreign dual or multiple residence is addressed through a series of sub-tests. Reference to the tax law of a foreign territory must be taken to include a reference to applicable tax treaties and therefore any treaty rules to resolve dual residence must be applied to decide if the company is dual resident before applying these tests.

Dual or multiple foreign residence is resolved, first, in favour of the place of effective management of the company.[182] The legislation thus adopts the language of Article 4(3) of the OECD Model Double Taxation Convention.[183] The draftsperson, however, misunderstood the meaning of 'place of effective management' in Article 4(3), as is demonstrated by the second rule which addresses the case where the place of effective management is in two or more territories.[184] In such a case, it is said that the company is resident in the territory where more than 50% of its assets are situated. The territory where more than 50% of its assets are situated is likewise deemed to be where the company is resident if its place of effective management is in none of the territories under whose laws it is resident.[185]

If none of these results in a single territory of residence, the third rule specifies that a company may elect to be treated as resident in a particular territory.[186] Where an election has not been made within the statutory time limit, an officer of HM Revenue & Customs may designate the territory of residence on a just and reasonable basis.[187]

A company with no territory of residence under the prime test is normally treated as resident in the territory where it is incorporated.[188] This could be the case for example, because it is only in a country with no system of corporate taxation or one which imposes tax on companies not by reference to domicile, residence or place of management, However, where the CFC is incorporated in the UK but resident in another territory under the tie-breaker provisions of a tax treaty with that territory and non-UK resident under CTA 2009 section 18, the CFC will be resident in that other territory.[189]

182 TIOPA 2010 s 371TB(2).

183 See **6.16** above.

184 TIOPA 2010 s 371TB(6). A company can have only one place of effective management: *Trevor Smallwood & Mary Caroline Smallwood Trustees of the Trevor Smallwood Trust v R & C Comrs; Trevor Smallwood Settlor of the Trevor Smallwood Trust v R & C Comrs*, [2008] UKSPC 669 at para 127.

185 TIOPA 2010 s 371TB(7).

186 TIOPA 2010 s 371TB(8).

187 TIOPA 2010 s 371TB(9).

188 TIOPA 2010 s 371TA(1)(b)(ii).

189 TIOPA 2010 s 371TA(2).

6.23 Transfer pricing – exemption for small or medium-sized enterprises

Profits of persons where there is common participation in the management control or capital fall to be adjusted in relation to transactions between them that are not on arm's-length terms.[190] This rule does not apply generally to small enterprises and is modified in the case of medium-sized enterprises.[191] These exceptions do not apply to transactions with persons resident in a 'non-qualifying territory'.[192] The exception applies whether or not that person is also a resident of a qualifying territory. For this purpose 'resident', in relation to a territory,

(a) means a person who, under the laws of that territory, is liable to tax there by reason of his domicile, residence or place of management; but
(b) does not include a person who is liable to tax in that territory in respect only of income from sources in that territory or capital situated there.[193]

6.24 Foreign dividends received by small companies

Dividends or other distributions received by a small company may be exempt from corporation tax if, among other requirements, the payer is a resident of (and only of) a qualifying territory at the time that the distribution is received.[194] For the purpose of CTA 2009 section 930, a company is a resident of a territory if, under the laws of the territory, the company is liable to tax there:

(a) by reason of its domicile, residence or place of management; but
(b) not in respect only of income from sources in that territory or capital situated there.[195]

6.25 Company liquidations and business cessations

The appointment of a liquidator with a view to the winding up of a company places the liquidator in control of the company's affairs and generally removes the powers of the directors and shareholders. In the case of a company incorporated outside the UK, the liquidator would typically be appointed under the law of the place of incorporation. Where such a company was

190 TIOPA 2010 Pt 4.
191 TIOPA 2010 Pt 4 Ch 3.
192 TIOPA 2010 s 167.
193 TIOPA 2010 s 167(5).
194 CTA 2009 s 930B(a).
195 CTA 2009 s 930C.

resident in the UK prior to the liquidators' appointment by reason of its central management and control having been exercised in the UK, CTA 2009 section 15 preserves the UK residence of the company, and HMRC view UK residence as continuing until the company ceases to exist.[196] The same rule applies to a company that ceases to carry on business.[197] HMRC state that the company will remain resident unless and until it starts business again and its central management and control is then outside the UK.198

196 HMRC International Manual INTM120100.
197 CTA 2009 s 1592(b).
198 HMRC International Manual INTM120100.

CHAPTER 7

Residence of partnerships

One likes to do business with a British firm. One knows where one is, if you see what I mean.

Graham Greene *Our Man in Havana*, Ch 1

7.01 Introduction

As the foregoing chapters have made clear, residence is a personal attribute – a quality which attracts to a person by virtue of the strength of the association with a particular place or country. Partnership is the relationship which subsists between persons carrying on a business in common with a view of profit.[1] In England and Wales, a partnership has no existence independent of its constituent members but, in Scotland, it is 'a legal person distinct from the partners of whom it is composed'.[2] The characterisation of a foreign legal entity as a partnership is by analogy to partnerships in the UK applied to the rights, legal rights and obligations under the governing foreign law.[3] Thus in principle any partnership that does not have legal personality under its governing law cannot have the quality of residence attributed to it. The direct tax treatment of partnerships is consistent with this approach by treating each partner as individually carrying on a notional trade in respect of the partnership trade actually carried on in common.[4] Residence or an analogous quality is, however, imputed by statute in the case of firms with a foreign element for limited purposes. First, the remittance basis is made applicable to the foreign profits of a trade carried on in partnership where the control and management of the partnership's trade is outside the UK.[5] Secondly, tax treaty protection from UK tax on the trading profits of partnerships resident outside the UK or

1 Partnership Act 1890 s 1.
2 Partnership Act 1890 s 4(2).
3 *Memec Plc v IRC* [1998] STC 754 (CA).
4 See generally, ITTOIA 2005 Pt 9.
5 ITTOIA 2005 s 857.

whose trade is controlled and managed outside the UK is overridden in the case of UK-resident partners.[6]

7.02 Control and management

Although a partnership, lacking in legal personality, cannot, in principle, have a residence, the Court of Appeal in *Padmore v Inland Revenue Commissioners*[7] observed that under the predecessor to ITTOIA 2005 Part 9 a residence is ascribed in the legislation to some partnerships. This residence is by reference to a test of control or management of the trade or business. Under the predecessor legislation, the partnership, rather than each partner, was assessed to income tax on its trading profits. Fox LJ also observed that the test for partnerships was statutory, unlike the judge-made test for companies.[8] Despite the different origins of the corporate and partnership tests, there has been little disagreement that the same analysis applies to question whether the control and management of a partnership carried on outside the UK as that which the courts have formulated for ascertaining the residence status of companies.

In *Padmore* the partnership was governed by the laws of Jersey. The overwhelming majority of the partners were resident in the UK. The business of the partnership was carried on from its offices in St Helier, Jersey; and its day-to-day business is dealt with by two managing partners who were Jersey residents. General meetings of the partners were held in Jersey or Guernsey (but nowhere else) four times a year, or more frequently as occasion demanded. At those meetings policy matters were discussed and the decisions taken were thereafter implemented by the Jersey resident managing partners. On those facts, it was common ground that the control and management of the business of the partnership was situated abroad.

Similarly in *Newstead (HM Inspector of Taxes) v Frost*,[9] a Bahamian partnership established to exploit the services and intellectual property of the entertainer David Frost, a UK resident, outside the UK was found by the Special Commissioners as a fact, without analysis of the legal principles, to be controlled and managed abroad on the basis that the partnership meetings and all the activities of the partnership took place outside the UK.[10]

Specific examination of the relationship between the partnership and corporate principles by the First-tier Tribunal in *Mark Higgins Rallying (a firm) v Revenue & Customs*[11] resulted in the conclusion that:

6 ITTIOA 2005 s 858.
7 *Padmore v Inland Revenue Commissioners* [1989] STC 493 (CA).
8 At p 499. See Chapter 6 on the residence of companies.
9 *Newstead (HM Inspector of Taxes) v Frost* (1975–1981) 53 TC 525.
10 At p 533.
11 *Mark Higgins Rallying (a firm) v Revenue & Customs* [2011] UKFTT 340 (TC).

'[T]he appropriate test for the location of control and management of the business of a partnership is that adopted by the courts in relation to residence of companies. We note the same conclusion was reached by HMRC and stated in their Manual; also that it was the one argued for before us by the Partnership.'[12]

In October 1991 Mr Dixon and Mr Higgins, both Manxmen resident in the Isle of Man, entered into a partnership to combine Mr Dixon's management and commercial experience with Mr Higgins' driving skills. Mr Higgins relocated to the UK in 1993. No records were kept of any partners' meetings. The partners reconstructed a diary of partnership meetings from 1991 to 2006. Mr Dixon, a solicitor, was very aware of the need to maintain control and management of the partnership outside the UK. Mr Higgins was rather perplexed at the rules that Mr Dixon laid down, but bowed to Mr Dixon's professional knowledge in these matters. While in the UK, Mr Higgins did not discuss with Mr Dixon or make any decisions and would travel back to the Isle of Man, when he requested, for meetings to discuss major decisions and to sign contracts.

ITTIOA 2005 section 858(1)(a)(i) applies to partnerships resident outside the UK in addition to those whose trade is controlled and managed outside the UK. The meaning of residence in this provision has yet to be judicially construed, but it would seem unlikely to add much to the analysis.

12 At para 51.

CHAPTER 8

Residence for stamp duty land tax

8.01 SDLT surcharge on non-UK residents purchasing residential property

Three separate regimes for taxing land transactions apply according to the country in which the land is situated. Transactions in land situated in England or Northern Ireland are liable to stamp duty land tax (SDLT).[1] The land and buildings transaction tax applies to land in Scotland[2] and land transaction tax, as its name implies, is a tax on transactions in land situated in Wales.[3]

Until 31 March 2021, SDLT the tax was chargeable equally on resident and non-resident purchasers of land situated in England or Northern Ireland. From 1 April 2021 higher rates apply to non-resident purchasers than those applicable to residents.[4] This change coincides with the UK departure from the European Union (EU) and the end of the transition period on 31 January 2021.Until that time, such discrimination against non-residents was prohibited by EU law and by the terms of the Withdrawal Agreement.[5] Although separate land tax regimes apply to Scotland and Wales, the SDLT charge in England and Northern Ireland distinguishes between residents of the UK and non-UK residents rather than discriminating on the basis of residence in the countries that constitute the UK.

The stated purpose of the differential was to ensure that UK residents can get on the housing ladder while keeping the UK an open and dynamic economy.[6]

1 Finance Act 2003 s 48(1).
2 Land and Buildings Transaction Tax (Scotland) Act 2013.
3 Land Transaction Tax and Anti-Avoidance of Devolved Taxes (Wales) Act 2017.
4 Finance Act 2021 s 88 and Sch 16, inserting new s 75ZA and Sch 9A into Finance Act 2003.
5 The Agreement on the Withdrawal of the United Kingdom of Great Britain and Northern Ireland from the European Union and the European Atomic Energy Community, [2020] OJ L29/7. See Chapter 10 on non-discrimination on the basis of residence and nationality in EU law.
6 HM Treasury: *Stamp Duty Land Tax, non-resident surcharge consultation* (February 2019), para 2.9.

In introducing the higher rate, the Treasury rejected the use of the existing statutory residence test (SRT).[7] It regards the SRT as 'a complex piece of legislation, involving several interconnected tests which consider closeness of connection to the UK as well as periods of time spent in and out of the UK.' For this purpose, the Treasury wanted the test for individuals to be as simple as possible, arguing that most people buying homes do not use a professional tax adviser. It should be capable of application by a conveyancing solicitor, they proposed. In addition, the Treasury stated that the SDLT, as a transactional tax, applies on completion of the purchase. The annual nature of the SRT, which applies to a tax year was not relevant to such a tax.[8]

Simplicity was not a stated aim in relation to companies. In that context, the Treasury view was that the existing rules, discussed in Chapter 6, 'are long standing, and will be familiar to persons who control and run companies as well as professional advisers such as solicitors, accountants and tax practitioners.'[9] The existing income tax residence rules for trusts were proposed to be used for SDLT but are not included in the legislation.[10] Again, simplicity was not a stated objective.

The SDLT residence rules, in keeping with other statutory provisions on residence, distinguish between individuals, companies and trusts. In addition, there are two different SDLT residence rules for individuals. One applies where individuals only are involved in the land purchase. The other applies where companies, partnerships and settlements are involved. A separate rule applies to employees of the Crown. Residence for the purpose of deciding whether a SDLT transaction is a 'non-resident transaction' are in Schedule 9A to the Finance Act 2003.[11] The legislative drafting does not make for easy navigation of the rules. For example, the rules deem individuals to be 'UK resident' while companies are deemed to be 'non-resident'. In the case of trusts and settlements, the transaction is instead deemed to be a 'non-resident transaction'.

8.02 SDLT: residence of individuals –basic rule

Presence in the UK is a key determinant of whether an individual is 'UK resident' for a specific land transaction. As with the SRT, an individual is present in the UK on a day if they are present at the end of that day.[12] Unlike

7 See Chapter 2.

8 HM Treasury: *Stamp Duty Land Tax, non-resident surcharge consultation* (February 2019), paras 2.7 and 2.8.

9 HM Treasury: *Stamp Duty Land Tax, non-resident surcharge consultation* (February 2019), para 3.7.

10 HM Treasury: *Stamp Duty Land Tax, non-resident surcharge consultation* (February 2019), paras 3.33 and 3.42. See Chapter 5 on the residence of trusts.

11 Inserted by Finance Bill 2021 Sch 16 para 5.

12 FA 2003 Sch 9A para 4(4).

the SRT, there are no exceptions to the physical presence. Thus a person who is not present in the UK for circumstances beyond their control may not qualify as a UK resident for this purpose. Similarly, there are no exceptions for highly mobile individuals in international sea or air transport, nor for individuals in transit overnight abroad.[13] While the surcharge only applies to non-land in England and Northern Ireland, presence anywhere in UK and not just days spent in England or Northern Ireland are counted.[14]

An individual is 'UK resident' for a specific land transaction by being present in the UK on at least 183 days during any continuous period of 365 days that falls within the 'relevant period'.[15] The 'relevant period' starts on the day 364 days before the effective date of the chargeable transaction, and ends on the day 365 days after the effective date of the chargeable transaction.[16] Unlike the SRT which relies on presence in the UK during a tax year, the SDLT rule effectively allows a person to qualify as a UK resident through presence in any 365-day period measured over a two-year period, one year before and one year after completion of the purchase. In some cases, an individual may be non-resident under the SRT but resident for STLT.

The effect of counting days both before and after the chargeable transaction is that individuals who are living outside the UK may purchase a dwelling while outside but qualify as UK resident for the SDLT on the purchase if they move to the UK after the purchase. Similarly, individuals living in the UK would still qualify as resident if they made a purchase after leaving. The mechanical nature of the rules mean that the exact application will vary according to particular circumstances and travel patterns.

A special rule applies where the purchase is made by spouses or civil partners. If the land is purchased by spouses or civil partners jointly and they are living together[17] when the purchase is completed, then, if one of them is UK resident under the basic rule and the other is not, the otherwise non-resident spouse or civil partner is deemed to be UK resident.[18] This rule applies even if there is another purchaser with them.[19] Confusingly, the rule does not apply to any other joint purchasers with the spouses or civil partners. The residential status of any other joint purchasers must be determined by reference to the other purchasers alone. It does not matter where the spouses or civil partners live together when the purchase is completed. It does not apply to spouses or civil partners who intend to live together but do not yet do so. The UK property

---

13 See Chapter 2, para **2.15** for the SRT rule.
14 HMRC Stamp Duty Land Tax Manual [SDLTM09880].
15 FA 2003 Sch 9A para 4(1).
16 FA 2003 Sch 9A para 4(1).
17 Individuals who are married to, or are civil partners of, each other are treated as living together unless they are separated under a court order, by deed of separation, or in fact separated in circumstances in which the separation is likely to be permanent (FA 2003 Sch 9A paras 6(5) and 12(4) with Income Tax Act 2007 s 1011).
18 FA 2003 Sch 9A para 12(1) and (2).
19 FA 2003 Sch 9A para 12(2)(a).

purchased need not constitute the home of the buyers in such cases. In contrast, a couple intending to live together in the UK and purchasing a home there would not qualify for this beneficial treatment.

8.03 Crown employment

Employees of the Crown qualify for separate treatment. 'Crown employment' for this purpose is employment under the Crown of a public nature, the earnings from which are payable out of the public revenue of the UK or of Northern Ireland.[20] Civil servants, members of the armed forces and diplomats are included. This definition corresponds with that in ITEPA 2003 section 28, which treats the earnings of such employees as taxable if the duties are performed outside the UK, and if the employee is not resident under the SRT. Civil servants are all Crown employees regardless of seniority or whether they have a technical or policy function.[21] An employee who is seconded to a foreign government that reimburses his remuneration remains a Crown employee. In *Caldicott v Varty*,[22] a tax inspector was seconded to the Fijian tax authority. The High Court held that he was paid out of public funds even though a part of his salary was reimbursed by the government of Fiji. He remained employed under the Crown even though his name appeared on a list of Fijian tax officials.

Crown employees are treated as present in the UK at the end of a day if they are present in a country or territory outside the UK for the purpose of performing duties of that employment.[23] A spouse or civil partner of a Crown employee who performs such duties overseas will qualify for the same treatment if the spouse or civil partner and the Crown employee are living together.[24] This special treatment only apples if it is claimed on the land transaction return.[25]

8.04 SDLT: residence of individuals – modified basic rule

The basic rule is modified in four cases which involve other categories of purchaser. These categories are first, when the purchaser is a company, or if there is more than one purchaser and the purchasers include a company,[26] and second, when the purchaser is acting as a trustee of a unit trust scheme or, if

20 FA 2003 Sch 9A para 6(4).

21 *Graham v White* (1971) 48 TC 163, a case concerning an individual who supervised mechanical and engineering operations by workmen at military establishments and was responsible to professional engineers or superior officers for the work supervised.

22 *Caldicott v Varty* (1976) 51 TC 403.

23 FA 2003 Sch 9A para 6(1).

24 FA 2003 Sch 9A para 6(2).

25 FA 2003 Sch 9A para 6(2).

26 FA 2003 Sch 9A para 5(3)(a).

there is more than one purchaser, the purchasers include any person acting as a trustee of a unit trust scheme.[27]

The third case concerns land purchases by partnerships. A land purchase for the purpose of a partnership is treated as a purchase by the partners for SDLT purposes.[28] Thus, the modified rule applies where the purchaser is acting on behalf of a partnership, or if there is more than one purchaser acting on behalf of a partnership.[29]

The fourth case is where the purchase is for certain discretionary trusts. The modified rule also applies if the purchaser is acting as a trustee of a settlement, or, if there is more than one purchaser, they include an individual who is acting as a trustee of a settlement, and, under the terms of the settlement, no beneficiary is entitled to occupy the dwelling or dwellings for life, or to income earned in respect of the dwelling or dwellings.[30] In general, this would include trusts where there is no life interest in the land or interest in possession of the land.

In these special cases a modified, simpler test applies: an individual is 'UK resident' in relation to a chargeable transaction if the individual is present in the UK on at least 183 days during the period that begins with the day 364 days before the effective date of the chargeable transaction and ends with the effective date of the chargeable transaction.[31]

8.05 SDLT: residence of companies – basic rule

A company is 'non-resident' in relation to a chargeable transaction if it is not UK resident for the purposes of the Corporation Tax Acts on the effective date of the chargeable transaction.[32] Unlike individuals who are deemed UK resident in the prescribed circumstances, companies are deemed non-resident. The residence of companies for corporation tax is discussed in Chapter 7.

For corporation tax purposes, a company is either resident or non-resident for an accounting period. Where residence is determined by reference to central management and control,[33] then acts of management throughout the period and not just at the time of the chargeable transaction will be relevant. The same will be true where the residence of dual resident companies is resolved by reference to the place of effective management.[34] In the case of treaties where the traditional place of effective management test has been replaced by the

27 FA 2003 Sch 9A para 5(3)(b).
28 FA 2003 Sch 15 para 2.
29 FA 2003 Sch 9A para 5(4).
30 FA 2003 Sch 9A para 5(5).
31 FA 2003 Sch 9A para 5(1). The same rules relating to presence in the UK and the effect of marriage or civil partnership as apply to the basic rule also apply to these special cases (Sch 9A paras 5(6) and 5(7)).
32 FA 2003 Sch 9A para 7(1) and (2).
33 See Chapter 7, para **7.03** and following.
34 See Chapter 7, para **7.16**.

obligation of the competent authorities to endeavour to resolve dual residence by mutual agreement,[35] a company will remain dual resident if and until the competent authorities agree otherwise, such a company will be UK resident for corporation tax purposes. Because competent authority procedure seldom takes less than 12 months and is usually longer, a purchaser may not know the position at the time of the transaction. If the competent authorities agree that the company is resident in the other contracting state, then the company will have been non-resident at the time of the chargeable transaction.[36] Agreement that a dual resident company is UK resident for treaty purposes will not therefore change the non-resident surcharge for such a company.

This basic rule is subject to several exceptions.

8.06 SDLT: residence of companies – UK resident close companies

Special rules apply to UK resident close companies that are controlled by non-residents[37] unless the company is acting as trustee of a settlement.[38] A UK resident company is generally a 'close company' if:

- it is under the control of five or fewer participators; or
- it is under the control of any number of participators who are also directors; or
- five or fewer participators, or any number of participators who are directors, would receive more than 50% of the company's assets available for distribution to the participators as a whole on a winding-up.[39]

The definition of close company for SDLT purposes is, however, broader than the general definition under the Corporation Tax Acts. First, a company will be close even if it is controlled by one or more companies none of which is a close company and one of its five or fewer participators is not a close company.[40] This would include many corporate groups with a UK subsidiary that owns a dwelling in England or Northern Ireland. Secondly, a company will be close even if it is a public company whose shares are quoted on a recognised stock exchange and, as such, would not be close.[41]

A UK resident company that is treated as close for SDLT purposes is deemed to be non-resident if it meets the 'non-UK control test' in relation to a

35 See Chapter 7, paras **7.16** and **7.18**.
36 CTA 2009 s 18(3).
37 FA 2003 Sch 9A para 7(3).
38 FA 2003 Sch 9A para 11(1)(e). See paras 2A.08 and 2A.09 on the deemed residence of trusts and settlements.
39 CTA 2009 s 439. The definition is complex: See CTA 2009 Pt 10 Ch 2 for fuller details.
40 FA 2003 Sch 9A para 8(2) which excludes CTA 2009 s 444(2).
41 FA 2003 Sch 9A para 8(3) which excludes CTA 2009 s 447.

chargeable transaction.[42] Thus the company will be non-resident if any one of a number of participators is non-resident for SDLT purposes.[43]

The rights of others may be attributed to a person in determining control for corporation tax purposes.[44] These attribution rules are modified for SDLT purposes.[45] First, the rights of partners are not attributed to each other, thereby relaxing the rules for partnerships.[46] Second, and in contrast, the rights of spouses and civil partners living together are not attributed to each other when one is non-resident.[47] Thus, while a non-resident spouse or civil partner may be deemed to be UK resident if they purchase land in England or Northern Ireland jointly, the non-resident spouse or civil partner remains non-resident for the purpose of deciding whether a UK resident company is a non-resident controlled company.

The attribution rules are also modified in the case of participants with minor (de minimis) interests in a company. An interest of less than 5% in a company is minor. The interest is by reference to possession or entitlement to acquire:

- share capital or issued share capital in the company;
- voting rights in the company;
- share capital in the company that entitles the income of the company if it were to be distributed;
- rights in the company that entitle assets of the company which would be available for distribution among the participators if the company were wound up or otherwise.[48]

The rules that deem UK companies to be non-resident if they are foreign controlled almost certainly infringes the non-discrimination rules in Article 24(5) of tax treaties that follow the OECD Model.[49] Special rules for these companies that are collective investment vehicles are discussed in paragraph 2A.07.

8.07 SDLT: collective investment vehicles

A UK resident close company that is non-resident controlled will not be deemed non-resident[50] if it is in one of two excluded categories of tax favoured property investment vehicles, the PAIF and the company UK REIT.[51]

42 FA 2003 Sch 9A para 9(1).
43 FA 2003 Sch 9A para 9(2) to 9(5). This does not apply to a participator who is a general partner in a limited partnership (para 9(3)(b)).
44 CTA 2009 ss 450 and 451.
45 FA 2003 Sch 9A para 10(1).
46 FA 2003 Sch 9A para 10(2).
47 FA 2003 Sch 9A para 10(3).
48 FA 2003 Sch 9A para 10(4), (5) and (6).
49 The modern UK treaty negotiating position is to exclude Art 24(6) from its treaties with the result that they will not apply to SDLT. See J Schwarz, *Schwarz on Tax Treaties* (7th edn, Wolters Kluwer, 2025), Ch 16.
50 See para 2A.06 for the deemed non-residence of such companies.
51 FA 2003 Sch 9A para 7(3)(c).

A Property Authorised Investment Fund (PAIF)[52] is an open-ended investment company within Part 4A of the Authorised Investment Funds (Tax) Regulations 2006.[53] These funds enjoy exemption from SDLT in certain circumstances.[54] A body corporate that is a 51% subsidiary of a PAIF is similarly excluded.[55]

Real Estate Investment Trusts (REITs) within CTA 2010 Part 12 and their shareholders enjoy beneficial corporation tax treatment. Elective treatment may apply to UK resident companies that are not open-ended investment companies and whose ordinary share capital is listed on a recognised stock exchange.[56] The company must carry on a qualifying property rental business.[57] The exclusion extends to both a standalone company REIT and members of a group UK REIT.[58]

Co-Ownership Authorised Contractual Schemes (COACSs) are not deemed 'non-resident' for SDLT.[59] They involve a pool of assets held by a depositary and managed on behalf of investors by contract among the parties but treated as a company for SDLT purposes. However, if the scheme is constituted under a contract governed by the law of an EEA State and authorised under the law of that EEA State,[60] then it is deemed to be 'non-resident' for SDLT even if it is managed by a UK resident body corporate.[61]

8.08 SDLT: trusts, settlements and similar arrangements

The rules applicable to the residential status of trustees and settlements is primarily determined by the legal nature of the rights under the settlement. HMRC regard any trust arrangement other than a bare trust as a settlement for SDLT.[62] Different regimes apply to various trust relationships.

Although the Treasury proposed the use of the existing statutory residence rules for trusts,[63] no such extension of those definitions was included in the legislation. The residence of trusts, in the absence of legislation, is somewhat obscure. In *Dawson v IRC*,[64] the House of Lords ruled that a UK resident trustee, who was one of three trustees, the other two of which were not UK

52 FA 2003 Sch 9A para 11(1)(a).
53 FA 2013 Sch 7A para (2)(2); Authorised Investment Funds (Tax) Regulations 2006, SI 2006/964, as amended, Pt 4A.
54 FA 2013 Sch 7A para 1.
55 FA 2003 Sch 9A para 11(1)(b) and 11(2)(b). See CTA 2010 Pt 24 Ch 3 for the meaning of 51% subsidiary.
56 CTA 2010 ss 524 and 528.
57 CTA 2010 s 529.
58 FA 2003 Sch 9A paras 11(1)(c) and (d); 11(2)(c) and (d).
59 FA 2003 Sch 9A para 15(1).
60 See FA 2013 s 102A(7).
61 FA 2003 Sch 9A para 15(1).
62 HMRC Stamp Duty Land Tax Manual [SDLTM31720].
63 ITA 2007 ss 475 and 476; TCGA 1992 s 69. See Chapter 6.
64 *Dawson v Inland Revenue Commissioners* [1989] STC 473(HL).

resident, was not liable to income tax on foreign source income. The decision rested on a narrow point, namely that the single UK trustee could not be said to be 'entitled to the income' because the trustees jointly were the 'person' entitled to the income. Lord Keith observed that there might be merit in making the liability depend upon the centre of administration of the trust and the place of residence of the majority of the trustees, as was the statutory position with capital gains tax, but Parliament has not done that.[65] This would appear to support the view that the residence of a trust is where the trustees, or a majority of them are resident.

8.09 Bare trusts

In the case of trustees of a bare trust acquiring a new lease, residence is by reference to the beneficiary or beneficiaries of the trust and not the trustee or trustees.[66] A bare trust exists where the beneficiary or beneficiaries are absolutely entitled to the property against the trustees, including where the beneficiary would be absolutely entitled, but for disability or age preventing the beneficiary from holding the legal title.[67] This includes the case where the purchasers include trustees of a bare trust. Where there is more than one purchaser including the bare trust and if the trustees are treated as purchaser of the whole of the interest acquired,[68] the entire transaction is either a resident or a non-resident transaction by reference to the status of the beneficiary or beneficiaries.[69] The special rule for new leases is needed because, FA 2003 Schedule 16, paragraph 3(3) treats the trustee as acquiring a new lease. In other cases, it is the beneficiary of a bare trust who is the acquirer of the interest in land in the normal course.

8.10 Life interest and interest in possession trusts

A similar approach applies to the purchase by certain life interest settlements. Thus, if under the terms of the settlement a beneficiary is entitled to occupy the dwelling or dwellings for life (a life interest trust), or to income earned in respect of the dwelling or dwellings (an interest in possession trust), then the residential status of the purchaser is by reference to the residence of the beneficiary and not that of the trustees.[70] Again, the residential status of the

65 Ibid at 479.
66 FA 2003 Sch 9A, para 13(2).
67 HMRC Stamp Duty Land Tax Manual [SDLTM09940].
68 By FA 2013 Sch 16 para 3(3).
69 FA 2003 Sch 9A para 13(2).
70 FA 2003 Sch 9A paras 14(1) and (2).

beneficiary will determine whether the transaction as a whole is resident or non-resident even if there are other purchasers with the trustees.

8.11 Alternative property finance

FA 2013 contemplates two forms of alternative property finance that do not involve the payment of interest. In the first, a financial institution purchases an interest in land that is held on trust for the institution and the economic purchaser as beneficial tenants in common. The institution then grants a lease to the economic purchaser, and the parties agree that the economic purchaser is entitled to have the whole interest in the land transferred to it.[71] The second involves similar arrangements where a financial institution purchases an interest in land and sells that interest to the economic purchaser who grants a legal mortgage to the institution over that interest.[72]

Where the purchase of land is by a financial institution as part of either of these alternative property finance arrangements, the financial institution making the purchase is deemed non-resident in relation to the transaction if the person with whom it enters into the arrangements is non-resident in relation to that transaction.[73]

8.12 Unit trusts

Trustees of a unit trust scheme are generally deemed to be a company, and the rights of unit holders as shares in that company for SDLT.[74] This does not apply for purposes of the increased rates for non-resident transactions.[75] Consequently, the residence of the trustees of the unit trust scheme is engaged in determining whether the transaction is a non-resident transaction.

8.13 SDLT: compliance with non- resident surcharge

A purchaser must deliver a land transaction return within 30 days of the effective date of the transaction.[76] This simple rule is made complex by the fact that the residence of a purchaser for STLT will be dependent in part, at least in some cases, on facts that arise after the date on which the return must be submitted

71 FA 2013 s 71A(1).
72 FA 2013 s 73(1).
73 FA 2003 Sch 9A para 16(2) and (4).
74 FA 2013 s 101(1).
75 FA 2013 s 101(7). Similarly, settlement under a unit trust scheme is not within the rules for settlements with a life interest in the dwelling (FA 2003 Sch 9A para 14(3)).
76 FA 2013 s 76(1).

to HMRC. In the case of individual purchasers who, on the date the return is due, do not qualify as UK resident under paragraph 4(1) but might do so in the remainder of the two-year period over which UK presence is measured, the return must be delivered on the assumption that they are not present in the UK during that time.[77] Thus the return must be submitted and the tax paid on the basis that the individual is not UK resident. If the individual subsequently satisfies the requirement and becomes UK resident, then the return may be amended at any time within two years after the transaction.[78]

No equivalent provision is made for companies. In particular, a dual resident company that the competent authorities subsequently determine to be resident in another contracting state under a treaty and therefore non-resident could only be addressed through the normal assessment machinery.

Residence is tested at the date of substantial performance of the contract. Where the later completion of the transaction is itself a chargeable notifiable transaction that later transaction will be a non-resident transaction if the substantial performance of the contract was a non-resident transaction.[79]

8.14 Record keeping for individuals

HMRC record keeping requirements for the statutory residence test are extensive.[80] The approach to record-keeping for this purpose appears to be more tolerant. HMRC say:

> 'HMRC recognise that as a tax, SDLT is not something that the majority of customers encounter on a frequent basis nor is undertaking a property transaction something that is necessarily planned for.
>
> Furthermore, HMRC understand that although customers will or are likely to have access to records relating to their property purchase (such as contracts, completion statements, records of payments etc.), they may not have kept contemporaneous records of their location on a day to day basis, especially if their property purchase was undertaken at short notice.'[81]

Information they regard as helpful incudes:

- credit card and bank statements which indicate place of the purchaser's day-by-day expenditure;
- work diaries or planners, including timesheets or rosters;

77 FA 2003 Sch 9A para 18.

78 FA 2003 Sch 9A para 19. HMRC guidance on obtaining repayment published online 1 April 2021: https://www.gov.uk/guidance/apply-for-a-repayment-of-the-non-uk-resident-stamp-duty-land-tax-surcharge.

79 HMRC Stamp Duty Land Tax Manual [SDLTM09955].

80 See Chapter 11, para **11.4** and Appendix 2.

81 HMRC Stamp Duty Land Tax Manual [SDLTM09955].

- mobile phone usage and bills pointing to the individual's presence in a country;
- general overheads – utility bills which may demonstrate that the individual has been present in the UK, for example, telephone bills or energy bills; and
- membership and usage of clubs, for example, sports, health or social clubs.

An indication of their use of modern information powers is hinted by the statement that 'HMRC will however take a pragmatic approach, in particular to considering a purchaser's digital footprint as evidence of a presence in the UK.'[82]

82 HMRC Stamp Duty Land Tax Manual [SDLTM09955].

CHAPTER 9

Domicile

If I should die, think only this of me:
That there's some corner of a foreign field
That is forever England …

Rupert Brooke, *The Soldier*

9.01 Introduction

The concept of domicile has long served as a determinant of liability to inheritance tax and as a modifying factor in relation to income and capital gains taxes. Despite the abolition of domicle as a factor that impacts on the territorial scope of UK taxation by Finance Act 2025, and its replacement with the concepts discussed in Chapter 3, the concept remains relevant for the foreseeable future:

First, individuals who claimed the remittance basis as being not domiciled will continue to have foreign income and gains that accrued prior to 6 April 2025 remain taxable on the remittance basis on those amounts.[1] Such individuals also have the opportunity to benefit from a 'temporary repatriation facility' which permits unremitted income and gains from prior years to be taxed at concessionary rates in the 2025/26, 2026/27 and 2027/28 tax years.[2]

Second, such individuals may be entitled to rebase foreign-situated assets held before the abolition of the remittance basis for capital gains tax.[3]

Certain individuals who were not UK domiciled and who ceased to be UK resident before the long-term UK resident regime commenced may qualify as not long-term UK residents in certain circumstances.[4]

Since publication of the decisions of the Special Commissioners started in 1995, numerous cases have been reported concerning the domicile of

1 Finance Act 2025 s 40(2).
2 Finance Act 2025 s 41 and Sch 10.
3 Finance Act 2025 s 42 and Sch 11.
4 See Chapter 3, **3.15.**

individuals.[5] Only one[6] has been appealed by a taxpayer (unsuccessfully) to the High Court or the Upper Tribunal, and none have grappled with the essential elements of the law of domicile which has shown much stability. In *Gaines-Cooper* it was argued that the Special Commissioners made an error of law if their conclusion was not the only true and reasonable conclusion on the basis of the facts found *and the unchallenged evidence*. This was not found to be the case. Arguments on the law of domicile advanced by the taxpayer were likewise rejected. All have turned on the facts and surrounding circumstances examined in great detail by the Commissioners. They all make interesting reading, but a comparison of the facts of one domicile case with the facts of another domicile case is of limited assistance in deciding the domicile of any particular person.[7]

The nature of domicile

9.02 Historical background

The concept of domicile (or domicil, as some prefer to call it) originated in the Roman Empire when, following the downfall of the Republic, Italy was divided into a number of individual townships known as *municipia* and the Empire was fragmented into numerous provinces. Each province and *municipium* possessed its own jurisdiction and, to a large extent, its own divergent internal law which was administered and enforced by magistrates. Most inhabitants of the Empire were connected by citizenship with one or more of these provincial or municipal communities and/or with Rome itself.

The link of citizenship could arise in various ways – by *origo* (the place within the Empire to which a person's father or, if he was illegitimate, his mother belonged), by adoption, by election or by manumission – and that presented three possibilities. A person might be a citizen of one place, a citizen of more than one place[8] or a citizen of none. This inevitably created difficulties. Given that, as stated, each province or *municipium* had its own system of law, to which system should a person in each of those situations be

5 *Anderson (executor of Anderson dec'd) v IRC* (1997) Sp C 147; *F & Anor (as personal representatives of F deceased) v Commissioners of Inland Revenue* (1999) Sp C 219; *Civil Engineer v IRC* (2001) Sp C 299; *Surveyor v IRC* (2002) Sp C 339; *Executors of Moore dec'd v IRC* [2002] UKSC SPC335; *Executors of Winifred Johnson Dec'd v HMRC* (2005) Sp C 481; *Gaines-Cooper v HMRC* [2006] UKSPC SPC568; *Jeremy Coller v HMRC* [2023] UKFTT 212 (TC); *Ameet Shah (executor, estate of Anantrai Maneklal Shah) v HMRC* [2023] UKFTT 539 (TC); *Ian Charles Strachan v HMRC* [2023] UKFTT 617 (TC); *Aubrey Weis v HMRC* [2025] UKFTT 348 (TC).

6 *Gaines-Cooper v HMRC* [2007] EWHC 2617 (Ch).

7 Cf Lord Justice Mummery in *Agulian & Anor v Cyganik* [2006] EWCA Civ 129 para 49.

8 St Paul, for example, was a citizen of Tarsus in Cilicia and a citizen of Rome (Acts 21: 39; 22: 27).

subject? The answer supplied by Rome was, in the first situation, the law of the person's place of citizenship, and, in the second situation, the law of their *origo*. In the third situation, however, a different determinant was needed and the determinant created was 'domicile' – the place in which a person had made their permanent home.

That concept of domicile was one of the concepts of Roman law, which, in the thirteenth century, was enthusiastically revived by the 'post-glossators' jurists who were attached to the Italian universities and who were engaged in developing the Roman law to meet the nation's changing needs.[9] Italy had by then emerged from the barbarism and feudalism into which the civilised world had been plunged following the fall of the Roman Empire in the fifth century and had become a land of independent, cosmopolitan cities – Bologna, Florence, Genoa, Milan, Padua, Pisa, etc – all of which were subject generally to Roman law, but each of which had diverse laws of its own which gave rise to conflict as commercial intercourse between the cities increased. As a basis for the resolution of such conflicts, the post-glossators developed a set of principles, known to legal historians as 'statute theory', and it was into these that the revived concept of domicile was introduced.

A 'statute' in the terminology of the post-glossators was any legislative or customary local law which was found to be contrary to Roman law in general; and the statute theory proceeded from the premise that all such laws were either 'real', 'personal' or 'mixed'. A law which concerned things other than moveables was 'real',[10] a law which concerned persons and moveables was 'personal', and a law which concerned acts (such as the making of a contract) was 'mixed' as it generally concerned both persons and things. Real statutes were seen as essentially territorial and as having no application beyond the territorial bounds of the locality in which they were found. Mixed statutes were seen as partially territorial in that they applied to all acts done within the territorial bounds of the locality in which they were found but could give rise to litigation elsewhere. Personal statutes, on the other hand, were seen as non-territorial and as applicable to any person *domiciled* within the locality in which the laws were found, wherever that person might be. Thus a Bologna-born merchant whose permanent home was in Florence would remain subject to Florentine personal laws while visiting, say, Padua, and neither Bolognan nor Paduan personal laws would apply to him.

The statute theory – the basis of today's 'private international law' or 'conflict of laws' as it is often called – was neither as simple nor as effective as it might appear and it was much refined by French jurists in the sixteenth century and Dutch jurists in the seventeenth century. Its subsequent development is beyond the scope of this work and it is sufficient to say that, despite all the changes

---

9 In the eleventh century the jurists of Italy had taken the *Corpus Juris* – the Justinian code of Roman law – and added to it glossae – explanatory notes. The jurists themselves came to be known as the 'glossators' and the revived and expanded Roman law became the general law throughout Italy and the legal code on which the post-glossators then worked.

10 From late Latin *realis* (Latin *res*), a thing.

which have taken place and despite the English and Scottish developments of the conflict of laws in the nineteenth century, the concept of domicile, and its use as the determinant of the system of personal law to which persons should be subject wherever they might be, has remained intact to the present day in the common law jurisdictions of the UK, the Commonwealth and the United States of America. To such nations, possessing as they do within their territorial boundaries a number of diverse legal systems, domicile still presents, as it once presented to Italy, the best determinant of the relevant personal law. Ironically, in the nineteenth century, Italy itself and most other countries in Europe rejected the test of domicile in favour of the test of nationality, and Japan and many South American states followed suit.

9.03 The two roles of domicile

The brief picture of domicile's origins given at **9.02** above should have sufficed to show that domicile is essentially a conflict of laws concept employed in determining the system of personal law which should be applied where a person has connections with more than one jurisdiction. Personal law is that part of law which, to some degree, governs the validity of marriage, the effect of marriage on the proprietary rights of husband and wife, divorce and nullity of marriage, legitimacy, legitimation and adoption, wills of moveables and intestate succession to moveables. It follows, therefore, that, whenever a question arises in the English courts concerning any of these matters, it must be determined according to the law of the domicile of the person concerned and not (unless English law happens to be the law of their domicile) according to English law, the law of the territory in which they happen to be, or the law of the nation of which the person is a citizen.

Example

Alan, a citizen of Eriador (where wills require the attestation of three witnesses), dies on holiday in Mordor (where wills require the attestation of four witnesses) but, at the time of his death, is domiciled in Gondor under whose laws he has made a will attested by only one witness as is permitted under Gondorian law. His will is contested in the English courts on the grounds that two witnesses are required under English law or, alternatively, that three are required under Eriadorian law or, alternatively, that four are required under Mordorian law. The suit fails.[11]

The rationale for this lies in the fact that (conceptually, at any rate) domicile, at any given moment in a person's life or at the moment of his death, singles

11 The territories used in this example are some of the fictitious territories created by J R R Tolkien as a setting for *The Lord of the Rings*.

out, from among all the territories in the world, the one territory in which – irrespective of where that person happens to be or happens to reside or ordinarily reside – that person has their real home; and, once that person's real home has been identified, the law of that territory, and of no other, is the law which should be applied in all matters which relate to them as a person.

One of those matters is the transfer of capital to another – dispositions which reduce the value of a person's estate upon death or, in certain circumstances, during lifetime – and it is upon such transfers of value that, under UK revenue law, inheritance tax is charged. It is entirely appropriate, therefore, that – except as regards any part of a person's estate which is situated in the UK – the determinant of liability to tax on capital transfers should be the same as the determinant of the personal law governing those transfers (ie domicile).

There is, however, a second and more cogent reason why a person's domicile is a more appropriate determinant of liability to inheritance tax than residence. Inheritance tax is a cumulative charge on transfers of value made by a person upon death *and* during the previous seven years, and there is also a seven-year cumulation period in respect of lifetime chargeable transfers.[12] The effectiveness of the inheritance tax system depends, therefore, on a link of the greatest possible strength being used to attach a person to the UK, and domicile is just such a link. Residence may more easily be snapped, ordinary residence is only a little stronger, but the bonds of domicile are very difficult to break – and, as is explained later.[13] The confinement of UK taxation of income and capital gains to the taxation of remittances in the case of income and gains generated overseas by a person who is not domiciled in the UK is further parliamentary recognition of the strength of the link between person and territory which domicile represents. This principle has been eroded over time by expansion of the scope of deemed domicile by legislation.[14]

9.04 The five principles of domicile

Domicile, being a common law concept, is not defined in the Taxes Acts. In 1858, however, Lord Cranworth said: 'By domicile we mean home, the permanent home,'[15] and, ever since, that has been regarded as a basic (if deceptively simple) definition of the term. Although the idea of a permanent home is indeed central to the concept of domicile, the meaning of 'permanent home' in this context is not necessarily the ordinary meaning of the term. There are, as will be shown, instances in which the courts will decide that a person's permanent home is in some faraway territory in which the person has never set foot and with which there may be no direct personal connection. This

12 IHTA 1984 s 7 as amended by FA 1986.
13 At **9.16** below.
14 See **9.16**, **9.17** and **9.18**.
15 *Whicker v Hume* (1858) 7 HL Cas 124 at 160.

is because domicile, though founded on fact, is not merely a finding of fact but a conclusion of law which is reached by application of a set of legal principles.

The principles referred to are five in number, and the **first principle** is that no one shall, at any time, be without a domicile.[16] The necessity for this becomes apparent once we remind ourselves that domicile is, in English law, the sole determinant of the personal law to which a person is to be subject. Indeed, it is one of the weaknesses of legal systems which have opted for nationality as a determinant of the personal law that a person may be stateless and may thus not possess the required connecting link. This is not to say, of course, that assigning a domicile to every person never presents difficulties: it frequently does, but the courts have developed additional principles to overcome these problems.

The **second principle** is that no one can simultaneously have more than one operative domicile.[17] The justification for this is that domicile, being the sole determinant of the personal law, must, by its very nature, be exclusive, otherwise a further determinant will be needed. This exposes another weakness in systems which have taken nationality as the determinant of the personal law, for many persons have dual nationality. The adjective 'operative' has been introduced into the above statement of principle because, as will be explained,[18] there are three kinds of domicile and one of these, domicile of origin, will, if displaced by either of the others, become dormant but will, in the event of either of the others being lost, instantly revive. It should be noted that, in English law, domicile is regarded as a purely objective concept which remains unaffected by the subject matter of the point at issue.[19] In theory, therefore, there should be no question, in English law, of a person having one domicile for taxation purposes and another for, say, the purposes of divorce. As explained below, however, there are certain situations in which that may be possible – though not through any abandonment of the objective approach.

The **third principle** is said to be that domicile must relate to a territory subject to a single system of law, whether or not the limits of that territory coincide with national boundaries. This, so far as the UK is concerned, would mean that a domicile could arise only in Northern Ireland, Scotland or England and Wales.

However, the Taxes Acts speak not of domicile in Northern Ireland or Scotland or England and Wales but of domicile 'in the United Kingdom'.[20]

The **fourth principle** is that a change of domicile may never be presumed.[21] As Jenkins LJ has said:

---

16 *Udny v Udny* (1869) Lr 1 Sc & Div 441 at 457, per Lord Westbury.

17 *IRC v Bullock* [1976] STC 409 at 414, per Buckley LJ.

18 See **9.06** below.

19 It is understood that a subjective or 'multiple concept' view of domicile is increasingly being adopted in the United States.

20 Eg, ICTA 1988 ss 65(4), 192 and 207 and TCGA 1992 s 12(1).

21 See *Moorhouse v Lord* (1863) 10 HL Cas 272 at 286, per Lord Chelmsford.

> 'Change of domicile, particularly where the change is from the domicile of origin to a domicile of choice (as distinct from a change from one domicile of choice to another) has always been regarded as a serious step which is only to be imputed to a person upon clear and unequivocal evidence.'[22]

In other words, a change of domicile will always have to be proved and, as Lord Chelmsford has said:

> '... the burden of proof unquestionably lies upon the party who asserts the change.'[23]

The question of the degree of proof required is considered at **7.15** below.

The **fifth principle** is that domicile must be determined according to the English concept of domicile. As Lindley MR said in *Re Martin*:[24]

> 'The domicil ... must be determined by the English Court ... according to those legal principles applicable to domicil which are recognised in this country and are part of its law.'[25]

The significance of this rule lies in the fact that 'domicile' does not have a precise and universally accepted meaning. Not all jurisdictions accept the objective approach to domicile, others (such as Australia, New Zealand and the United States) do not accept English doctrines such as that of the revival of the domicile of origin,[26] and under some international conventions domicile is equated with habitual residence.[27]

Domicile of origin

9.05 Acquisition

English law recognises three kinds of domicile: domicile of origin; domicile of dependence; and domicile of choice. Every person will possess the first of these, and may, at different times, possess either of the others. *Henderson & Ors v Revenue and Customs*[28] graphically illustrates the interaction of all three kinds of domicile. The case concerned a claim by four individuals to have a domicile of origin in Brazil through a domicile of choice acquired by their grandfather as a result of a move from England to Brazil which was in place when their

22 *Travers v Holley* [1953] P 246 at 252.
23 *Moorhouse v Lord* (1863) 10 HL Cas 272 at 286.
24 [1900] P 211.
25 [1900] P 211 at 227.
26 See **9.06** below.
27 Art 5 of the 1955 Hague Convention to Regulate Conflicts between the Law of Nationality and the Law of Domicile attributes domicile with this meaning.
28 *Henderson & Ors v Revenue and Customs* [2017] UKFTT 556 (TC).

father was born. For the individuals to succeed, the grandfather would also need to not have abandoned that domicile of choice before their father turned 16 (which would have revived the grandfather's English domicile of origin and given their father an English domicile of dependence). In addition, if their father had a Brazilian domicile, he would need to have not acquired a domicile of choice in England before the four individuals were born. The taxpayers failed but the case usefully reveals the application of the rules to a peripatetic family of English origin: The grandfather, Ian was born in 1930 and went to Brazil in 1960 for work and married a Brazilian. The father, Nicholas, was born in Brazil in 1963. Ian and his wife, whose parents were of New Zealand origin, moved permanently to London in 1966. Nicholas spent a gap year in Brazil but lived primarily in England with army postings elsewhere. The First-tier Tribunal concluded that Ian never acquired a domicile of choice in Brazil and Nicholas consequently only ever had a domicile of origin in England. The reasons will be apparent from the discussion that follows.

The domicile of origin is the form of domicile which is imposed on every person at the moment of their birth. It is a link, forged by the law, which attaches a person to a particular system of law and which remains throughout life. Should a domicile of dependence or a domicile of choice be acquired, the link will be removed, but not destroyed; rather it will be held at readiness to reattach the person instantly to the original system of law should the domicile of dependence cease or the domicile of choice be abandoned.

Except in the case of a foundling (when the domicile of origin imposed is that of the place where the child is found), the basis of imposition of a domicile of origin is parentage. If a child is born legitimate and during the father's lifetime, the domicile of origin imposed is that of the father at the time of the child's birth.[29] If a child is born illegitimate,[30] or born legitimate but after the father's death,[31] the domicile of origin imposed is that of the mother.

One problem which could arise in this connection springs from the fact that the question of legitimacy is itself a matter of personal law. As the determinant of the appropriate person law is the child's domicile and as the child's domicile cannot be determined until the question of its legitimacy has been settled, it can be seen that, unless both parents are of the same domicile, an endless legal loop is created. Various solutions to the problem have been proposed[32] but there is no authority on the question in English law.

It seems clear that in the event of an illegitimate child being legitimated the child's domicile of origin will remain unaffected since, under the Legitimacy Acts, legitimation does not operate retrospectively.[33] In the event of a child becoming adopted, however, it would appear that a new domicile of origin

29 *Udny v Udny* (1869) LR 1 Sc & Div 441 at 457, per Lord Westbury.

30 *Udny v Udny* (1869) LR 1 Sc & Div 441 at 457, per Lord Westbury.

31 This is apparently unsupported by any English authority.

32 Eg, by R H Graveson in *Private International Law* (7th edn, Sweet and Maxwell) at pp 195–196.

33 See **9.08** below for the domicile of dependence which legitimation creates.

will be acquired since adoption involves the complete severance of the legal relationship between parent and child and the establishment of a new one between child and the adoptive parent.[34]

The Law Commission and the Scottish Law Commission have recommended that the domicile of origin be abolished and that, in future, a child's domicile should be determined from the outset under revised domicile of dependence rules.[35]

9.06 Displacement and revival

A domicile of origin, being a domicile imposed by operation of law independently of a person's will, can never be extinguished by an act of will or by mere abandonment. It will continue to be operative, whether its possessor wishes it to be operative or not, until it is displaced by the acquisition of either a domicile of dependency or a domicile of choice. This is well illustrated by the leading case of *Bell v Kennedy*.[36]

Mr Bell was born in 1802 of Scottish parents who were domiciled by choice in the island of Jamaica. Accordingly, he possessed a Jamaican domicile of origin. Following the death of his mother, Bell, at the age of two, was sent to Scotland to be cared for and educated. When he was ten years old his father died and left him his Jamaican estate. Mr Bell completed his education in Scotland, travelled for a while in Europe, then, shortly after reaching his majority, returned to Jamaica to cultivate the estate that had been left to him. The estate prospered and Mr Bell became a wealthy and important personage, attaining membership of the island's Legislative Assembly. He married and fathered three children. In 1834, however, the law was changed with regard to slavery and the change was to culminate in the complete emancipation of slaves in 1838. Mr Bell strongly disapproved of the change and that, coupled with his failing health, decided him upon a permanent return to the UK. Accordingly, in 1837, he sold the estate and left the island for good. Initially, he and his immediate family resided with his mother-in-law in Edinburgh and Mr Bell set about finding a suitable estate, preferably in Scotland but possibly across the border, in England, which he could purchase and in which he and his family could settle down. Before he had succeeded in this, however, his wife died. At that time, a woman acquired the domicile of her husband upon marriage and, accordingly, in order to resolve a dispute which had arisen concerning Mr and Mrs Bell's daughter's succession to Mrs Bell's share in goods held in common between Mr and Mrs Bell at the date of Mrs Bell's death, it became necessary

34 Lowe and Douglas, *Bromley's Family Law* (10th edn, Oxford University Press, 2006) p 408.

35 The Law Commission Working Paper No 88 and the Scottish Law Commission Consultative Memorandum No 63, 'Private International Law, The Law of Domicile' (1985), para 4.22. See **9.08** below.

36 *Bell v Kennedy* (1868) LR 1 Sc & Div 307.

to determine Mr Bell's domicile at the date of his wife's death. The court held that his domicile was his domicile of origin (ie Jamaica). Lord Cairns said:

> 'The birth-domicile of [Bell] in Jamaica continued, at all events till 1837, and the onus lies upon those who desire to shew that there was a change in this domicile ... to prove that that change took place. The law is, beyond all doubt, clear with regard to the domicile of birth, that the personal status indicated by that term clings and adheres to the subject of it until an actual change is made by which the personal status of another domicile is acquired ... It appears to me ... that so far from [Mr and Mrs Bell's daughter and her husband] having discharged the onus which lies upon them to prove the adoption of a Scottish domicile, they have entirely failed in discharging that burden of proof, and that the evidence leads quite in the opposite direction. There is nothing in it to shew that [Bell's] personal status of domicile as a native and inhabitant of Jamaica has been changed on coming here by that which alone could change it, his assumption of domicile in another country.'[37]

Lord Colonsay had this to say:

> 'I think it is very clear that Mr Bell left Jamaica with the intention of never returning ... But I do not think that his having sailed from Jamaica with that intent extinguished his Jamaica domicile ... He could not so displace the effect which law gives to the domicile of origin, and which continues to attach until a new domicile is acquired *animo et facto*.'[38]

Once a person has, however, *animo et facto* or through the act of the person on whom they are dependent, acquired a new domicile, the domicile of origin, though displaced, still does not die. It lives on dormant but ready to awake and come back into operation in the instant any other domicile is voluntarily abandoned. As Lord Westbury has said in *Udny v Udny*:[39]

> 'When another domicile is put on, the domicile of origin is for that purpose relinquished, and remains in abeyance during the continuance of the domicile of choice; but as the domicile of origin is the creature of law, and independent of the will of the party, it would be inconsistent with the principles on which it is by law created and ascribed to suppose that it is capable of being by the act of the party entirely obliterated and extinguished.'[40]

Colonel Udny acquired a domicile of origin in Scotland when he was born there of Scottish parents in 1779. His childhood was spent in Scotland but, after serving as an officer in the Guards, in 1812, he married and settled in London. There he resided for the next 32 years. In 1844, however, the Colonel 'having been involved for some time in pecuniary difficulties (owing chiefly to

37 *Bell v Kennedy* (1868) LR 1 Sc & Div 307 at 310, 316–317.
38 *Bell v Kennedy* (1868) LR 1 Sc & Div 307 at 323.
39 (1869) LR 1 Sc & Div 441.
40 (1869) LR 1 Sc & Div 441 at 458.

his connection with the turf) was compelled to leave England in order to avoid his creditors'.[41] He first went to Scotland and from there he arranged for the sale of the lease of the London house and 'everything that was in the house, including what had belonged to his mother, his sister, and his ... wife';[42] he then fled to Boulogne. It was in Boulogne that he formed a relationship that resulted in the birth of a child whose legitimation was in question.

Some doubt was expressed by the court whether Colonel Udny had ever, in fact, acquired an English domicile of choice. Nevertheless, the Lord Chancellor was of the opinion that:

> '... the English domicil of Colonel Udny, if it were ever acquired, was formally and completely abandoned in 1844 when he sold his house and broke up his English establishment with the intention never to return. And, indeed, his return to that country was barred against him by the continued threat of process by his creditors. I think that on such abandonment his domicil of origin revived. It is clear that by our law a man must have some domicil, and must have a single domicil. It is clear, on the evidence, that the Colonel did not contemplate residing in France ... Why should not the domicil of origin cast on him by no choice of his own, and changed for a time, be the state to which he naturally falls back when his first choice has been abandoned *animo et facto*, and whilst he is deliberating before he makes a second choice.'[43]

Both the Private International Law Committee[44] and now the Law Commission and the Scottish Law Commission[45] have recommended that the principle of revival be discarded and that an existing domicile should continue until a new domicile is acquired. This is the rule in the United States,[46] New Zealand[47] and Australia.[48]

The question of the precise point at which the domicile of origin will revive upon a domicile of choice being abandoned is fully discussed at **9.15** below.

Domicile of dependence

9.07 Married women

Until 1 January 1974 there were three classes of persons who could or would acquire a domicile of dependence: children, mentally disordered persons and

---

41 (1869) LR 1 Sc & Div 441 at 445.
42 (1869) LR 1 Sc & Div 441 at 445.
43 (1869) LR 1 Sc & Div 441 at 448.
44 First Report (1954) Cmd 9068, para 14.
45 The Law Commission Working Paper No 88 and the Scottish Law Commission Consultative Memorandum No 63, 'Private International Law, The Law of Domicile' (1985, HMSO), para 5.22.
46 *Re Jones' Estate* 192 Iowa 78, 182 NW 227 (1921).
47 Domicile Act 1976 s 11 (New Zealand).
48 Domicile Act 1982 s 7 (Australia).

married women. Now, only the first two classes remain, for, by the Domicile and Matrimonial Proceedings Act 1973 section 1, the rule at common law that every woman acquired from her husband his domicile immediately upon her marriage was swept away.[49] The Act provides that the domicile of a married woman as at any time on or after 1 January 1974:

> '… shall, instead of being the same as her husband's by virtue only of marriage, be ascertained by reference to the same factors as in the case of any other individual capable of having an independent domicile.'[50]

So far as any woman who married on, or has married since, 1 January 1974 is concerned, the position is quite straightforward. As the subsection quoted makes plain, the woman has the same capacity as her husband or any other non-dependent person for acquiring a domicile of choice. It will, of course, usually be the case that the domicile of a husband and his wife will normally be the same, but this will now merely be because of their independent choice to live together permanently in the same place. Such a choice is not always made at the time of the marriage, or if made then, may not be implemented by residence until later. In that event, each may, under the Act, retain different domiciles.

Example

Marie-Louise is domiciled in Belgium. While attending art college in Manchester in 1985 she marries a fellow student, Henri, who is domiciled in France. Upon the completion of their respective courses they are resolved to settle permanently in Monaco. Until that decision is implemented by residence in Monaco, Marie-Louise will retain her Belgian domicile and Henri will retain his French domicile. Thereafter they will each acquire a Monagesque domicile of choice. Had they married before 1 January 1974, Marie-Louise would, upon her marriage, have acquired a French domicile of dependence and then, when they settled in Monaco, a Monagesque domicile of dependence.

The position of a woman who married before 1 January 1974 is set out in subsection (2) of the Act:

> 'Where immediately before [1 January 1974] a woman was married and then had her husband's domicile by dependence, she is to be treated as retaining that domicile

49 The author's view is that domicile of dependence of married women is, in any event, inconsistent with Art 14 (prohibition of discrimination) read with Art 1 (protection of property) to the First Protocol of the European Convention on Human Rights. See Irish Supreme Court in *W v W* 1993 IR 476, a case under the non-discrimination provisions of the Irish Constitution.

50 DMPA 1973 s 1(1).

> (as a domicile of choice, if it is not also her domicile of origin) unless and until it is changed by acquisition or revival of another domicile on or after [1 January 1974].'[51]

The principal difficulty to which this provision gives rise was dealt with in *IRC v Duchess of Portland*.[52] In 1948, the taxpayer, a Canadian citizen with a domicile of origin in Quebec, married Lord William Cavendish-Bentinck (subsequently the Duke of Portland) in England and became Lady William Cavendish-Bentinck (subsequently the Duchess of Portland). Thereupon she acquired from her husband an English domicile of dependence which displaced her Quebec domicile of origin, but she was resolved to return to live in Canada should her husband predecease her and she hoped to persuade him to live in Canada on his retirement. Throughout her marriage, the Duchess of Portland maintained her links with Canada, returning there to visit friends and relatives for between ten and 12 weeks each year and (since about 1964) owning and maintaining there at her own expense her family home in Metis Beach, Quebec. The Duchess of Portland's first visit to Canada following the enactment of the Domicile and Matrimonial Proceedings Act 1973 was in July 1974, and following that visit she claimed that, under section 1(2) of the Act, her domicile of dependence had been changed by the revival of her Quebec domicile of origin. Had her claim succeeded she would have become exempt under ICTA 1970 section 122(2)(a) from liability to tax on income accruing to her in Canada but not remitted to the UK.

The basis of the Duchess of Portland's claim was that the domicile of choice which, under DMPA 1973 section 1(2), she acquired on 1 January 1974 was merely a *deemed* domicile of choice and that the strict test applicable to the abandonment of a true domicile of choice should not be applied in deciding whether or not her deemed domicile of choice had been abandoned. Instead, she claimed, the more lenient test applicable to the abandonment of a domicile of dependency was appropriate. Nourse J agreed that DMPA 1973 section 1(2) was a deeming provision but said:

> '... that which is deemed in a case where the domicile of dependency is not the same as the domicile of origin is the retention of the domicile of dependency as a domicile of choice. I think that that must mean that the effect of the subsection is to reimpose the domicile of dependency as a domicile of choice. The concept of an imposed domicile of choice is not one which it is very easy to grasp, but the force of the subsection requires me to do the best I can. It requires me to treat the taxpayer as if she had acquired an English domicile of choice, even though the facts found by the commissioners tell me that that would have been an impossibility in the real world. In my judgment it necessarily follows that the question whether, after 1 January 1974, the taxpayer abandoned her deemed English domicile of choice must be determined by reference to the test appropriate to the abandonment of a

51 DMPA 1973 s 1(2).
52 [1982] STC 149.

> domicile of choice and not by reference to the more lenient test appropriate to the abandonment of one of dependency.'[53]

It was pointed out in *IRC v Duchess of Portland* that, if the Duke and Duchess had married on or after 1 January 1974 the effect of DMPA 1973 section 1(1) would have been to preserve the Duchess's domicile of origin. Nourse J admitted that it was so and said:

> 'It seems clear that a woman living in England with her husband who was married before 1 January 1974 can only free herself from the shackles of dependency by choosing to leave her husband for permanent residence in another country. That is a very limited freedom and it is less than that available under s 1(1) to those who marry on or after 1 January 1974. Be that as it may, Parliament did not, as it might have done, provide that a woman who was married before 1 January 1974 was to be treated as if she had never acquired her domicile of dependency. Section 1(2) having taken the form which it has, by treating the married woman as retaining her domicile of dependency as a domicile of choice, I regret that I have no choice but to attach to it all the consequences which the law has long recognised the latter domicile to have.'[54]

A second difficulty which arises in relation to DMPA 1973 section 1(2) concerns the position after 1 January 1974 of a woman who, having married before that date, had left or had been abandoned by her husband before that date and had settled permanently in some country other than that of her domicile of dependence. In the absence of some new act on her part on or after 1 January 1974, does the woman retain her domicile of dependence as her domicile of choice or does she immediately acquire as her domicile of choice the country in which she settled permanently during her domicile of dependency? This question was also answered, albeit *obiter*, in *IRC v Duchess of Portland*. The problem, said Nourse J, is to be resolved 'consistently with the rule which would have applied if the husband had died before 1 January 1974'.[55] The rule he referred to was established in *Re Cooke's Trustees*[56] and *Re Scullard*,[57] and is that where a husband and wife have been living apart, the intent and act of the wife in permanently making her home elsewhere creates a domicile of choice upon the death of her husband without the need for any additional act on her part, or, if the country in which she has settled is her domicile of origin, revives her domicile of origin without the need for any such act. The application of the rule is straightforward.

53 [1982] STC 149 at 154.
54 [1982] STC 149 at 156.
55 [1982] STC 149 at 155.
56 (1887) 56 LT 737.
57 [1956] 3 All ER 898.

Example

In 1952, Tom, who was, and continued to be, domiciled in England, married Ingrid, who had a domicile of origin in Germany. In 1968 Ingrid left Tom and made her permanent home in Switzerland. Upon her marriage, Ingrid acquired an English domicile of dependence. This endured until 1 January 1974, but, on that date, in accordance with the rule in *Re Scullard's Estate*,[58] she automatically acquired a domicile of choice in Switzerland. Had Ingrid, upon leaving Tom, made her permanent home in Germany rather than Switzerland, her domicile of origin would have automatically revived on 1 January 1974.

Nourse J summed up as follows the procedure that DMPA 1973 section 1(2) requires one to adopt in determining the domicile of a woman who was married before 1 January 1974:

> '... first ... look at the state of affairs prevailing on 1 January 1974 to see whether there has been any automatic change on that date [as in the above example]. If there has not ... look at events after that date in order to see whether any change has occurred subsequently.'[59]

9.08 Children

Until 1 January 1974, it was the rule at common law that a minor, whether married or not, was totally incapable of acquiring by their own act an independent domicile of choice.[60] A female child who, before then, married before attaining her majority acquired her husband's domicile as a domicile of dependence and, if widowed before that date, reacquired the domicile she had immediately before her marriage.[61]

On 1 January 1974, however, the Domicile and Matrimonial Proceedings Act 1973 came into effect and, with application only to England and Wales and Northern Ireland,[62] confined this rule to unmarried children under the age of 16.[63] Since then, any child reaching the age of 16 or marrying under that age, has been capable of acquiring an independent domicile of choice; and the same applied to any child who, at that date, was already over the age of 16 or, if then still under the age of 16, was then already married.[64]

58 [1956] 3 All ER 898.

59 *IRC v Duchess of Portland* [1982] STC 149 at 155.

60 *Forbes v Forbes* (1854) Kay 341; *Harrison v Harrison* [1953] 1 WLR 865.

61 *Shekleton v Shekleton* [1972] 2 NSWR 675.

62 Not Scotland. Under Scottish law the relevant respective ages are 14 in the case of a boy, 12 in the case of a girl.

63 DMPA 1973 s 3.

64 Because no English domiciled child has the capacity to marry below that age, however, the parts of the rule which relate to persons who are married under the age of 16 is of application only to foreign domiciled children whose marriages are recognised by the courts in this country – as, for example in *Mohamed v Knott* [1968] 2 All ER 563.

The present position is, then, that every child acquires at birth a domicile of origin[65] and cannot, so long as they remain unmarried and below the age of 16, displace that domicile of origin by a domicile of choice acquired by their own act of will. There is, however, nothing to prevent their domicile of origin being displaced by an act of will on the part of one of their parents, and if this occurs the new domicile they acquire will be a domicile of dependence.

The primary rule is that, upon any change in the domicile of a child's father after the child's birth, a legitimate or adopted child will acquire their father's new domicile as a domicile of dependence unless their parents[66] are living apart and they either have then a home with their mother and not with their father or having had a home with their mother have not since then had a home with their father.[67] This is because, upon a separation, a child acquires a domicile of dependence from the parent with whom they make their home and, should they subsequently make their home with the other parent, they will (subject to a mother's right *not* to communicate her domicile to a child who is dependent upon her – see next paragraph) acquire a new domicile of dependence from that parent, but, should they cease to have a home with either parent, their last-acquired domicile of dependence will continue. A legitimate, legitimated or adopted child who shares their time between the homes of both parents will acquire and retain throughout the arrangement the domicile of their father.

Where a child is illegitimate or was born after the death of their father, they will prima facie acquire as a domicile of dependence any new domicile acquired by their mother whether they have a home with her or not,[68] unless the mother elects, bona fide and in the interests of the child, that the child's domicile shall not change with her domicile.[69]

Where one or both of a child's parents die during a child's period of dependency, the rules are as follows.

Where a legitimate or adopted child's father dies after the child is born, the child acquires (if they have not acquired it already[70]) the domicile of their

65 See **9.05** above.

66 Adoptive parents in the case of an adopted child (Children Act 1975 Sch 1, para 3 as repealed and re-enacted in the Adoption Act 1976 s 39(1) and the Adoption (Scotland) Act 1978 s 39(1)).

67 *D'Etchegoyen v D'Etchegoyen* (1888) 13 PD 132, DMPA 1973 s 4(1)–(2).

68 DMPA 1973 s 4(4) and *Johnstone v Beattie* (1843) 10 Cl & Fin 42.

69 In *Re Beaumont* [1893] 3 Ch 490 at 496, Stirling J said, 'Change in the domicile of an infant which … may follow from a change of domicile on the part of the mother, is not to be regarded as the necessary consequence of a change of the mother's domicile, but as the result of the exercise by her of a power vested in her for the welfare of the infants, which in their interest she may abstain from exercising, even when she changes her own domicile.' Where, however, a mother exercises her power in her own interest (eg to take advantage of a law of succession more beneficial to herself), such an exercise of her power will be ineffective (*Potinger v Wightman* (1817) 3 Mer 67).

70 The child might already have acquired their mother's domicile as a domicile of dependence if their parents had separated before their father's death and if the child had, upon the separation, made their home with their mother.

mother as a domicile of dependence[71] which will then change as her domicile changes – subject, as explained above, to her right to elect that it shall not be so. The same will be true of an illegitimate child who, before their father's death, has been legitimated, for such a child will, upon legitimation, have received their father's domicile as a domicile of dependence. The death of the father of an illegitimate child who has not been legitimated will have no effect.

Where a child's mother dies, the death will have no effect on the child's domicile unless the child was either born illegitimate and has never been legitimated or has (or last had) a home with their mother following a separation of their parents. In either event, the child will continue to have their dead mother's domicile as a domicile of dependence unless and until, in the case of a legitimate or legitimated or adopted child only, they make a home with their father.[72]

Where a child's parents both die, the domicile of dependence which the child possessed at the date of their deaths will continue; though a child's guardian has no capacity to change the domicile of their ward.[73]

A domicile of dependence will continue until *animo et facto* they abandon the country of that domicile. Thereupon their domicile of origin will revive until it is displaced by a domicile of choice.[74]

Example

Susan is born of an English domiciled father and thus acquires an English domicile of origin by operation of law. When she is eight years old she and her parents move to Denmark and her father acquires there a domicile of choice which is then automatically communicated to Susan as a domicile of dependence. Susan continues to live with her parents until she is 24 when she marries a Norwegian and moves to Oslo where she intends to spend the rest of her life. Her Danish domicile of dependence will endure until she leaves Danish territorial waters, whereupon her English domicile of origin will revive. Upon arriving in Norway, however, her domicile of origin will be displaced by her Norwegian domicile of choice.

It should be noted that it is usually easier to establish the abandonment of a domicile of dependence than to establish the abandonment of a domicile of choice.[75]

The Law Commission and the Scottish Law Commission have proposed that the domicile of any person under the age of 16 should be determined according to where the child has their home. If their home is with both parents, their

71 *Potinger v Wightman* (1817) 3 Mer 67.
72 DMPA 1973 s 4(3).
73 See Dicey and Morris, *The Conflict of Laws* (13th edn, Sweet & Maxwell), Vol 1, p 141.
74 *Re Macreight, Paxton v Macreight* (1885) 30 ChD 165.
75 *Harrison v Harrison* [1953] 1 WLR 865.

domicile, they say, should be the same as, and change with, that of their parents if their domiciles are the same, or with that of their mother if their domiciles are different. If their home is with only one parent, their domicile, they say, should be the same as, and change with, the domicile of that parent. And in any other case, the child's domicile should, they say, be the country with which they are, for the time being, most closely connected.[76]

9.09 Persons suffering from mental disorder

The position of a person suffering from mental disorder is lacking in direct authority so far as the question of their domicile is concerned. Until a child reaches the age of 16 or marries under that age, the rules governing their domicile will be those already discussed at **9.05** and **9.08** above. If, however, a child becomes of unsound mind and that state continues beyond their 16th[77] birthday, the law would appear to be that their domicile will continue to change with the parent from whom they last acquired a domicile of dependence, but that where they become of unsound mind after they have attained the age of 16 or married under that age, they will permanently retain whatever domicile they then possessed and that domicile will be incapable of change either by their own act or by that of those who are entrusted with their care.[78] The degree of mental unsoundness which is required before these rules will have effect is not settled, but it is arguable that the test to be applied should be whether or not the person is capable of forming the necessary intention to bring about a change in domicile.[79]

The Law Commission and the Scottish Law Commission have recommended that the domicile of an adult *incapax* should not be frozen at the onset of their incapacity but should be changed as necessary so that their domicile is always that of the country with which they are at any time most closely connected.[80]

Domicile of choice

9.10 Acquisition

As has been explained at **9.07** to **9.09** above, a domicile of choice can be acquired only by a person who is not incapacitated either by age or by

76 The Law Commission Working Paper No 88 and the Scottish Law Commission Consultative Memorandum No 63, 'Private International Law, The Law of Domicile' (1985, HMSO), para 4.18.

77 In Scotland, 14 in the case of a boy, 12 in the case of a girl.

78 *Sharpe v Crispin* (1869) LR 1 P & D 611 at 615, per Sir J P Wilde.

79 See **9.12** below.

80 The Law Commission Working Paper No 88 and the Scottish Law Commission Consultative Memorandum No 63, 'Private International Law, The Law of Domicile' (1985, HMSO), para 6.9.

unsoundness of mind. There are no formal steps to be taken for a person of full age and capacity to acquire a domicile of choice. As the former HMRC guidance put it:

> 'To do so, you must broadly leave your current country of domicile and settle in another country. You need to provide strong evidence that you intend to live there permanently or indefinitely.'[81]

In *Udny v Udny*,[82] Lord Westbury described a domicile of choice as:

> '… a conclusion or inference which the law derives from the fact of a man fixing voluntarily his sole or chief residence in a particular place, with the intention of continuing to reside there for an unlimited time.'[83]

Both elements must be present. As Lord Chelmsford put it in *Bell v Kennedy*:[84]

> '… a new domicile is not acquired until there is not only a fixed intention of establishing a permanent residence in some other country, but until also this intention has been carried out by actual residence there.'[85]

These two elements are known, respectively, as the *animus manendi* (the intention to remain) and the *factum* (the fact of residence) and, as foregoing dicta make clear, both are essential. Before considering each element individually, however, one point must be made. The 'country' to which both the *animus* and the *factum* relate must, for the purpose of determining whether a domicile of choice has been acquired under common law, be 'a territory subject to a distinctive legal system.'[86]

This follows from the third principle of domicile discussed at **9.04** above but, as explained there, the problem which arises when discussing domicile in the context of UK taxation is that, under the Taxes Acts, the question to be determined is whether a person is domiciled 'in the UK' (ie a territory which is *not* subject to a distinctive legal system). It is important to refer to the earlier discussion, therefore, and to bear in mind that where a reference is made to a 'country' or 'territory' in the following paragraphs, it is possible that, for the purposes of this work, the country or territory referred to may be the UK collectively and not necessarily Northern Ireland, Scotland or England and Wales individually.

81 HMRC6 (April 2009), para 4.3.2.
82 (1869) LR 1 Sc & Div 441.
83 (1869) LR 1 Sc & Div 441 at 458.
84 (1868) LR 1 Sc & Div 307.
85 (1868) LR 1 Sc & Div 307 at 319.
86 *Re Fuld's Estate (No 3)* [1968] P 675 at 684, per Scarman J reiterating the formula in *Henderson v Henderson* [1967] P 77 at 79.

9.11 Residence

The meaning of the term 'residence' has already been explored at some depth in the earlier chapters of this work but here a distinction must be drawn between residence as a connecting factor in its own right for the purposes of UK taxation and residence in the context of the acquisition of the connecting factor of domicile. In *IRC v Duchess of Portland*,[87] Nourse J said:

> 'Residence in a country for the purposes of the law of domicile is physical presence in that country as an inhabitant of it ... [I]n a case where the domiciliary divides his physical presence between two countries at a time ... it is necessary to look at all the facts in order to decide which of the two countries is the one he inhabits.'[88]

The Duchess of Portland had claimed that, by spending some 10 to 12 weeks each year in Quebec visiting relatives and maintaining her links with Canada (the land of her birth and the country to which she hoped eventually to return), she had acquired a domicile of choice in Canada. She spent the rest of her time living with her husband in England. Nourse J said:

> 'On those facts it appears clear to me that since 1948 the taxpayer has been physically present in this country as an inhabitant of it. Her physical presence in Quebec has been for periods of limited duration and for the purpose of maintaining her links with the country to which it is her intention ultimately to return. That is not enough to have made her an inhabitant of Quebec. In my judgment it is clear that she was resident in England on 1 January 1974 and that that residence was not displaced when she went to Canada in July 1974 or at any other time during the material period.'[89]

It has been shown that residence for tax purposes (ie as a territorial connecting link per se), is a quality of the person which – despite judicial asseverations to the contrary – may be attributed to a person not according to its ordinary meaning but according to a special, forensic meaning derived from case law precedents. It will be recalled, for instance, that the celebrated Mr Lysaght, who had a settled place of residence in Ireland, was attributed with UK residence status merely by reason of his regular monthly business trips to the UK during the course of which he stayed with his brother or at the Spa Hotel in Bath.[90] It has also been demonstrated that, because residence in its taxation context is a qualitative attribute, a person may (as in the case of Lysaght) be resident in two or more countries at the same time.[91] It is clear from the judgment of Nourse J, however, that neither of these possibilities is open so far as residence in the context of the acquisition of a domicile of choice is concerned. A person *may*

87 [1982] STC 149.
88 [1982] STC 149 at 155.
89 [1982] STC 149 at 155–156.
90 See **3.12** above.
91 See **3.21** above.

be resident in a particular country for both taxation purposes *and* domicile purposes, but he will not necessarily be so. Residence for domicile purposes involves actual inhabitance of a country,[92] dwelling within its borders rather than merely paying it visits, however extensive and regular those visits might be: and where a person inhabits two different countries, the only one in which he will be regarded as resident for domicile purposes is the one in which, on the balance of the facts, he is shown to have his 'chief residence'.[93]

The length of a person's residence in a particular country may be of great importance in determining whether or not a person has acquired a domicile of choice in that country, but it is not in itself determinative of the matter. As Lord Chelmsford said in *Bell v Kennedy*:[94]

> 'It may be conceded that if the intention of permanently residing in a place exists, a residence in pursuance of that intention, however short, will establish domicile.'[95]

This principle was reiterated (with the insertion of an interesting additional clause) by Nourse J in *Re Clore (No 2)*:[96]

> '... if the evidence [of intention] is there, particularly perhaps where the motive is the avoidance of taxes, the necessary intention will not be held to be missing merely because the period of actual residence is a short one.'[97]

The fact of residence does, however, raise a presumption of domicile in the country of residence[98] and this presumption grows with the length of the period of residence so that, in some instances, it will be sufficient to override declarations of contrary intention[99] and will require a person's actual removal elsewhere if it is to be rebutted.[100] In *Udny v Udny*,[101] Lord Chelmsford said:

> 'Time is always a material element in questions of domicil; and if there is nothing to counteract its effect, it may be conclusive upon the subject.'[102]

Anderson v Laneuville[103] provides an interesting illustration of the point. The case concerned Anderson, a person born in 1768 with an Irish domicile of origin who, at the age of 67 (by which time he had acquired an English domicile

92 *IRC v Duchess of Portland* [1982] STC 149 at 155, per Nourse J.
93 *Re Fuld's Estate (No 3)* [1968] P 675 at 682, per Scarman J.
94 (1868) LR 1 Sc & Div 307.
95 (1868) LR 1 Sc & Div 307 at 319.
96 [1984] STC 609.
97 [1984] STC 609 at 615.
98 *Bruce v Bruce* (1790) 2 Bos & P 229; *Bempde v Johnstone* (1796) 3 Ves 198.
99 *Stanley v Bernes* (1830) 3 Hagg Ecc 373; *Re Marrett, Chalmers v Wingfield* (1887) 36 Ch D 400.
100 *Hodgson v De Beauchesne* (1858) 12 Moo PC 285.
101 (1869) LR 1 Sc & Div 441.
102 (1869) LR 1 Sc & Div 441 at 455.
103 (1854) 9 Moo PC 325.

of choice) traced, and thereafter until his death some 24 years later, cohabited with, in France, a widow, Madame Laneuville, who, some 46 years earlier, had risked her life in helping him to escape the Terror of the revolution in France where he was then being educated. Anderson had, it seems, expressed some intention of returning to England should Madame Laneuville have predeceased him, but on appeal from the Prerogative Court of Canterbury, that one fact was held to carry insufficient weight to counteract the effect of the length of Anderson's residence in France, and that long period of residence was held to lead inevitably to the conclusion that Anderson had died domiciled in France.

Thus it was in *Re Furse, Furse v IRC*.[104] William King Furse was born in Rhode Island in 1883 and had a Rhode Island domicile of origin. At the age of four, he was brought to England by his father but, after completing his education here, he returned to America, married and remained in employment there until 1916. He then left America to serve in the British army in the 1914/18 war. Upon demobilisation in 1919 he returned to New York where his wife had purchased a house and he found employment there. In 1923 Furse and his wife and children moved to England and bought a farm in West Hoathly. There Furse lived until his death 40 years later. From time to time between 1923 and the early 1950s, Furse and his wife contemplated a return to America and in the 1940s actually inspected a farm in Maryland. In the early 1950s Furse decided, however, that he would not return to America unless he became incapable of leading an active life on his farm in England. Fox J, declaring that Furse died domiciled in England, said:

> '… the facts … show a man deeply settled in England. He came to England at the age of four; he died in England at the age of 80. Of the intervening 76 years he spent 58 in England (in the sense that England was his normal place of abode in those years) and three or four in the British army … [He] was wholly integrated into the English community in which he lived. There is no doubt at all, as I see it, that the life which he was living in England was the life he wanted to go on living to the end of his life … In my view, by the time of his death, the balance of probabilities is that he can have had no real intention of leaving; a fact which is emphasised by the vagueness of his expressed intentions.'[105]

There was, to use Lord Chelmsford's words, nothing (or nothing sufficiently concrete in the way of intention or surrounding circumstances) to counteract the effect of time, and time was, therefore, conclusive on the subject. This is not to say, however, that residence of long duration will alone suffice to establish domicile. It will not. As the previous HMRC guidance correctly pointed out:

> 'Living in another country for a long time, although an important factor, is not enough in itself to prove you have acquired a new domicile.'[106]

104 [1980] STC 596.
105 [1980] STC 596 at 606.
106 IR20 (July 2008), para 4.5.

This follows from what Cottenham LC said in *Munro v Munro*:[107]

> 'Residence alone has no effect, per se, though it may be most important as a ground from which to infer intention.'[108]

In both *Anderson v Laneuville*[109] and *Re Furse, Furse v IRC*,[110] that was where the significance of the long residence of Anderson and Furse lay. All the evidence suggested that, despite their vague assertions of a possible return to their native lands, Anderson and Furse would have remained where they were, however long they had lived; and the courts, therefore, permitted the *animus* of true intention to be inferred from the *factum* of residence.

Where, however, there is evidence to the contrary – something sufficiently concrete to counteract the effect of the duration of residence – the duration of residence will not be conclusive upon the subject as *Ramsay v Liverpool Royal Infirmary*[111] illustrates. George Bowie (the validity of whose will was in question) was born in Glasgow in 1845 and acquired from his father a Scottish domicile of origin. Upon reaching the age of 37 he gave up his employment as a commercial traveller and steadfastly refused to work again throughout the remainder of his life. For ten years he 'lived on the bounty' of his mother and sisters in Glasgow, then, in 1892, he moved to lodgings in Liverpool and for the next 21 years sponged instead on his brother. Upon his brother's death, Bowie moved into his brother's house and for the next eight years sponged on his sister until she died in 1920. He remained at his brother's house and died in Liverpool (where he had arranged to be buried) seven years later. Bowie boasted of being a Glasgow man but during the 36 years he lived in England he refused to return to Scotland, even for his mother's funeral. He left England only twice, once to visit America and once to holiday in the Isle of Man. On those facts, the House of Lords held unanimously that Bowie had *not* acquired a domicile of choice in England but that his Scottish domicile of origin was still operative at the date of his death. Their lordships were convinced that declarations by Bowie to the effect that he would never return to Scotland were mere posturing and that, had Bowie's source of funds dried up, he would, in fact, have gone back there. That, plus the fact that there was no evidence to show that Bowie had made his permanent home in England was, in their view, sufficient to quash the inference of intention to which Bowie's 36 years of residence in England would otherwise have given rise. Lord Macmillan said:

> 'Prolonged actual residence is an important item of evidence of … volition, but it must be supplemented by other facts and circumstances indicative of intention. The residence must answer a qualitative as well as a quantitative test.'[112]

---

107 (1840) 7 Cl & Fin 842.
108 (1840) 7 Cl & Fin 842 at 877.
109 (1854) 9 Moo PC 325.
110 [1980] STC 596.
111 [1930] AC 588.
112 [1930] AC 588 at 598.

IRC v Bullock[113] provides a modern (and much more convincing) illustration of the application of this principle. Group Captain Bullock had a domicile of origin in Nova Scotia but came to England in 1932 and joined the Royal Air Force. He intended to return to Canada on completing his service but, in 1946, he married an Englishwoman some three years his junior. Between then and 1960, Bullock and his wife made several trips to Canada and, upon leaving the RAF in 1959, Bullock would have liked them to move there permanently. His wife did not wish to do so, however, so Bullock took up civilian employment in England until 1961 when an inheritance enabled him to retire completely. Until 1966, Bullock continued to try to persuade his wife to move with him to Canada, but thereafter resigned himself to the fact that she would never do so. In that year, however, he made a will under Nova Scotia law in which he declared that his domicile was and would continue to be the Province of Nova Scotia and that he would return and remain there upon his wife's death. Bullock retained his Canadian nationality and passport, never acquired British nationality or a British passport, refused to vote in local or parliamentary elections, maintained close contact with Canadian relatives and friends, and was a regular reader of a Toronto newspaper. On these facts the Commissioners found that Bullock was not domiciled in England and the Court of Appeal (reversing Brightman J's judgment in the High Court) upheld the Commissioners' finding. Bullock's residence in England, though over 40 years in duration, was accompanied at all times by a clear and definite intention to return to Canada upon the substantial possibility of his wife predeceasing him, and that was sufficient to counteract the effect of the element of time.[114]

9.12 Intention

The acquisition of a domicile of choice requires not only residence (in the sense of actual habitation of the chosen territory) but also an intention to make that territory 'the permanent home'.[115] The problem of what is meant by 'permanent' has lain at the root of many a case concerning domicile. Lord Chelmsford took a strict view of the matter. In *Moorhouse v Lord*[116] he said:

---

113 [1976] STC 409. See also *IRC v Cohen* (1937) 21 TC 301 where a person with an English domicile of origin who went to Australia at the age of 18 and did not return to England until 32 years later was nonetheless held to have retained his English domicile of origin throughout. Overturning the Commissioners' finding that Henry Cohen had acquired an Australian domicile of choice and never abandoned it, Finlay J held (at 315) that the true inference from the facts was that Henry Cohen 'intended to reside and to reside for a long time in Australia, but … he intended to reside there so long only as his business made that necessary, and his business connection with Australia ceased in 1911'.

114 See also *Henkes v Revenue & Customs* [2020] UKFTT 159 (TC) which involved an individual with a foreign domicile of origin who lived in England from the age of 23 for over 50 years.

115 *Whicker v Hume* (1858) 7 HL Cas 124 at 160, per Lord Cranworth.

116 (1863) 10 HL Cas 272.

'The present intention of making a place a person's permanent home can exist only where he has no other idea than to continue there without looking forward to any event, certain or uncertain, which might induce him to change his residence. If he has in contemplation some event upon the happening of which residence will cease, it is not correct to call this even a present intention of making it a permanent home. It is rather a present intention of making it a temporary home, though for a period indefinite and contingent.'[117]

But others thought that far too strict. In *A-G v Pottinger*,[118] Bramwell B said:

'There is not a man who has not contingent intentions to do something that would be very much to his benefit if the occasion arises. But if every such intention or expression of intention prevented a man having a fixed domicil, no man would ever have a domicil at all, except his domicil of origin.'[119]

The less absolute view of the nature of the necessary intention may be discerned in Lord Westbury's statement in *Udny v Udny*[120] that the residence which is the other necessary element in the acquisition of a domicile of choice:

'... must be a residence not for a limited period or particular purpose, but general and indefinite in its future contemplation.'[121]

It emerged even more openly when, in *Gulbenkian v Gulbenkian*,[122] Langton J said:

'The intention must be a present intention to reside permanently, but it does not mean that such intention must be irrevocable. It must be an intention unlimited in period, but not irrevocable in character.'[123]

And it is clearly discernible in the two widely-approved propositions concerning the acquisition of a domicile of choice made by Scarman J in *Re Fuld's Estate (No 3)*:[124]

'... a domicile of choice is acquired when a man fixes voluntarily his sole or chief residence in a particular place with an intention of continuing to reside there for an unlimited time.'[125]

---

117 (1863) 10 HL Cas 272 at 285–286.
118 (1861) 30 LJ Ex 284.
119 (1861) 30 LJ Ex 284 at 292.
120 (1869) LR 1 Sc & Div 441.
121 (1869) LR 1 Sc & Div 441 at 458.
122 [1937] 4 All ER 618.
123 [1937] 4 All ER 618 at 627.
124 [1968] P 675.
125 [1968] P 675 at 682.

> 'A domicile of choice is acquired only if it be affirmatively shown that the *propositus* is resident within a territory subject to a distinctive legal system with the intention, formed independently of external pressures, of residing there indefinitely.'[126]

'Permanent', it will be noted, has become 'indefinite' or 'unlimited' and the difference that brings about may clearly be seen by comparing the dictum of Lord Cairns in *Bell v Kennedy*[127] and that of Buckley LJ in *IRC v Bullock*.[128] Lord Cairns said:

> 'The question … is … Whether [Bell] … had determined to make, and had made, Scotland his home, with the intention of establishing himself and his family there, and ending his days in that country.'[129]

Buckley LJ said:

> 'I do not think that it is necessary to show that the intention to make a home in the new country is irrevocable or that the person whose intention is under consideration believes that for reasons of health or otherwise he will have no opportunity to change his mind. In my judgment, the true test is whether he intends to make his home in the new country until the end of his days *unless and until something happens to make him change his mind*.'[130]

Buckley LJ had not only the authority of Bramwell B to rely on in adding those final 11 words. In *Aikman v Aikman*,[131] Campbell LC (another nineteenth-century judge) had said that a mere intention to return to a man's native country on a doubtful contingency would not prevent residence in a foreign country putting an end to his domicile of origin.

Given that Scarman J and Buckley J have accurately stated the current judicial view of intention for domicile of choice purposes, however, the question then arises: what constitutes a 'doubtful contingency'; what is the 'something' which a person might have in contemplation without the necessary intention of indefinite or unlimited residence being found lacking? Scarman J has answered the question thus:

> 'If a man intends to return to the land of his birth upon a clearly foreseen and reasonably anticipated contingency, eg the end of his job, the intention required by law is lacking: but if he has in mind only a vague possibility, such as making a fortune (a modern example might be winning a football pool) or some sentiment about dying in the land of his fathers, such a state of mind is consistent with the

126 [1968] P 675 at 684.
127 (1868) LR 1 Sc & Div 307.
128 [1976] STC 409.
129 *Bell v Kennedy* (1868) LR 1 Sc & Div 307 at 311.
130 *IRC v Bullock* [1976] STC 409 at 415. [Author's italics.]
131 (1861) 4 LT 374 at 376.

intention required by law. But no clear line can be drawn; the ultimate decision in each case is one of fact.'[132]

And Buckley LJ has answered it in a similar manner:

> 'No doubt, if a man who has made his home in a country other than his domicile of origin has expressed an intention to return to his domicile of origin or to remove to some third country on an event or condition of an indefinite kind (for example 'if I make a fortune' or 'when I've had enough of it'), it might be hard, if not impossible, to conclude that he retained any real intention of so returning or removing. Such a man, in the graphic language of James LJ in *Doucet v Geoghegan*,[133] is like a man who expects to reach the horizon; he finds it at last no nearer than it was at the beginning of his journey.'[134]

In both these passages, however, the contingency contemplated is of a 'pipe dream' character. What if the contingency contemplated is something more specific? In the event, said Buckley LJ, the question to be asked is:

> '... is there a sufficiently substantial possibility of the contingency happening to justify regarding the intention to return as a real determination to do so on the contingency occurring rather than a vague hope or aspiration?'[135]

The facts of the case of *IRC v Bullock*[136] in which that test was propounded, have already been set out at **9.11** above and it is clear from those facts that the single contingency upon which Group Captain Bullock intended to return to Canada was the death of his wife. It was only his wife's refusal to live in Canada which was keeping the Group Captain here, and, as his wife was only two or three years his junior, there was a substantial possibility that she would predecease him. Accordingly, Buckley LJ held that his test question could be answered affirmatively: Group Captain Bullock did not have the necessary intention to make England his domicile of choice. When applied to the facts in *Re Furse, Furse v IRC*[137] (also set out at **9.11** above), however, Buckley LJ's test produced the opposite answer. William Furse was happy and content in England and the only contingency upon which he intended to return to America was his becoming physically incapable of taking an active interest in his farm. Fox J said:

> 'It seems to me that the intention of [Furse] was indeed to continue to reside in England for an unlimited period. His intention was to continue to live here for the rest of his life, save on the contingency which he expressed. That contingency is so

132 *Re Fuld's Estate (No 3)* [1968] P 675 at 685, per Scarman J.
133 (1878) 9 Ch D 441 at 457.
134 *IRC v Bullock* [1976] STC 409 at 416.
135 *IRC v Bullock* [1976] STC 409 at 416.
136 [1976] STC 409.
137 [1980] STC 596.

> vague that I do not think it can be regarded as imposing any clear limitation on the period of his residence. I do not believe that he was ever prepared to face up to such a limitation. The contingency is of the sort which Simon P in *Qureshi v Qureshi*[138] described as 'open-ended' … I think that, when [Furse] died in his 81st year, still in England and still with no arrangements made for leaving England, one could not realistically regard his permanent home as other than in England. He intended to live out his days here, save on a contingency so vaguely expressed that I do not think, against the history of his life, it could be regarded for practical purposes as limiting that intention.'[139]

It will have been noted that in many of the extracts from judgments given in this section the words 'present intention' are used. The force of the adjective 'present' emphasises that what must be considered is the state of a person's mind at the time when the acquisition of a domicile of choice is alleged to have taken place. Subsequent variations in that intention are irrelevant[140] unless accompanied or followed by appropriate action.[141]

It should not be overlooked, however, that evidence of a subsequent change of mind might, in some instances, lead the court to infer that the original intention to remain indefinitely in the country of choice was not as settled as the evidence of that original intention indicated.

Although actual residence and the intention to reside indefinitely must concur before a domicile of choice can be created, the intention may precede or succeed the commencement of residence. The person who decides to emigrate to Quebec will possess the intention which is one element in the creation of a Quebec domicile of choice before he establishes the residence which is the other essential element. The refugee escaping persecution may, on the other hand, establish residence before acquiring the intention to remain indefinitely in the land of current residence.

The only remaining point to be made concerning intention is that it is only the intention to remain indefinitely in a country which is relevant to the acquisition of a domicile of choice. If a person has that intention and there comes a time when the intention coincides with actual residence, a domicile of choice is acquired whether it was also the person's intention to acquire a domicile of choice or not. Thus, in *Re Steer*,[142] Mr Steer, an Englishman who established his permanent home in Hamburg and died there 50 years later, was held to have died domiciled in Germany even though, on one of his temporary visits to England, he had made a will in which he declared that although he was returning to Hamburg he had no intention of renouncing his English domicile of origin. The principle governing this matter was succinctly stated over a century ago:

---

138 [1971] 1 All ER 325 at 340.

139 *Re Furse, Furse v IRC* [1980] STC 596 at 606.

140 *Re Marrett, Chalmers v Wingfield* (1887) 36 Ch D 400.

141 See **9.15** below.

142 (1858) 3 H & N 594. See also *Re Lawton* discussed at **9.14** below.

> 'If the intention [to reside indefinitely in a particular country] exists and if it is sufficiently carried into effect certain legal consequences follow from it, whether such consequences are intended or not and perhaps even though the person in question may have intended the exact opposite.'[143]

9.13 Motive as evidence of intention

It will have been noted that the first of Scarman J's two propositions concerning the acquisition of a domicile of choice, quoted at **9.12** above contains the words 'fixes *voluntarily* his sole or chief residence', and that the second contains the words 'with the intention, *formed independently of external pressures*, of residing'. Those words draw attention to the fact that the acquisition of a domicile of choice presupposes a freedom of choice. As Lord Westbury put it in *Udny v Udny*:[144]

> 'There must be a residence freely chosen, and not prescribed or dictated by any external necessity … .'[145]

If it can be shown that a person resides where they do, not by choice but by constraint, the necessary intention will be lacking and no change of domicile will be imputed to the involuntary exile.

The most obvious example of residence by constraint rather than through choice is imprisonment in some country other than that of the existing domicile. No prisoner, during a term of imprisonment, will acquire a new domicile in the country of imprisonment, even if the imprisonment is for a very long term, for this residence is not a matter of choice.[146]

Another example of constraint is the persecution which may impel a person to flee his existing country of domicile for some other country. Although the residence in the country of refuge will be a matter of free choice, the inference at law will be that the refugee will return to their homeland upon it being safe to do so and they will, therefore, prima facie lack the intention to reside permanently in the country of refuge which would be necessary in order to acquire a domicile of choice in that country. It might be, of course, that a refugee will acquire such an intention during the course of their exile.[147]

A fugitive from justice is in much the same position as the refugee except that, if the crime is such that the fugitive will always (or for a very long time)

143 *Douglas v Douglas* (1871) LR 12 Eq 617 at 644–645.

144 (1869) LR 1 Sc & Div 441.

145 (1869) LR 1 Sc & Div 441 at 458.

146 *Re the late Emperor Napoleon Bonaparte* (1853) 2 Rob Eccl 606.

147 *De Bonneval v De Bonneval* (1838) 1 Curt 856. See also *Steiner v IRC* (1973) 49 TC 13 where a refugee from the Nazi persecution of Jews made his home in England in 1939 but was held not to have acquired an English domicile of choice here until about 1950 when the facts were such as to indicate that he had formed the intention of remaining permanently in England.

be liable to proceedings in the country from which they have fled, there will be a presumption at law that the country of refuge has been selected with the intention of residing there indefinitely.[148] The departure will have been a matter of constraint but the establishment of residence elsewhere will have been a matter of free choice.

'The demands of creditors' was one of Lord Westbury's examples of an external necessity which might result in a person residing where they would not otherwise reside.[149] So it was with Colonel Udny and his residence in France. But the fact that a person has fled the country to escape creditors will not necessarily mean that a domicile of choice cannot be acquired in the country to which the debtor has fled. It will depend on circumstances: the size of the debts, the likelihood of them ultimately being met, how long their discharge is likely to take, and the imminence of recovery proceedings.

The invalid who, although in no immediate danger of untimely death, settles for health reasons in a country other than the country of their existing domicile is regarded at law as doing so out of choice rather than out of constraint. In the case of *Hoskins v Matthews*,[150] for example, Turner LJ said that Mr Matthews, an Englishman who, at the age of 60, had gone to Florence suffering from a spinal injury and had died there 12 years later, was not, when he first took up residence in Florence,

> '… in any immediate danger or apprehension. He was, no doubt, out of health, and he went abroad for the purpose of trying the effect of other remedies and other climates. That he would have preferred settling in England I have little doubt, but I think he was not driven to settle in Italy by any cogent necessity. I think that in settling there he was exercising a preference, and not acting upon a necessity, and I cannot venture to hold that in such a case the domicil cannot be changed.'[151]

If, however, the change of environment is a matter of life or death, or if, death being imminent and inevitable, the change of climate will alleviate suffering, there will, it seems, be no presumption of a change in domicile.[152]

The 'tax exile' who, in order to escape the incidence of taxation in the country of existing domicile, settles in a country with a less harsh tax regime, will, it seems, be presumed to intend to remain in the new country permanently. In *Re Clore (No 2)*,[153] Nourse J said that even a short period of residence would be sufficient to establish a domicile of choice 'if the evidence is there, particularly perhaps where the motive is the avoidance of taxes'.[154]

---

148 *Re Martin, Loustalan v Loustalan* [1900] P 211.
149 *Udny v Udny* (1869) LR 1 Sc & Div 441 at 458.
150 (1856) 8 De GM & G 13.
151 (1856) 8 De GM & G 13 at 28–29.
152 See Lord Kingsdown's comments in *Moorhouse v Lord* (1863) 10 HL Cas 272 at 292.
153 [1984] STC 609.
154 [1984] STC 609 at 615.

In the *Clore* case, there were, according to Nourse J, three areas where the evidence supported Sir Charles Clore's acquisition of a domicile of choice in Monaco. One was the severance of the more important of his connections with England where Sir Charles had his domicile of origin. Another was the establishment of connections with Monaco including residence there. But the most important, in Nourse J's eyes, was that:

> '... the professional advice which Sir Charles received was given not solely with the immediate object of his acquiring a non-resident status for income and capital gains tax purposes, but with the long-term objective of his acquiring a foreign domicile. Further, unless the operation was to be at least partially counter-productive, it was essential that the new country should be one where no tax was payable. Monaco was chosen because it was the only tax haven with which Sir Charles was familiar and the only one which could have been acceptable to him.'[155]

Against the evidence in those three areas, however, was the evidence of four of his close friends who were unanimous in their testimony that Sir Charles was unhappy in Monaco and had never, in his heart of hearts, abandoned England. All his actions from mid-1978 until his death in London on 26 July 1979 were tentative and, right up to the time of his death, he was showing an interest in acquiring residential properties in France and Israel. Accordingly, Nourse J held that Sir Charles died domiciled in England. That decision must not, however, be allowed to obscure the fact that, because Sir Charles had resided in Monaco and his motive for residing there was tax avoidance, Nourse J accepted that there was a presumption at law that a domicile of choice had been acquired in Monaco. As with any presumption at law, however, the presumption to which a tax avoidance motive will give rise may be rebutted by other evidence, and in the *Clore* case it was rebutted by the evidence of parol declarations made by Sir Charles in his final years and testified to by his four friends.

It must finally be pointed out that the residence of a person in a country other than the country of their existing domicile will give rise to no presumption that a domicile of choice has been acquired in the new country if the person is there in pursuit of what Lord Westbury called 'the duties of office'.[156] These have been held to include the duties of a consul,[157] chief justice,[158] embassy attaché,[159] naval officer,[160] and army officer.[161] Such a negative presumption may, of course, be rebutted by evidence to the contrary.[162]

155 [1984] STC 609 at 614.
156 *Udny v Udny* (1869) LR 1 Sc & Div 441 at 458.
157 *Sharpe v Crispin* (1869) LR 1 P & D 611.
158 *A-G v Lady Rowe* (1862) 1 H & C 31.
159 *A-G v Kent* (1862) 31 LJ Ex 391.
160 *Re Patten's Goods* (1860) 6 Jur NS 151.
161 *Firebrace v Firebrace* (1878) 4 PD 63.
162 *Donaldson v Donaldson* [1949] P 363.

9.14 Proof of intention

As Scarman J said in *Re Fuld's Estate (No 3)*:[163]

> 'It is beyond doubt that the burden of proving the abandonment of a domicile of origin and the acquisition of a domicile of choice is upon the party asserting the change. But it is not so clear what is the standard of proof: is it to be proved beyond reasonable doubt or upon the balance of probabilities, or does the standard vary according to whether one seeks to establish abandonment of domicile of origin or merely a switch from one domicile of choice to another? Or is there some other standard? … The formula of proof beyond reasonable doubt is not frequently used in probate cases and I do not propose to give it currency. It is enough that the authorities emphasise that the conscience of the court … must be satisfied by the evidence. The weight to be attached to evidence, the inferences to be drawn, the facts justifying the exclusion of doubt and the expression of satisfaction will vary according to the nature of the case. Two things are clear – first, that unless the judicial conscience is satisfied by evidence of change, the domicile of origin persists: and secondly, that the acquisition of a domicile of choice is a serious matter not to be lightly inferred from slight indications or casual words.'[164]

Those statements were later endorsed by Orr LJ who, in *Buswell v IRC*,[165] said:

> 'I … accept the statements as accurate and would only add that in referring to the judicial conscience I am satisfied that Scarman J was not recognising the existence of some general standard of proof intermediate between the criminal and civil standards but was merely emphasising that in the application of the civil standard the degree of proof required will vary with the subject-matter of the case.'[166]

The approach to assessing evidence of intention was neatly expressed by Mummery LJ in *Agulian & Anor v Cyganik*:[167]

> '(1) Although it is helpful to trace … life events chronologically and to halt on the journey from time to time to take stock, this question cannot be decided in stages. [T]he court must look back at the whole of the deceased's life, at what he had done with his life, at what life had done to him and at what were his inferred intentions in order to decide whether he had acquired a domicile of choice in England by the date of his death. Soren Kierkegaard's aphorism that "Life must be lived forwards, but can only be understood backwards" resonates in the biographical data of domicile disputes.
>
> (2) Secondly, special care must be taken in the analysis of the evidence about isolating individual factors from all the other factors present over time and treating a particular factor as decisive.'

163 [1968] P 675.
164 [1968] P 675 at 685–686.
165 [1974] STC 266.
166 [1974] STC 266 at 273.
167 [2006] EWCA Civ 129 at para 49.

If the judicial conscience is to be satisfied that a change in domicile has taken place, the courts must subject every department of a person's life to the most searching scrutiny. The length and nature of residence in the country in which it is asserted that the person has acquired a domicile will, of course, be a factor of particular interest since, as has been explained,[168] residence gives rise at law to a presumption of domicile, and intention may be inferred from residence if the residence is of sufficient length and there is other evidence to support such an inference. Motives too must be examined for, as has been explained at **9.13** above, a person's motive in taking up residence in a country other than that of their existing domicile may give rise to an inference of, or against, a change in domicile. But the court's concern is never confined merely to residence and the motive for residence. As Lord Atkinson said of *Winans v A-G*[169] in *Casdagli v Casdagli*:[170]

> '… the tastes, habits, conduct, actions, ambitions, health, hopes, and projects of Mr Winans deceased were all considered as keys to his intention to make a home in England.'[171]

It is often said that if a person wishes to ensure that a change of domicile will withstand the scrutiny of the courts the person must not only take up residence in the country of choice but should purchase a property there and dispose of any property in the country that has been abandoned, apply for citizenship of the new country, obtain a passport in the new country and relinquish an existing passport, close all bank accounts in the abandoned country and open new accounts in the country of choice, relinquish credit cards and obtain new ones in the country of choice, resign any directorships in the abandoned country and acquire business interests in the country of choice, sever membership of clubs, societies, religious organisations etc in the abandoned country and join clubs etc in the country of choice, vote in the new country's elections,[172] become involved in its politics and socially integrated into its life, educate children in its schools, have a will drawn up under its laws and make arrangements to be buried or cremated there. Such a checklist has a certain value, being a list of factors to which particular significance has been attached in cases which have come before the courts at different times. But the approach is wrong. A person who has genuinely made a 'permanent home' in a new country will, in those and many other ways, manifest the reality of their intention to live out their days as an inhabitant of the land to which they have gone; but the person who is engaged in nothing more than a cosmetic exercise designed to conceal the fact that 'in spite of all temptations to belong to other nations,

168 See **9.11** above.
169 [1904] AC 287.
170 [1919] AC 145.
171 [1919] AC 145 at 178.
172 The fact that an individual is registered on the UK electoral roll as an overseas voter does not affect his domicile unless the individual wishes it to be taken into account: ITA 2007 s 835B.

he remains an Englishman'[173] is likely to betray his lack of genuine intention no matter how scrupulously he adheres to a list of 'dos and don'ts'. No one factor will, in itself, be decisive, and even a factor which seems of supreme significance when viewed in isolation may carry little weight when set against all other factors. Thus, for example, in *Wahl v A-G*,[174] the fact that a person with a German domicile of origin and German nationality had become a naturalised British subject was not regarded as being at all conclusive:

> 'I am far from saying that an application for naturalisation is not a matter to be carefully considered as part of the evidence in a case of domicile, but it must be regarded as one of the totality of facts and it cannot assume the dominant importance attached to it in the judgment of the trial judge … It is not the law either that a change of domicile is a condition of naturalisation, or that naturalisation involves necessarily a change of domicile.'[175]

In making his application for naturalisation, Wahl had made a statutory declaration to the effect that he intended to continue to reside permanently within the UK. That too formed part of the evidence of his intention and, since such declarations are frequently made by persons changing their domicile, their value must now be considered. In *F v IRC*[176] the executor of F, a former Iranian national who had died in 1993, appealed against the determination of the Revenue that he had been domiciled in the UK for the years of assessment 1986–87 to 1992–93 inclusive. F had operated an accountancy business in Iran. He had bought land with a view to developing it, owned three houses and had constructed a large family home. At the time of the Iranian revolution he had sent his wife and children to live in the UK while remaining himself in Iran. At the time of the US hostage crisis F had decided to remain outside Iran at the same time he had been placed on an exit barred list due to alleged outstanding tax liabilities. In 1980 he had been granted indefinite leave to remain in the UK. He had subsequently applied for naturalisation, falsely claiming that he had left Iran to escape religious persecution. Up until the time of his death, F had made efforts at getting the exit bar removed. He had continued to consider Iran as his home. The Court in allowing the appeal held that the Revenue had not discharged the burden of proof to demonstrate that F had not abandoned his Iranian domicile. Having regard to the evidence, it had always been F's intention to return to Iran permanently during the relevant years for assessment. His acquisition of British citizenship and a British passport had not affected his domicile of origin in Iran, and so *Wahl v A-G* applied. He had been keen to gain the necessary documentation that would enable him to continue to travel freely in the furtherance of his business interests and had been willing to lie in order to gain such documentation. His return to Iran had been precluded by the exit

173 W S Gilbert, *HMS Pinafore*, Act II.
174 (1932) 147 LT 382.
175 (1932) 147 LT 382 at 385, per Lord Atkin.
176 [2000] 1 WTLR 505.

bar. Such external pressures had prevented F from forming a free intention to acquire another domicile.

An example of the difficulties to which a written declaration might give rise is found in *Buswell v IRC*.[177] Leslie Buswell had a Transvaal domicile of origin acquired from his father who had a Transvaal domicile of choice. In 1928, when Buswell was seven years old, he and his parents moved to England so that Buswell could be educated here. Following his education and a brief period which Buswell spent as a teacher in Tenbury Wells, he was called up in 1941 and served in the Royal Indian Navy. Upon demobilisation in 1945, he took employment in India and remained there until 1952 when he returned to England where his father was living in a poor state of health. Once in England, he took employment with a publishing firm for six months, then obtained a position with British Olivetti Ltd which he held until 1963. In 1955, Buswell obtained a South African passport and elected for South African nationality when South Africa left the Commonwealth, and, in 1958, wrote to a cousin in South Africa saying he intended to return there one day. In 1961, he married an Englishwoman of means who was agreeable to settling eventually in South Africa, and, by her, had children who were educated in England but were registered as South African nationals. In 1968, Buswell and his wife visited South Africa (Buswell's first visit there for 40 years) and bought a property in which they thereafter spent some three months of each year. Buswell claimed that, for the years 1961/62 to 1967/68, he was 'not domiciled in the UK' for the purposes of ITA 1952 section 132 (now ITTOIA section 832)). That claim was resisted by the Inland Revenue on the grounds that, on 11 November 1952, Buswell had completed a Revenue questionnaire (Form P86) by answering 'Yes' to the question 'Do you propose to remain permanently in the UK?' and inserting a dash in answer to the next question: 'If not, how long do you expect to remain in this country?' The Commissioners attached great weight to those replies and accordingly found that Buswell had acquired an English domicile of choice. The High Court upheld the Commissioners' finding on appeal, but the Court of Appeal reversed it. Orr LJ said.

> 'The crucial question … is … whether the Commissioners, in coming to their conclusion, attributed to the answers on Form P86 a weight which in all the circumstances they could not reasonably bear. For this purpose it is necessary to consider both the terms of the questions asked on the form and the circumstances in which it may reasonably be supposed that [Buswell] answered them … [T]he form was not intended by the Revenue to ascertain domicile and it nowhere used that word … A person faced with … mutually exclusive questions, would, I think, be very likely to consider that he was not expected to say "I do not know" in answer to the second question, an answer which would have to be given if he said "No" to the first … I find … that, in attributing a decisive importance to [Buswell's] answers on the Form P86, given at a time when he had been back in this country for less than five months after an absence of ten years, and against the background to which

177 (1974) 49 TC 334.

> I have referred, the Commissioners acted "upon a view of the facts which could not reasonably be entertained".'[178]

Often a written declaration of intention will appear in a person's will, taking a form similar to that appearing in the will of Frank Lawton in *Re Lawton*:[179]

> 'Inasmuch as I am a British subject having my original domicile in England (which domicile I have never relinquished or abandoned) it is my wish and intention that this my will … shall be construed and operate so far as the case admits as if I were now and remained until my death domiciled in England.'[180]

The value of such a declaration was assessed by Romer LJ in *A-G v Yule and Mercantile Bank of India*[181] as follows:

> 'For myself, I am not prepared to attach any importance to a declaration by a man as to his domicile unless there is some evidence to show that the man knew what "domicile" means. A declaration by a man made orally or in writing that he intends to remain in a certain country will, if not inconsistent with the facts, be of assistance in determining the question whether he has become domiciled there. Domicile is, however, a legal conception on which the views of a layman are not of much assistance.'[182]

Lawton had, in fact, left England before he had attained the age of 21 and, having lived and worked in Argentina and Spain, retired to France where he died some 63 years later. Upjohn J held that, despite the declaration in his will, Lawton died domiciled in France.

Where the assertion of intention as to residence has been made orally, the testimony of the person to whom it was made is admissible as evidence of intention but, if made long after the assertion itself was made, will be treated with caution:

> 'To entitle such declarations to any weight, the court must be satisfied not only of the veracity of the witnesses who depose to such declarations, but of the accuracy of their memory, and that the declarations contain a real expression of the intention of the deceased.'[183]

Where the assertion is actually made by the person whose domicile is being determined during the court proceedings at which the determination of domicile is to be made, the assertion will, of course, carry very little weight indeed. In *Bell v Kennedy*[184] the Lord Chancellor said of Bell's own testimony:

---

178 (1974) 49 TC 334 at 362–363.
179 (1958) 37 ATC 216. See also *Re Steer* discussed at **9.12** above.
180 (1958) 37 ATC 216 at 218.
181 (1931) 145 LT 9.
182 (1931) 145 LT 9 at 17.
183 *Hodgson v De Beauchesne* (1858) 12 Moo PC 285 at 325.
184 (1868) LR 1 Sc & Div 307.

'… it is to be accepted with very considerable reserve. An Appellant has naturally, on an issue like the present, a very strong bias calculated to influence his mind, and he is, moreover, speaking of what was his intention some twenty-five years ago.'[185]

9.15 Change of domicile of choice

It should by now have become clear that the courts will not easily be satisfied that a domicile of origin has been replaced by a domicile of choice. The presumption of a domicile of origin's continuance is of the utmost strength and, compared with a domicile of choice:

'… its character is more enduring, its hold stronger and less easily shaken off.'[186]

This is because a domicile of origin is conferred on a person by operation of law whereas, as has been explained,[187] a domicile of choice is acquired merely *animo et facto*. Once acquired, however, a domicile of choice may be extinguished *animo et facto* also (ie by an intention and an act). The act is the leaving of the country of the domicile of choice and the intention is the intention not to resume permanent residence there. This last is technically referred to as an *animus non revertendi*. Such an *animus* does not, it should be noted, include within it a decision to reside permanently elsewhere. In *Udny v Udny*,[188] the Lord Chancellor summed up the whole matter as follows:

'… if the choice of a new abode and actual settlement there constitute a change of the original domicil, then the exact converse of such a procedure, viz the intention to abandon the new domicil, and an actual abandonment of it, ought to be equally effective to destroy the new domicil. That which may be acquired may surely be abandoned, and though a man cannot, for civil reasons, be left without a domicil, no such difficulty arises if it be simply held that the original domicil revives. That original domicil depended not on choice but attached itself to its subject on his birth, and it seems to be consonant both to convenience and to the currency of the whole law of domicil to hold that the man born with a domicil may shift and vary it as often as he pleases, indicating each change by intention and act, whether in its acquisition or abandonment; and, further, to hold that every acquired domicil is capable of simple abandonment *animo et facto* the process by which it was acquired, without its being necessary that a new one should be at the same time chosen, otherwise one is driven to the absurdity of asserting a person to be domiciled in a country which he has resolutely forsaken and cast off, simply because he may (perhaps for years) be deliberating before he settles himself elsewhere.'[189]

185 (1868) LR 1 Sc & Div 307 at 313.

186 *Winans v A-G* [1904] AC 287 at 290, per Lord Macnaghten; *F (F's Personal Representatives v IRC)* [2000] STC (SCD) 1.

187 See **9.10** above.

188 (1869) LR 1 Sc & Div 441.

189 (1869) LR 1 Sc & Div 441 at 450.

Just as a domicile of choice cannot be acquired *animo solo*, however, a domicile of choice cannot be abandoned unless the intention to leave the territory of the existing domicile of choice for good is accompanied by an actual departure from that territory. As Cotton LJ said in *Re Marrett*:[190]

> '... in order to lose the domicil of choice once acquired, it is not only necessary that a man should be dissatisfied with his domicil of choice, and form an intention to leave it, but he must have left it, with the intention of leaving it permanently.'[191]

The application of this principle is to be found in *Zanelli v Zanelli*.[192] The case concerned an Italian who, having married an English woman and lived with her in England, deserted her and returned to Italy. The wife petitioned for divorce in England claiming that the English courts had jurisdiction because immediately before deserting her, her husband was domiciled in England within the terms of the Matrimonial Causes Act 1973 section 13. The question before the court was whether that was so. It was accepted that, following the marriage, the woman's husband had acquired a domicile of choice in England and it was accepted also that, by the time of his desertion, he had formed the intention to return permanently to Italy. But did that bring about a loss of domicile of choice? Lord du Parcq decided that no, it did not:

> '... although the husband may have given up an intention to reside here, he certainly had not given up residence here. The *factum* had not occurred.'[193]

Accordingly, the woman's petition was granted and her divorce (which would not have been permitted under Italian law) was granted under English law.

The question of when the *factum* of departure does occur is not always an easy question to answer as *Re Raffenel's Goods*[194] illustrates. Madame Raffenel had a domicile of origin in England but, upon marrying a French naval officer, had acquired a French domicile of dependence. Following her husband's death, she decided to return permanently to England. She boarded ship at Calais with her children and baggage, having closed down her establishment in Dunkirk, but, before the ship left the harbour, became so ill that she had to disembark. She returned to Dunkirk where she later died. Sir Cresswell Cresswell said:

> 'I cannot think that the French domicil was abandoned so long as the deceased remained in the territory of France. It must be admitted that she never left France, and that intention alone is not sufficient.'[195]

---

190 (1887) 36 Ch D 400.
191 (1887) 36 Ch D 400 at 407.
192 (1948) 64 TLR 556.
193 (1948) 64 TLR 556.
194 (1863) 3 Sw & Tr 49.
195 (1863) 3 Sw & Tr 49.

Although that case was concerned with abandonment of a domicile of dependence, Lord du Parcq, in the case of *Zanelli v Zanelli*[196] which (as explained above) concerned the abandonment of a domicile of choice, expressly approved the decision in *Re Raffenel's Goods*[197] and drew no distinction between the two types of domicile in this connection. Speaking of Zanelli's desertion of his wife he said:

> '… he cannot be said to have lost his domicile of choice even at the moment when he stepped into the train with his ticket in his pocket. Having regard to what was decided … in *Re Raffenel's Goods* … I do not think that, even when he stepped on board the ship which was to carry him to the Continent, he had yet lost his domicile of choice.'[198]

It should be noted, however, that in that case, Asquith LJ went even further:

> 'To change an English domicile of choice there must be both *animus* and *factum*, the *animus* being the formation of the intention, and the *factum* consisting in some outward and visible act evincing it such as leaving this country or, *perhaps more accurately, arriving in another*.'[199]

And on the strength of that dictum, Baker J held, in *Leon v Leon*,[200] that a person who had displaced his domicile of origin in British Guiana (now Guyana) by a domicile of choice in England but had then left England for good and returned to British Guiana, had:

> '… kept his English domicile until he reverted to his domicile of origin on his arrival in British Guiana in August 1964.'[201]

This, it is suggested, was stretching Sir Cresswell Cresswell's dicta in *Re Raffenel's Goods*[202] too far. Surely, the domicile of origin of both Zanelli and Leon revived as soon as their respective ships left the territorial waters of the UK, not when they docked on the shores of their respective homelands.

It was said at the outset of this section that the *animus* required to effect the abandonment of a domicile of choice is an *animus non revertendi* (ie an intention not to return). It must now be emphasised that (despite recent

196 (1948) 64 TLR 556.
197 (1863) 3 Sw & Tr 49.
198 (1948) 64 TLR 556.
199 (1948) 64 TLR 556 at 557 [Author's italics].
200 [1967] P 275.
201 [1967] P 275 at 282. These words must not be taken as some sort of authority for the proposition that presence in the domicile of origin is necessary for that domicile's revival. As *Tee v Tee* [1974] 1 WLR 213 clearly shows, it is not.
202 (1863) 3 Sw & Tr 49.

indications of some relaxation in this view)[203] such an *animus* does *not* cover a case of mere irresolution (*sine animo revertendi*). A person who leaves the country of their existing domicile of choice in a state of indecision as to whether or not to return there retains their existing domicile of choice until such time as the indecision hardens into a decision never to return. This is illustrated by *Fielden v IRC*.[204] Fielden had an English domicile of origin but, in or about 1935, this was displaced by a Michigan domicile of choice when he married a Michigan resident and settled in that state of America with the intention of remaining there permanently. In 1943, Fielden and his wife moved to Burnley in Lancashire with the intention of helping in his father's ailing business, and they bought a house there. In 1947, Fielden became a director of his father's company and later became chairman and managing director. It seems that he then decided that he owed it to his father to remain in England until he was satisfied the business could continue successfully without him, but he asserted that, upon his retirement, he would return to America, though not necessarily to Michigan. At the time the case was heard, however, he was still living in Burnley, 22 years after leaving America. The Commissioners decided that, by 1954/55, the first of the years for which his domicile was in question, Fielden's English domicile of origin had revived, but they also found that his Michigan domicile of choice had been retained for some years after his return to England, probably until 1947. This was, it is suggested, because for those years he was merely *sine animo revertendi* to Michigan, not *animo non revertendi* to Michigan. Later, however, his intention to return to America in general became too vague to prevent him being regarded as *animo non revertendi* and thereupon his domicile of origin revived. The Commissioners' findings were upheld by Cross J who said:

> '... it is not necessary, in order to retain a domicile of choice after a change of residence, to have an unwavering intention of returning to live in the place of domicile in all circumstances ... When [Fielden] came to England in 1943, he came under the stress of circumstances. He wanted to help his country and his father in the war; and the Commissioners have found – I think quite rightly found – that he did not there and then lose his Michigan domicile of choice. It would not, I think, matter for this purpose whether he then had an intention to go back as soon as possible to Michigan after the war, or simply to go back to some place in the United States after the war. But then one finds that after the war he buys a house here, that when he goes to the United States it is only for a short stay, and that he remains here continuously until the present time ... [H]e re-acquired his English domicile of origin about 1947 ... because ... such intention as he may thereafter have had of

203 In *Re Flynn* [1968] 1 WLR 103 Megarry J said (*obiter* at 113) that 'mere negative absence of any intention' to resume residence, rather than a positive intention not to return, would suffice to bring a domicile of choice to an end, and this was approved in *Qureshi v Qureshi* [1971] 2 WLR 518 at 530; but see *Executors of Winifred Johnson Dec'd v HMRC* [2005] UKSPC 481.

204 (1965) 42 TC 501.

going to live somewhere in the United States after his retirement was really too vague and uncertain to prevent the re-acquisition of his English domicile of origin.'[205]

If a person leaves a domicile of choice *animo revertendi* but subsequently abandons the intention to return, the domicile of origin will, of course, thereupon revive.[206]

Finally, it should be noted that where a person *animo et facto* abandons one domicile of choice and *animo et facto* acquires another, the domicile of origin will revive for the duration of the interval, however brief, between the abandonment and the acquisition.[207]

9.16 Deemed domicile to 5 April 2017

In introducing the capital transfer tax (which was renamed 'inheritance tax'), the Finance Act 1975 section 45 provided that, under any of three sets of circumstances a person who was not domiciled in the UK under the common law rules described in this chapter was nevertheless to be treated as domiciled in the UK for most purposes of the tax. The provision relating to one of those three sets of circumstances was repealed by Finance (No 2) Act 1983 section 12 and the provisions describing the remaining two sets of circumstances were substantially re-enacted as the Inheritance Tax Act 1984 section 267(1)(a) and (b).

Section 267(1)(a) and (3) provided that a person not domiciled in the UK at the time of a transfer of value etc ('the relevant time') is to be treated as domiciled in the UK at that time if he was domiciled in the UK on or after 10 December 1974 and within the three years immediately preceding the relevant time.

In the absence of statutory definition to the contrary, 'year' means a period of 12 calendar months consisting of 365 days or 366 days in a leap year.[208]

The effect of this provision was to postpone (for inheritance tax purposes only) a person's acquisition of a domicile in some country outside the UK to a date three years after the date on which, according to common law rules, the acquisition of the new domicile actually took place. Thus, any transfer of value made by the person within the three years immediately following his acquisition of an overseas domicile will remain potentially subject to inheritance tax regardless of the *situs* of the asset.

205 (1965) 42 TC 501 at 507–508.

206 *Tee v Tee* [1973] 3 All ER 1105.

207 *Harrison v Harrison* [1953] 1 WLR 865. The proposal of The Law Commission and the Scottish Law Commission is that this should cease to be so and that an abandoned domicile of choice should continue until a new domicile is acquired (Working Paper No 88 and Consultative Memorandum No 63, para 5.22).

208 *IRC v Hobhouse* [1956] 1 WLR 1393.

This rule had no rational basis and is transparently directed at keeping within the inheritance tax net for a period of time anyone who leaves the UK permanently. Superficially, it paralleled a Revenue practice prior to the Statutory Residence Test in Finance Act 2014, regarding the residence status of a person who left the UK for permanent residence abroad, ie that a decision on that person's claim to have become non-resident and not ordinarily resident in the UK would be postponed for three years and that during those three years the person's tax liabilities would be calculated on the basis that they remain UK resident; but, in the case of residence, a decision at the end of three years that the person had become non-resident on departure is then applied retrospectively to the date of departure and all assessments are revised accordingly. There was, however, nothing similarly provisional about the three-year postponement of non-domiciled status.

Unlike section 267(1)(a), section 267(1)(b) was a more rational piece of legislation, designed to place a non-domiciled person who has lived in the UK for a specified number of years on an equal footing with the UK-domiciled taxpayer.[209] It (and section 267(3)) provided that a person not domiciled in the UK at the time a transfer of value etc takes place ('the relevant time') is to be treated as domiciled in the UK at that time if the individual was resident in the UK on or after 10 December 1974 and in not less than 17 of the 20 years of assessment ending with the year of assessment in which the relevant time falls. It should be noted, however, that, for the purposes of this provision:

> '… the question of whether a person was resident in the UK in any year of assessment shall be determined as for the purposes of income tax.'[210]

Chapters 2 and 2 should, therefore, be studied in this context in relation to years after 5 April 2013, and previous editions of this work for years up to that date. In deciding whether an individual was deemed domiciled under section 267, any election to be treated as domiciled in the UK under sections 267ZA and 267ZB is ignored.[211]

The provision itself had two effects. The first is to bring persons who have never been domiciled in the UK into the inheritance tax net. The second (and often overlooked) effect is, unless the change of domicile took place on 6 April, to keep a person who has been, but is no longer, domiciled in the UK within the inheritance tax net for up to almost a year longer than section 267(1)(a) would keep that person there.

Members of the House of Commons (Members of Parliament) and House of Lords (Peers) are deemed domiciled in the UK for the purposes of income tax, inheritance tax and capital gains tax.[212]

---

209 See Official Report, Standing Committee A, 13 February 1975, cols 1645–1646.
210 IHTA 1984 s 267(4).
211 IHTA 1984 s 267(5). See **9.17**.
212 Constitutional Reform and Governance Act 2010 s 41(1)–(3). See also Chapter 2, at **2.27**.

9.17 Deemed domicile from 6 April 2017 to 5 April 2025

Finance (No 2) Act 2017 comprehensively reformed the tax treatment of individuals who are not domiciled in any part of the UK at common law. A major extension of the deemed domicile legislation was proposed in Summer Budget of July 2015 and the consultation that followed.[213] Two targets of this reform were identified: first, non-domiciled individuals who have been resident in the UK for 15 out of the preceding 20 years, and, second, individuals who were born in the UK, who have a UK domicile of origin but have acquired a foreign domicile and are resident in the UK. Broadly, both categories of individuals who were not domiciled in any part of the UK would no longer qualify as such for UK tax purposes. Individuals who ceased to be domiciled in the UK continued to remain UK domiciled for three years after giving up a UK domicile for inheritance tax purposes.[214] Similarly Members of the House of Commons (Members of Parliament) and House of Lords (Peers) continued to be deemed domiciled in the UK for the purposes of income tax, inheritance tax and capital gains tax.[215]

The deemed domicile provisions applied to income tax, capital gains tax[216] and inheritance tax.[217] The rules are to similar effect in each case but there are notable differences for income tax, capital gains tax purposes on the one hand, and for inheritance tax purposes on the other. The rationale of reducing the time that non-UK domiciled residents could continue to reside in the UK before being put in the same tax position as UK domiciled residents produced haphazard outcomes for individuals in its interaction with both the case law and statutory residence tests. A close study of Chapters 2 and 3 will indicate that individuals with relatively modest connections to the UK may become resident. Such individuals will inevitably also have substantial residential connections with other countries. The prospects of double taxation are significantly increased as a result.

Income tax and capital gains tax

An individual not domiciled in the UK at common law at a time in a tax year, was treated as domiciled in the United Kingdom for income tax and capital gains tax purposes at that time if that individual had been UK resident for at

213 HMRC Technical Note, Technical briefing on foreign domiciled persons changes announced at Summer Budget 2015 (8 July 2015); HM Treasury Consultation document, Reforms to the taxation of non-domiciles; further consultation (19 August 2015); HM Treasury Consultation document, Reforms to the taxation of non-domiciles (30 September 2015).

214 IHTA 1984, s 267(1)(a).

215 Constitutional Reform and Governance Act 2010, s 41(1)–(3). See also Chapter 2, at **2.27**.

216 ITA 2007 s 835BA(1), inserted by F(No 2) A 2017 s 29(1).

217 IHTA 1984 s 267(1), amended by F(No 2) A 2017 s 30(1).

least 15 of the 20 tax years immediately preceding the relevant tax year.[218] Thus individuals who ceased to be resident from 6 April 2018 continued to be treated as UK domiciled unless and until they were non-UK resident for at least six tax years in the 20 tax years before the relevant tax year. A transitional rule permitted individuals who had not been UK resident in any tax year from 6 April 2017 to 5 April 2025 and including the year when their domicile is to be determined (a 'relevant tax year'), to not be UK domiciled for this purpose.[219]

An individual not domiciled in the UK at common law at a time in a tax year, was also treated as domiciled in the United Kingdom for income tax and capital gains tax purposes at that time if (a) the individual was born in the United Kingdom, (b) the individual's domicile of origin was in the United Kingdom, and (c) the individual was UK resident for the relevant tax year.[220] Consequently, a UK born individual who originally had a domicile of origin in any part of the UK but who subsequently acquired a foreign domicile (of choice or dependence) will be deemed to be UK domiciled in any tax year when they were UK resident. This rule will apply, for example, to a child born in England of English parents who emigrated from the UK to Australia as a family and remain there permanently. If in adulthood, that child returned to the UK, for example for a one-year short-term work assignment, that child was deemed domiciled during that tax year of UK residence.

The consequence of deemed domicile status was essentially the loss of access to the remittance basis for foreign income and gains. Some complexities of such a loss of status were addressed in Finance (No 2) Act 2017 Sch 8.

Inheritance tax

An individual not domiciled in the UK at common law at a time in a tax year before 6 April 2025, was treated as domiciled in the United Kingdom for inheritance tax purposes at that time if the individual was resident in the United Kingdom for at least 15 of the 20 tax years immediately preceding the relevant tax year, and for at least one of the four tax years ending with the relevant tax year.[221] This differed from the income tax and capital gains tax test in that an individual person who would otherwise satisfy the 15 of 20 tax years test was not deemed domiciled if they were non UK resident in that tax year and had been non-resident for the previous three consecutive tax years.

An individual not domiciled in the UK at common law at a time in a tax year, was treated as domiciled in the United Kingdom for inheritance tax purposes at that time if the individual was a 'formerly domiciled resident' for the tax year.[222] A 'formerly domiciled resident' was an individual (a) who was born in

218 ITA 2007 s 835BA(2) and (4) ('Condition B').
219 ITA 2007 s 835BA(5).
220 ITA 2007 s 835BA(2) and (3) ('Condition A').
221 IHTA 1984 s 267(1)(b).
222 IHTA 1984 s 267(1)(aa).

the United Kingdom,(b) whose domicile of origin was in the United Kingdom, (c) who was resident in the United Kingdom for the relevant tax year, and (d) who was resident in the United Kingdom for at least one of the two tax years immediately preceding the relevant tax year.[223] Thus the difference between deemed domicile of UK born individuals was that for inheritance tax purposes, the individual must have been UK resident in at least two tax years. Income tax and capital gains tax required residence in only one year.

Thus in the example of a child born in England of English parents who emigrated from the UK to Australia as a family and remained there permanently, if in adulthood, that child returned to the UK, for example for a one-year short-term work assignment, that child would not be deemed domiciled during a single tax year of UK residence. However, a one-year short-term work assignment to the UK that straddles two tax years, making the individual resident in both,[224] resulted in deemed domicile for inheritance tax in the second year of residence.

A transitional rule permitted individuals who have not been UK resident in any tax year from 6 April 2017 and including the year when their domicile was to be determined (a 'relevant tax year'), to be not UK domiciled for this purpose.[225] As a result, individuals who were not UK domiciled at common law and who ceased to be resident from the 2017/18 tax year and who dis not again become UK resident were not domiciled in the UK for inheritance tax from 6 April 2017. Such individuals who ceased to be resident after 5 April 2018 needed to wait until they no longer had been resident for 15 of the 20 preceding tax years to cease to be deemed domiciled.

The broad effect of deemed domicile was that property situated outside the UK no longer qualified for exclusion from inheritance tax. This is subject to detailed rules in Finance (No 2) Act 2017 section 30.

Deemed domicile and the statutory residence test

The question whether an individual was UK resident in any given tax year is answered by reference to the law in that year. Thus, for years up to 5 April 2013 the case law tests discussed in previous editions of this work will apply. FA 2013 Schedule 45, paragraph 1(4) makes clear that the Statutory Residence Test, discussed in Chapter 2 applies thereafter.

One consequence of the residence rules is that residence at any time in a tax year, no matter how short, will make the individual resident for that year. An individual who qualifies for split year treatment under FA 2013 Schedule 45 Part 3, in a given tax year, was likewise resident for the whole of that tax year for purposes of the deemed domicile rules.[226] Depending on the time of arrival

223 IHTA 1984 s 272.

224 See 'Fulltime work in the UK', discussed in Chapter 2 at **2.14**.

225 F(No 2) A 2017 s 30(10).

226 See Chapter 2, at **2.31**.

and departure from the UK, it was possible to become deemed domiciled with a little over 12 years of actual living in the UK.

9.18 Elective UK domicile for spouses and civil partners

On 24 October 2012 the EU Commission requested the UK to review inheritance taxation of transfer between spouses. The Commission noted that UK legislation provided that transfers between domiciled spouses or civil partners were exempt from inheritance tax. However, transfers between domiciled and non-domiciled spouses or civil partners are not exempt from inheritance tax. Furthermore, in the latter case the rules on the nil rate band applicable to subsequent transfers differ and may result globally in a higher taxation. In the Commission's view, this difference in tax treatment was discriminatory and contrary to EU law (Article 18 TFEU).[227]

FA 2013 provided a legislative response in the form of an election by the non-domiciled spouse or civil partner of a UK-domiciled individual to choose to be treated as UK domiciled for the purposes of the IHTA 1984.[228] In determining whether a person making an election under this section was UK domiciled, the deemed domicile rules in section 267 are ignored.[229] An election could be made in writing to HMRC in two circumstances:

Firstly, a lifetime election could be made to be treated as UK domiciled by an individual, if at any time from 6 April 2013 and during the period of seven years ending with the date on which the election was made, he or she had a spouse or civil partner who was UK domiciled.[230] A lifetime election took effect on the date specified in the notice of election which had to be on or after 6 April 2013 and within the period of seven years of the date of election. On the effective date, the individual making the election must have been married to, or in a civil partnership with, the spouse or civil partner who was then domiciled in the United Kingdom.[231]

Secondly, a death election may be made if at any time from 6 April 2013 an individual died, and within the period of seven years ending with the date of death the deceased was: (a) domiciled in the United Kingdom; and (b) the spouse or civil partner of the person who would, by virtue of the election, be treated as domiciled in the United Kingdom.[232] This election could be made by the deceased person's personal representatives.[233] A death election could only be made within two years of the death of the deceased or such longer period

227 EU Commission MEMO/12/794 Case No 2010/2111. See Chapter 10 on the EU fundamental freedoms.
228 FA 2013 s 177, inserting s 267ZA and s 267ZB.
229 IHTA 1984 s 267ZA(8).
230 IHTA 1984 s 267ZA(1) and (3).
231 IHTA 1984 s 267ZB(3), (4) and (5).
232 IHTA 1984 s 267ZA(1) and (4).
233 IHTA 1984 s 267ZA(2).

as an officer of Revenue and Customs allowed.[234] A death election took effect on a date specified in the notice, which have been on or after 6 April 2013 and within the period of seven years ending with the date of death of the deceased. On the effective date, the person who was to be treated as UK domiciled by virtue of the election must have been married to, or in a civil partnership with, the deceased who was then UK domiciled.[235]

Any such election was irrevocable.[236] It did not affect the application of a tax treaty,[237] and it did not affect a person's domicile for the purposes of sections 6(2) or (3) or 48(4).[238] Thus, the individual did not become liable to inheritance tax in respect of excluded property situated outside the UK.

Although the election was irrevocable, it ceased to have effect if the electing person was resident outside the UK for more than four full consecutive tax years.[239] As part of the extension of deemed domicile for tax purposes discussed in **9.16**, one consequence of deemed domicile resulting from UK residence for 15 out of 20 years, was that the period of non-residence before the election ceased to have effect after six years.

9.19 Domicile for tax treaty purposes

Where (whether under these deemed domicile rules or not) a person is regarded under UK law as domiciled in the UK but is regarded under the law of a foreign state with which the UK has a double tax treaty covering estate and inheritance taxes as domiciled in that foreign state, the provisions of the treaty will apply so as to ensure that the person is treated by both the UK and the foreign state as being domiciled only in one of the territories for the purpose of that treaty. In this context, the meaning of domicile in such treaties only refers to common law domicile and not to statutory deemed domicle.[240] Article 4(2) of the OECD 1982 draft double taxation convention on estates and inheritances provides for this to be achieved by a series of tests identical to those applied to determine fiscal residence as described at **2.45** above. A number of these treaties are, however, old and contain a variety of provisions addressing fiscal domicile quite differently from the OECD Model.

234 IHTA 1984 s 267ZB (6).
235 IHTA 1984 s 267ZB(3), (4) and (5).
236 IHTA 1984 s 267ZB(9).
237 IHTA 1984 s 267ZA(6)–(8). See **9.18**.
238 IHTA 1984 s 267ZA(5).
239 IHTA 1984 s 267ZA(8).
240 IHTA 1984 ss 158 and 267(2).

CHAPTER 10

Compliance and appeals

'The bell', said Noggs, as though in explanation; 'at home?'
'Yes.'
'To anybody?'
'Yes.'
'To the tax-gatherer?'
'No! Let him call again.'

Charles Dickens *Nicholas Nickleby*, Ch 2

10.01 Introduction

This chapter examines the residence and domicile aspects of compliance and dispute resolution in relation to income, capital gains corporation taxes and inheritance tax. Stamp duty land tax compliance is discussed in Chapter 8, paras **8.13** and **8.14**.

Absence from the territory of the UK does not relieve compliance obligations or provide a defence against proceedings in the UK for the recovery of tax payable under an assessment. Any person chargeable to income tax or capital gains tax for a year of assessment and who has not received a notice requiring a return for that year of his total income and gains, must give to an officer of HMRC notice that he is so chargeable within six months from the end of that year.[1] Notice is not required in respect of certain classes of income where tax is deducted at source.[2] In *Whitney v IRC*,[3] Lord Wrenbury considered the obligation which ITA 1918 section 7(3) imposed on every person chargeable with supertax (a form of income taxation which no longer exists) to give notice that he was so chargeable, and said of Mr Whitney, an American citizen and a resident of New York who had received dividends in respect of shares in a UK corporation:

1 TMA 1970 s 7.
2 TMA 1970 s 7(3).
3 (1924) 10 TC 88.

> If … I am right in thinking that the non-resident alien is chargeable in respect of property in the UK, it was his duty to give that notice.[4]

In *IRC v Huni*,[5] for example, a Swiss national who was not resident in the UK argued that a notice to make a return for supertax purposes served on him at his Paris address was invalid since it had been served outside the territory of the UK. It followed, he said, that he could not have failed to make a return within the terms of the legislation (FA 1910 in relation to supertax) and that the Commissioners had, therefore, no jurisdiction to make an assessment to the best of their judgment. Furthermore, he contended, irrespective of the validity of the assessment, the notice of assessment (also served on him at his Paris address) was as invalid (on the same grounds) as had been the notice requiring him to make a return. Rowlatt J did not agree. He said:

> 'A great deal has been said in the course of this argument about a non-resident and about an alien, but I think I am confronted with the question as to the operation of this Statute without the realm … In the words of the Statute there is no distinction drawn between aliens or residents or non-residents or anything of that sort; the question really is as to whether the Statute is to be cut down so as not to serve notices abroad. Now the principle involved here is the principle that Acts of Parliament are prima facie not to be construed so as to assume jurisdiction without the realm – extra-territorial jurisdiction – so as to make the jurisdiction extra-territorial. And of course where it comes to the case of creating a duty abroad or creating an offence abroad – both of which of course can be done by Parliament – … the Courts are bound to look narrowly at the Statute to see whether that is what is meant. But I apprehend there is no difficulty of that sort in the way if what the Statute really directs is the mere service of a notice, and that is all it is. There is no international difficulty in serving a notice abroad … It may have consequences, but it is a mere notice … I think there is involved in this machinery the mere giving of a notice as a preliminary to the Commissioners proceeding to do something which they are entitled to do … and that I ought not to limit the words of this Section so as to make this notice as a mere notice null and void.'[6]

That being so, the assessment which followed Mr Huni's failure to make the return required of him was valid. Accordingly, Rowlatt J turned to the question of the notice of assessment:

> 'The Respondent says that the notice of assessment is bad too, because it was served on him abroad. That I cannot think is bad. If a man has been validly assessed in England, what principle of international law is to be invoked by way of reflection to limit the words of the Statute which says that he may be told he has been assessed, I cannot conceive.'[7]

4 (1924) 10 TC 88 at 114.
5 (1923) 8 TC 466.
6 (1923) 8 TC 466 at 474.
7 (1923) 8 TC 466 at 474.

This judgment was approved by the House of Lords in the *Whitney* case[8] where Mr Whitney had advanced arguments against his assessability similar to those which had been advanced by Mr Huni. Lord Wrenbury said:

> 'There was sent to the Appellant by post addressed to him in the United States a notice under Section 7(2) requiring him to make a return. It is contended that there was no right to send him a notice so addressed. The case, it is contended, is similar to the case of service of a writ out of the jurisdiction. I do not agree ... It is not a step in a judicial proceeding, but a step which will create *inter partes* a state of things in which judicial proceedings can subsequently be taken in default of compliance. I think the notice was duly served. In my opinion *IRC v Huni* was rightly decided.'[9]

If notice is to be served validly under the Taxes Acts, therefore, all that is required is that it be served at the 'usual or last known place of residence' of the person on whom it is served, whether that place of residence be in the UK or an address overseas.[10]

The provisions described above relate to income tax and capital gains tax, but similar provisions exist in relation to corporation tax and inheritance tax.

10.02 Assessment of non-residents

Notwithstanding the above, the UK adopts two domestic law mechanisms of ensuring compliance with its direct tax laws in the international context by imposing obligations on persons other than the taxpayer. Firstly, in the case of non-residents, a UK representative may be jointly liable with the non-resident in relation to trade income.[11] Secondly, the system of deduction of tax at source by the payer of certain items of income is extended to persons whose 'usual place of abode' is outside the UK which often, but not always, coincides with non-residence.

Deduction of tax at source – 'usual place of abode'

10.03 ITA 2007 imposes obligations on payers to deduct tax at source on certain amounts paid to persons whose 'usual place of abode is outside the UK'. This includes certain yearly interest[12], royalties, or sums payable periodically, in respect of a relevant intellectual property right,[13] and 'non-

8 (1924) 10 TC 88.
9 (1924) 10 TC 88 at 113.
10 TMA 1970 s 115.
11 ITA 2007 Pt 14, Chs 2B and 2C; TCGA 1992 Pt 7A for non-corporates and CTA 2010 Pt 22 Ch 6 for companies.
12 ITA 2007 s 874.
13 ITA 2007 s 906.

resident landlord income'.[14] The expression is not defined in the legislation and, like its counterpart expressions, residence, ordinary residence and domicile requires interpretation.

HMRC practice in this area is somewhat imprecise with slightly different expositions of their practice in different parts of their published guidance.

HMRC International Tax Manual explains that '[th]e term 'usual place of abode' is used in the legislation because the purpose of the legislation is to provide an effective way of collecting tax due from someone who is usually outside the UK and/or does not have a taxable presence in the UK.[15] Usual place of abode, it says, 'means principal place of business or the place where the person is normally to be found. It is not the same as tax residence'. The HMRC Property Income Manual suggests: 'Usual place of abode' is not identical in meaning to residence, or ordinary residence, but a person who is not resident in the UK should normally be treated as having their usual place of abode outside the UK'.[16]

One HMRC explanation of the usual place of abode in the context of 'non-resident' landlords in the Property Income Manual[17] reads:

> '1) Individuals have a usual place of abode outside the UK if they usually live outside the UK. You should still regard the term as applying to them even if in a particular year they are resident in the UK for tax purposes, as long as the usual place of abode is outside the UK. (For example the individual may count as resident in the UK in a particular year because of a six months' visit, or a visit of a shorter time when he has a place of abode available in the UK). Do not treat someone as having their usual place of abode outside the UK if they are only temporarily living outside the UK, say for six months or less.
>
> 2) Companies that have their main office or other place of business outside the UK, and companies incorporated outside the UK, will normally have a usual place of abode outside the UK. However if the company is treated as resident in the UK for tax purposes, do not treat it as having a usual place of abode outside the UK.
>
> 3) Trustees have a usual place of abode outside the UK if all the trustees have a usual place of abode outside the UK.'

In relation to interest payments, the HMRC Savings Income Manual comments in relation to trustees:

> 'Trustees, including personal representatives, have a usual place of abode abroad if each trustee, considered as an individual or a company as the case may be, has a usual place of abode there. So if one trustee does not have a usual place of abode abroad, neither does the trust.'[18]

14 ITA 2007 s 971.

15 INTM505020.

16 PIM4810 with PIM4800.

17 PIM4810 with PIM4800. Cf the International Manual INTM370060. Also see Savings Income Manual re interest SAIM9080.

18 SAIM9080.

While it may have been true under the case law test that a person whose usual place of abode was in the UK was resident in the UK, it did not follow that a person whose usual place of abode was outside the UK was *not* resident in the UK.[19] The effect of the statutory residence test[20] is to disconnect the two connecting factors entirely from each other. In imposing a test of 'usual place of abode' (rather than a test of residence) in this context, it may be observed that a person on whom it places the onus of applying the test (ie any person making payment) will rarely be in possession of such facts as are required for the determination of the residence status of the person to whom payment is being made, whereas the determination of such a person's usual place of abode may arguably be capable of determination by mere enquiry and observation.

In *Haslope v Thorne*,[21] Lord Ellenborough CJ considered the term 'place of abode' in the context of a rule of court which required the place of abode of the deponent of an affidavit to be inserted in the affidavit and came to the conclusion that it meant 'the place where the deponent was most usually to be found'.[22] Thus, the place where a man 'lives with his family and sleeps at night' will always be 'his place of abode in the full sense of that expression'.[23] That does not presuppose, however, that the living and sleeping will take place in a house or flat or even a hotel room: a yacht,[24] a caravan,[25] a tent or bender,[26] and even a car[27] may constitute a person's place of abode!

---

19 See Chapter 2.

20 See Chapter 2.

21 (1813) 1 M & S 103.

22 (1813) 1 M & S 103 at 104. In accordance with that principle, the usual place of abode of a company will presumably be its principal place of business.

23 *R v Hammond* (1852) 17 QB 772 at 780, 781, per Lord Campbell CJ.

24 In *Bayard Brown v Burt* (1911) 5 TC 667, it was accepted that an ocean-going yacht anchored in territorial waters was the place of abode of Mr Bayard Brown, its owner and occupier.

25 In *Makins v Elson* [1977] STC 46, it was held that a wheeled caravan jacked up and resting on bricks, with water, electricity and telephone services installed, was a dwelling house.

26 In *Hipperson v Electoral Registration Officer for the District of Newbury* [1985] 2 All ER 456, Sir John Donaldson MR (at 462) rejected the submission that women living in tents, vehicles and benders (a form of tent) on Greenham Common in furtherance of their protest concerning cruise missiles could not be said to have a home in the camp: 'It may be unusual to make one's home in a tent, bender or vehicle, but we can see no reason in law why it should be impossible.'

27 In *R v Bundy* [1977] 2 All ER 382, the motor car in which a certain Mr Bundy had been living rough was held to be his place of abode when sited but not while in transit. The court held, at 384, that the term '"place of abode" … connotes, first of all, a site. That is the ordinary meaning of the word "place". It is a site at which the occupier intends to abide. So there are two elements in the phrase "place of abode", the element of site and the element of intention. When the appellant took the motor car to a site with the intention of abiding there, then his motor car on that site could be said to be his "place of abode", but when he took it from that site to move it to another site where he intended to abide, the motor car could not be said to be his "place of abode" during transit.'

10.04 Claiming non-resident, treaty non-resident or non-domiciled status

For income and capital gains tax purposes, following the Finance Act 2008 it was normally necessary for an individual who is resident but not domiciled in the UK to claim such status (ITA 2007 section 809B). Where such individuals were liable to notify chargeability to tax, they would in consequence normally be required to complete a self-assessment tax return. Where a return is to be filed, the claim must be made in the return.[28] Provision for the making of such claims is made in the 'non-residence' pages of the return. Whether a claim to treaty non-residence is necessary is obscure.[29] Despite this legal obscurity, the non-resident pages of the return provide the same mechanism for treaty non-residence as for non-residence under domestic law or not domiciled status to be claimed or asserted.

Taxpayers have always needed to maintain records to demonstrate their status. The formulaic nature of the statutory residence test and the many numerical thresholds place a premium on accurate, detailed records to substantiate the contents of tax returns. HMRC views on record keeping for this purpose are set out in HMRC Residence and FIG Regime Manual FIG21900.

10.05 Administration of residence and domicile status of individuals

The administration of the residence and domicile status moved closer to a pure self-assessment approach as a result of operational changes announced by HMRC on 25 March 2009.[30] HMRC no longer accepted initial non-domicile claims on form DOM 1 (domicile questionnaire) or form P86 (arrival form). Form DOM 1 was withdrawn completely.[31] From that date, until the Form P86 was withdrawn on 1 June 2010, individuals did not need to fill in boxes 12 to 17 which ask questions about domicile on the P86 when submitting it. If individuals chose to fill in those boxes HMRC ignored the content when processing the form. Any DOM 1 forms received by HMRC by close of business 25 March 2009 were processed but any received after that date were returned unexamined.

Consequently, individuals have been required to self-assess their residence and domicile for income tax and capital gains tax purposes each year and questions about domicile status are dealt with by way of enquiry into a claim to non-domicile status either as a stand-alone enquiry, or as part of a wider enquiry.

28 TMA 1970 s 42.
29 See TIOPA 2010 s 6.
30 HMRC 2009 Brief 17/09.
31 The use of the form has been discussed in several tribunal decisions.

Where an individual had already submitted a form DOM 1 or P86 and obtained an initial view from HMRC about their domicile status HMRC practice was that it would be unusual for them to open an enquiry into domicile status in the few years after that, unless new information becomes available that indicates their initial view was incorrect or there has been a change in circumstances. They also indicate that initial views from HMRC can become less and less useful as an indicator of domicile status with the passage of time, circumstances and intentions change.

On 11 April 2013, HMRC published a revised form P85 (departure form) for use by taxpayers leaving the UK who wish to claim tax relief or a repayment of tax. The revised form takes into account elements of the statutory residence test.

10.06 Inheritance tax accounts

HMRC indicate that an individual setting up a non-resident trust who considers they are non-UK domiciled is not obliged to submit an inheritance tax account to HMRC. If the settlor is non-UK domiciled then no inheritance tax is due. But if an inheritance tax account is submitted in these circumstances, HMRC will continue its existing practice and only open an enquiry into that return if the amounts of inheritance tax at stake make such an enquiry cost effective to carry out. At present that limit is £10,000.

As was previously the case, where HMRC has expressed an opinion on the domicile status of a settlor for inheritance tax purposes they will not normally seek to reconsider that opinion unless new information becomes available that indicates their initial opinion was incorrect or there has been a material change in the circumstances of the settlor. They warn that when they make a decision it applies only to the date of the transaction concerned. So if circumstances change, that individual's domicile may need to be considered again at another point in time.

10.07 Domicile enquiries

For 2008/09 and later years up to 2024/25, in order to make a valid claim to the remittance basis, individuals are required to state on their self-assessment tax return the grounds for their entitlement by stating either that they are not domiciled in the UK (or up to 2012/13, that they are not ordinarily resident in the UK (or both)). If HMRC decide to enquire into an individual's domicile status this will be by way of a TMA 1970 section 9A enquiry into their self-assessment tax return. (Alternatively, in appropriate cases, HMRC may enquire into an individual's domicile status by way of an IHTA 1984 Part VIII enquiry into an inheritance tax return.) Where a claim to the remittance basis is not challenged for that year it does not mean HMRC necessarily accept the individual's domicile is outside the UK and does not prevent HMRC from later opening an enquiry to consider the domicile status of the individual in relation to that, or any earlier year.

Enquiries aimed at establishing an individual's domicile are, by their very nature, examinations of an individual's background, lifestyle, habits and intentions, possibly over the course of a lifetime. Consequently, any such enquiries conducted by HMRC will, where necessary, extend to areas of individuals' and their families' affairs that may not normally be regarded as relevant to their UK tax position. HMRC Remittance Basis and Domicile manual includes a section which explains the nature of a domicile enquiry and the sorts of questions an individual will need to answer as part of that enquiry.[32]

Where HMRC have expressed a view on an individual's domicile status for income tax or capital gains tax purposes, as a result of an enquiry, then that view will also apply for inheritance tax purposes at that time. Likewise an HMRC view expressed for inheritance tax purposes, following an IHTA 1984 Part VIII enquiry, will also apply for income tax and capital gains purposes at that time only.

Gulliver v Revenue and Customs,[33] concerned an application for a closure notice relating to a domicile enquiry. TMA 1970 section 28A allows a taxpayer to apply to the Tribunal for a direction that HMRC issue a closure notice, which the Tribunal must give unless it is satisfied that there are reasonable grounds for not issuing the notice. HMRC had opened an enquiry into Mr Gulliver's tax return for the 2013/14 tax year, for which the only outstanding issue was his domicile for that year. Mr Gulliver, the Group Chief Executive of HSBC plc, and a UK national with a UK domicile of origin, had an international business career with significant amounts of time living in the Far East. In 2002, he established a discretionary trust for the benefit of his family. At the time, his permanent home and the centre of his business and social life was Hong Kong. HSBC had asked him to undertake a specific assignment in London that was expected to last for two years after which he would return home to Hong Kong. In 2003 the then Inland Revenue agreed that Mr Gulliver, in funding the trust, had not made a transfer of value for inheritance tax purposes. This agreement implied recognition that he was not domiciled in the UK at the time, based on information provided.

In refusing the application, the First-tier Tribunal rejected the argument that, having determined that Mr Gulliver acquired a domicile of choice in Hong Kong, HMRC were stuck with the consequences. The presumption that his domicile of choice continued meant that HMRC bore the burden of showing that he abandoned that domicile of choice which was not supported by the evidence he had provided. The Tribunal ruled that the previous agreement was no impediment to HMRC enquiring, in relation to 2013/14, that Mr Gulliver never acquired a Hong Kong domicile of choice. The Tribunal noted that in 2003, a 'risk based approach' was taken to requests for confirmation of

32 RDRM23070 and RDRM23080.

33 *Gulliver v Revenue and Customs* [2017] UKFTT 222 (TC).

the inheritance tax treatment of lifetime transfers that took into account the amount of tax potentially in issue, and the chance of the taxpayer concerned being UK domiciled on the basis of the information provided. The amount of tax in issue was only £4,735 and there was not a high risk of Mr Gulliver being UK domiciled, based on the information provided.

The decision also highlights the onerous nature of domicile enquiries. HMRC requested large amounts of information and documents by way of notice under FA 2008 Schedule 36. Answers to 123 questions and the provision of 33 categories of document were not limited to matters arising after the date of the Inland Revenue confirmation in 2003 and involved a searching examination of a number of aspects of his personal and professional life dating back to 1981.

An enquiry into the tax return of an individual who claims to be domiciled outside the UK inevitably raises the relevance to the enquiry of information on foreign income, gains and property of the individual subject to the enquiry. In principle, such items are not relevant to the accuracy of a return in the absence of a rule or transaction that engages those items such as a remittance. Where the enquiry is into the domicile of the individual, their foreign income, gains and property will become relevant if ultimately the individual is UK domiciled. Four cases have come before the First-tier Tribunal where HMRC disputed the taxpayer's domicile and at the same time issued information notices under to Finance Act 2008 Schedule 36 paragraph 1, requiring the taxpayer to provide information on foreign income and gains in the course of the enquiry into domicile.[34] Such an information notice can require a taxpayer to provide information or documents that are 'reasonably required … for the purpose of checking the taxpayer's tax position.' In each case, the taxpayer sought a final or partial closure notice to end the enquiry and to decline to provide the income. In *Embiricos* the First-tier Tribunal judge ordered that the closure notice should be given and allowed the appeal against the information notice on the basis that the information demanded was not reasonably required pending determination of the taxpayer's domicile. The judge decided that it was not necessary for the taxpayer's self-assessment to be amended in order to issue a closure notice. Amendment would have a computational element that needs information on foreign income and gains. In *Executors of Mrs R W Levy*, they declined to order a closure notice and ruled that the information was required for purposes of the enquiry. In *Henkes* and *Perlman*, the judges considered that, on the evidence of domicile before him, a final closure notice need not be given and upheld the information notices. A more complex order was made in relation to partial closure covering only the domicile issue which turned on the outcome of appeals that had since been made in the *Embiricos* case.

34 *Embiricos v Revenue & Customs* [2019] UKFTT 236 (TC), [2019] SFTD 795; *The Executors of Mrs R W Levy v Revenue & Customs* [2019] UKFTT 418 (TC), [2019] SFTD 1045; *Henkes v Revenue & Customs* [2020] UKFTT 159 (TC); *Perlman v Revenue and Customs* [2021] UKFTT 219 (TC).

The Court of Appeal in *Embiricos v Revenue & Customs*[35] reversed the First-tier Tribunal decision, agreeing with the Upper Tribunal (UT)[36] that HMRC do not have the power to issue a partial closure notice in respect of a domicile and remittance basis claim without specifying the increased tax due because of their conclusion on domicile. Lady Justice Simler ruled that a partial closure notice could only be given in respect of a matter on which HMRC could issue a final closure notice. If a conclusion of the question has computational consequences, then its elements are not separate matters. Domicile was held to be relevant and constituent element of a quantifiable liability rather than a separate matter.[37]

Other strategies adopted in order to not disclose foreign income and gains in these cases have likewise been unsuccessful. In *Embiricos*, during the enquiry into his return, the taxpayer requested that the domicile issue be referred to the tribunal for determination pursuant to TMA 1970 section 28ZA. This provision permits any matter, any question arising in connection with the subject matter of the enquiry to be referred to the tribunal for its determination prior to closure of the enquiry. Such referrals must be given jointly by the taxpayer and HMRC, which HMRC refused to do.[38]

In *Henkes*, on appeal, the First-tier Tribunal was asked to determine the taxpayer's domicile by way of preliminary issue on the basis of the information already provided. HMRC considered the information as insufficient for this purpose. The judge decided that he had jurisdiction and exercised his discretion to hear the preliminary issue,[39] and went on to decide that the taxpayer was UK domiciled and, consequently, the information on foreign income and gains was required. Even if the taxpayer was not UK domiciled, there were sufficient grounds that the information on income and foreign gains was reasonably required. [40]

Abolition of domicile as a connecting factor and its replacement with residence-based tests will mean that enquiries into long-term UK residents or qualifying new residents will be focused only on evidence that addresses the requirements of the Statutory Residence Test, albeit going back for many years.[41]

---

35 *Embiricos v Revenue and Customs* [2022] EWCA Civ 3, [2022] STC 232 CA, [2022] BTC 1.

36 *Revenue and Customs v Embiricos* [2020] UKUT 370 (TCC), [2021] STC 201 (UT), [2021] BTC 507.

37 In the author's view, the decision may be regarded as *per incuriam* and open to challenge because the effect of Art 8 of the European Convention on Human Rights (right to privacy) was not taken into consideration. These privacy rights were not drawn to the attention of the court or tribunals at any stage. In the author's view the requirement for proportionality is not satisfied if a partial closure notice is not available in these circumstances.

38 *Revenue and Customs v Embiricos* [2020] UKUT 370 (TCC), at para 19.

39 *Henkes v Revenue & Customs* [2020] UKFTT 159 (TC), at para 134.

40 [2020] UKFTT 159 (TC), at para 175.

41 In contrast, for example, in *Strachan v HMRC* [2023] UKFTT 617 a 2,945-page document bundle plus three witnesses and in *Aubrey Weis v HMRC* [2025] UKFTT 348 (TC), a 2,088 page bundle of documents plus witness statements were before the Tribunal.

10.08 ITEPA 2003 directions re foreign employment income

Employers of employees who are not UK resident but work in the UK or are qualified new residents who work outside the UK and have qualifying foreign employment income to which relief for foreign employment Chapter 5C of Part 2 of ITEPA 2003 applies are able to ask for a direction pursuant to ITEPA 2003 section 690DD and 690E which permits them not to apply PAYE to qualifying payments made by those employees.

For years before 2025/25 employers of employees who are not UK resident or, if resident but not domiciled, work outside the UK and have foreign earnings when the remittance basis applies within ITEPA 2003 section 26A, are able to ask for a direction pursuant to ITEPA 2003 section 690 to 690C which permits them not to apply PAYE to certain employment income of those employees. An HMRC officer is permitted to treat the remittance basis as applicable even if no claim has been made by an employee.[42] This is necessary to permit such directions to be made as under the self-assessment system, claims are made after the relevant tax year has ended and is a minor modification to an otherwise complete self-assessment system.

10.09 Certificates of residence

Where a UK resident is entitled to relief from foreign taxes by operation of a tax treaty, the foreign tax authority will usually require HMRC to certify that the person is a UK resident within the meaning of the treaty. Some fiscal authorities may also require HMRC to confirm that the person fulfils other conditions. HMRC practice is set out in their International Manual. They will issue a certificate of residence in most cases. Requests are normally only refused if there is no doubt that the customer would not be entitled to benefits. HMRC may decide to make a spontaneous exchange of information with the foreign tax authority where such entitlement is questioned.[43]

HMRC may also, on request, issue a 'letter of confirmation' instead of a certificate of residence that they regard a person as UK resident for purposes other than claiming relief from foreign taxes under a Treaty such as relief from foreign taxes under the domestic law of the foreign state or, prior to Brexit, EU law (such as under the EU Interest and Royalties Directive).[44]

HMRC officers will not carry out a detailed review of residence when they receive a request for a certificate of residence. The officer will usually be able to certify residence, as long as they can see that the 'customer' is (or was for the period requested) liable to UK tax by virtue of their residence (eg by checking the customer's tax returns or, if no such returns have been submitted

42 ITEPA 2003 s 690(2A).
43 HMRC International Manual, para INTM162010.
44 HMRC International Manual, para INTM162140.

yet, the information provided with the request). If HMRC do not have enough information to determine whether a customer is liable to UK tax by virtue of their residence or, despite the self-assessments made by the customer, there are reasonable grounds for believing that the customer may not in fact be a resident of the UK, the request may be refused if sufficient doubt remains even after correspondence on the issue. A certificate of residence is not a formal determination of UK residence. It is simply confirmation that, to the best of HMRC's knowledge, the person is, or was for the period in question, liable to tax by virtue of UK residence. HMRC still have the right to enquire into a customer's self-assessment tax return when it is received.[45] Individuals may apply online for a certificate.[46] Other persons generally need to apply in writing.

10.10 Appeals

Up to the tax year 2007/08, a special procedure for dealing with disputes as to domicile or ordinary residence[47] required the Commissioners of Revenue & Customs to determine such disputed domicile or ordinary residence. Their decision was then subject to appeal to the Special Commissioners. This procedure was repealed in 2008.[48] For the tax years 2008/09 and thereafter, appeals in relation to these issues will be dealt with under normal self-assessment provisions and appeal.

The Special and General Commissioners were abolished and replaced by the First-tier Tribunal and the new Upper Tribunal of the Tax Chamber with effect from 1 April 2009.[49] In addition, an internal review by HMRC is available. If a taxpayer gives notice of appeal to HMRC, the taxpayer may either require HMRC to review the matter or take it directly to the First-tier Tribunal. HMRC may also offer an internal review.[50] A decision of the First-tier Tribunal may be appealed to the Upper Tribunal but only with the permission of either the First-tier or Upper Tribunal.[51] In addition, the Tribunal may review its own decisions and in doing so may correct or set them aside.[52]

---

45 HMRC International Manual, para INTM162040.

46 https://www.gov.uk/guidance/get-a-certificate-of-residence.

47 ITEPA 2003 Pt 2 and Ch 6, TCGA 1992 s 9(2).

48 FA 2008 Sch 7 paras 23, 54 and 77.

49 See generally Transfer of Tribunal Functions and Revenue & Customs Appeals Order, SI 2009/56.

50 TMA 1970 s 49B.

51 TCEA 2007 s 11(1) and Tribunal Procedure (First-tier) (Tax Chamber Rules) 2009, SI 2009/273, reg 39.

52 TCEA 2007 s 10 and Tribunal Procedure (First-tier) (Tax Chamber Rules) 2009, SI 2009/273, regs 37, 38 and 41.

10.11 Evidential burden on appeal

As early as 1876, in *Cesena Sulphur Co Ltd v Nicholson*[53] the court held that the burden of proof to show that a company was resident in the UK was on the Revenue and said, at p 105:

> 'I admit that the onus of proving residence lies upon the Crown … and if the Crown fails to satisfy the Court that the place of residence is within the jurisdiction, or within the area of taxation, you cannot say that the company should be taxed.'

Several recent cases have involved a consideration of the evidential burden. The Revenue have unsuccessfully argued that the burden of proof simply lies with the taxpayer, relying on section 50(6) of the Taxes Management Act 1970 which provides:

> '56(6) If, on an appeal, it appears to the majority of the Commissioners present at the hearing, by examination of the appellant on oath or affirmation, or by other lawful evidence, that the appellant is overcharged by any assessment, the assessment shall be reduced accordingly, but otherwise every such assessment shall stand good.'

Firstly, in *Untelrab Ltd & Ors v McGregor (HMIT)*[54] the Special Commissioners, on the authority of *Cesena* concluded that the burden of proving residence lies on the Crown. In their view, section 50(6) was not relevant in the context of that appeal because it was not a case where the appellants were saying that they had been overcharged by an assessment but where they were saying that the Revenue had no jurisdiction to assess them at all.[55]

Secondly, in *Wood v Holden*[56] the Court of Appeal upheld Park J in the High Court in relation to shifts in the evidentiary burden even where TMA 1970 section 50(6) applies. Once the taxpayer, on appeal, has 'done enough to raise a case that [the company] is not resident in the UK', the burden must then pass to the Revenue to produce some material to show that, despite what appears from everything which the taxpayer has produced, the company is actually resident in the UK. Chadwick LJ said this:[57]

> 'It is a feature of tax litigation – not least where the litigation arises from a tax avoidance scheme – that, in the first instance, the facts are likely to be known only to the taxpayer and his advisers. The revenue will not have been party to the transaction; and will know only those facts which have been disclosed by the taxpayer or others; following, perhaps, the exercise of the Revenue's investigatory powers. I have no doubt that there are cases in which the evidence before the special commissioners is so unsatisfactory that the only just course for them to take is to hold that the taxpayer

---

53 (1876) 1 TC 88.
54 (1995) Sp C 55.
55 At para 68.
56 [2006] EWCA Civ 26.
57 [2006] EWCA Civ 26, at para 33.

> has not discharged the burden of proof which section 50(6) of TMA 1970 has placed upon him. But, equally, I have no doubt that the judge was correct, for the reasons which he gave, to hold that the present case was not one of those cases. There was no reason to think that the material facts had not been disclosed; and the commissioners did not hold that it was for that reason that they were unable to decide the question of residence.'

In *News Datacom Ltd v Atkinson (HMIT)*[58] the Special Commissioners followed the guidance of Chadwick LJ in *Wood v Holden* and accordingly, proceeded on the basis that it was for the appellants there to show that the assessments had been wrongly made. They accepted that the evidential burden can shift to HMRC but did not reach a decision purely on grounds relating to the burden of proof in the *Wood v Holden* sense. They held the company to be not resident in the UK without a failure to discharge the evidential burden.[59]

The position is the same for individuals. Unsatisfactory evidence provided by taxpayers features in an increasing number of cases. In *Daniel v HMRC*,[60] the burden of proving that he was non-resident, having previously been UK resident, generally lay with the taxpayer. The decision in *Daniel* is also a salutary reminder of the kind of evidence needed to discharge this burden. His claim to non-residence was largely on the basis that he was working full time abroad. The Tribunal found that Mr Daniel's evidence was mainly generalisations of having worked full time or anything approaching it, more about what 'he could have done [by way of work], not what he actually did'. His claimed pattern of work – essentially, none done when in London, but every available hour worked when elsewhere – was not credible. More importantly, every piece of objective evidence in this case, such as fax and email correspondence, presentations, letters, and computers, was unavailable. There was no documentary evidence available of the work he did and where it was undertaken, his frequent travel, or of living in his holiday home in the south of France.

The same fate befell Mr and Mrs Rumbelow who contended that they ceased to be UK resident for five tax years when they rented an apartment in Belgium and subsequently owned a house in Portugal.[61] They asserted that they left the UK in April 2001 for a settled purpose, namely, to live permanently overseas for Mrs Rumbelow's health, to retire and to improve quality of life. Distinct changes to the pattern of life, they said, amounted to a distinct break and when returning to the UK they did so as visitors. The Tribunal found that there was no evidence of residence in Belgium or Portugal or absence from the UK. They had no contemporaneous record or documentary evidence of their movements. The rough schedule they produced was at odds with records kept by their solicitors in relation to transactions they had undertaken. Accordingly, they

---

58 (2006) Sp C 561.
59 See para 155.
60 *Daniel v Revenue & Customs* [2014] UKFTT 173 (TC) at para 120.
61 *Rumbelow & Anor v Revenue & Customs* [2013] UKFTT 637 (TC).

failed to demonstrate an intention of anything more than extended holidays abroad.[62]

Although these cases deal with facts that arose prior to the enactment of the statutory residence test, the same requirement for taxpayers exists under that legislation. Individuals are likely to find the record-keeping requirements even more onerous under the statutory residence test. The very detailed statutory rules impose strict boundaries and call for records that may not necessarily be produced or maintained under normal living or working patterns. HMRC views on what is required are set out in their Residence and FIG Regime Manual.[63]

10.12 Discovery assessments

Taxpayers claiming to be non-resident on their self-assessment returns need to carefully consider their status in making such a claim. An officer or the Board may make an assessment to recover the lost tax, if an officer of the Board, or the Board, 'discovers' that: (1) assessable income or chargeable gains have not been assessed to tax; (2) an assessment to tax has become insufficient; or (3) excessive relief has been given.[64]

Where a tax return has been filed, discovery assessments can only be made if either the loss of tax is because of the careless or deliberate behaviour (previously, fraudulent or negligent conduct) of the taxpayer or his agent; or, at the time HMRC ceased to be entitled to enquire into the return (or completed such an enquiry), the officer could not reasonably have been expected, on the basis of the information then available to him, to have been aware of the loss of tax.[65] Careless or deliberate behaviour also affects the ability of HMRC to make such assessments beyond the normal four-year time limit.

In *Daniel v HMRC*[66] one of the central questions was whether Mr Daniel's claim to non-resident status on his tax return was 'negligent conduct'. The test is whether a reasonable man filing his tax return, and applying the right legal test, would have claimed non-UK residence when reviewing the facts.[67] His claim to non-resident status was primarily that he was employed 'full-time abroad' within paragraphs 2.2 and 2.3 of IR20. While the burden of proof that he was non-resident lay with Mr Daniel, the burden of proof regarding whether he was negligent in doing so was on HMRC. HMRC would not discharge this burden if: (a) Mr Daniel had an honest and tenable basis for making this claim;

62 Other cases that turned on unreliable or inadequate taxpayer evidence include *Charman v Revenue & Customs* [2018] UKFTT 765 (TC) and *Da Silva v Revenue & Customs* [2020] UKFTT 163 (TC) (ordinary residence).

63 RFIG21910 to RFIG21940.

64 TMA 1970 s 29(1); FA 1998 Sch 18 para 41.

65 TMA 1970 s 29(3), (4) and (5); FA 1998 Sch 18 paras 42, 43 and 44.

66 *Daniel v Revenue & Customs* [2014] UKFTT 173 (TC).

67 *Daniel v Revenue & Customs* [2014] UKFTT 173 (TC at para 155).

or (b) he had sought to act on IR20 guidance (as he had done) and had a tenable claim to have satisfied the IR20 criteria.

The Tribunal accepted that the 'full-time working abroad' test in IR20 was a difficult one, in the sense that it involved a slightly vague definition that must be applied in different ways in different circumstances, with the result that there is inevitably an element of difficulty. The test, was not so difficult that no taxpayer could be expected to apply the test properly.[68]

The relevant facts 'unquestionably' involved 'the reality that there were countless weeks' during the period in question when 'plainly the Appellant had not worked full-time abroad'. Furthermore, he must have been aware that his role had been intermittent. The Tribunal 'simply [did] not accept that his evidence that he read documentation relating to a large transaction on which he worked for over 14 solid weeks can have been realistic or that he can have believed it himself'.[69] Although Mr Daniel may not have been given the very clearest of advice by his accountants, the Tribunal concluded that he must have known that his work had to be 'full-time' in a reasonably conventional sense. The Tribunal noted that he appeared to concentrate on the 91-day UK presence test, and did not appraise his work pattern.

In *Strachan v HMRC*,[70] the question arose whether the taxpayer had a domicile of origin in England or in Scotland and whether he had acquired a domicile of choice in Connecticut and subsequently in Massachusetts. Although the burden of proving that a person has changed their domicile rests on that person, and it is easier to show a change from one domicile of choice to another domicile of choice than it is to show a change to a domicile of choice from a domicile of origin,[71] one of the assessments related to a year before the four-year time limit.[72] In relation to that year, the Tribunal held that the burden rested on them to prove, not only that Mr Strachan had been careless, but that the carelessness had brought about the loss of tax, and they were unable to do so.[73]

10.13 Requirement to correct historic offshore non-compliance

Finance (No 2) Act 2017 section 67 and Schedule 18 introduced draconian measures to require any past 'offshore tax non-compliance' existing on 5 April 2017. Offshore tax non-compliance means tax non-compliance involving under declared income tax, capital gains tax or inheritance tax that relates to income arising outside the UK, assets situated or held outside the UK, activities carried

---

68 *Daniel v Revenue & Customs* [2014] UKFTT 173 (TC at para 157).
69 *Daniel v Revenue & Customs* [2014] UKFTT 173 (TC at para 155).
70 *Strachan v HMRC* [2023] UKFTT 617 (TC).
71 See paras 153 to 159 and the cases cited therein.
72 Taxes Management Act 1970 s 34.
73 At para 12.

on outside the UK, or anything having a similar effect.[74] Failure to correct by 30 September 2018 will result in penalties of up to 200% of the under-declared tax plus 10% of the value of an offshore asset.[75] In addition, HMRC may publish the personal details of any person subject to a penalty, including, name, address, place of business and amount of penalty.[76]

HMRC guidance indicates that non-compliance may result from incorrect decisions about residence or domicile.[77]

10.14 Judicial review

Judicial review is the process whereby the courts supervise public bodies to determine the lawfulness of a decision, action or failure to act in relation to the exercise of a public function. Civil Procedure Rules Part 54 rule 54.1(2)(a)(ii). In the context of this work, the primary ground for judicial review is that HMRC published practice has created a legitimate expectation that a person would be entitled to a particular treatment and it would amount to an abuse of power for HMRC to act in a way so as to breach that expectation.[78]

The First-tier Tribunal, on a statutory appeal, cannot give effect to these public law principles. As a result, jurisdiction rests exclusively with the High Court. The effect is that where a taxpayer relies on HMRC practice, there are, in effect two tracks of legal remedy that may be pursued. One is a statutory appeal to the First-tier Tribunal, which has jurisdiction to consider the question of residence as a matter of law, and the other is an application to the High Court for judicial review, which has jurisdiction to consider whether HMRC may be compelled to apply their published practice to the taxpayer. This means that taxpayers disputing HMRC views will need to initiate both procedures. Although applications for permission to seek judicial review are made to the Administrative Court, powers given by section 31A of the Senior Courts Act 1981 permit the transfer of judicial review proceedings to the Tax and Chancery Chamber of the Upper Tribunal.

There is no set rule for determining whether the appeal to the First-tier Tribunal or the judicial review application should be heard first. In *Daniel v Revenue & Customs Comrs*,[79] it was Mr Daniel's position that he left the UK on 5 March 1999 in order to take up full-time employment abroad followed by a sale of shares in the following tax year. HMRC issued to the appellant a

---

74 F(No 2) A 2017 Sch 18, Pt 1.

75 F(No 2) A 2017 Sch 18, Pt 2.

76 F(No 2) A 2017 Sch 18, para 30.

77 https://www.gov.uk/guidance/requirement-to-correct-tax-due-on-offshore-assets#the-scope-of-the-rtc-rule, accessed 16 February 2018. See *Perlman v Revenue and Customs* [2021] UKFTT 219 (TC) where a notice to correct related to domicile was issued.

78 *R v Inland Revenue Commissioners (ex parte Preston)* [1985] AC 835. See also Chapter 1, para **1.23**.

79 *Daniel v Revenue & Customs Comrs* [2012] EWCA Civ 1741.

determination to the effect that he had been resident and ordinarily resident in the UK during the relevant year and a discovery assessment to tax on the gain resulting from the sale. The Court of Appeal confirmed that there is no hard and fast rule and that the appropriate course must inevitably be determined on a case-by-case basis.[80] The guiding principle is which route permits the matter to be resolved more quickly and cheaply.[81] In Daniel's case there was an underlying factual dispute between the taxpayer and HMRC which could only be conclusively resolved by the First-tier Tribunal. Resolution of the judicial review claim in such a case would not dispose of the dispute. If the taxpayer loses his judicial review claim, he will then have to pursue his statutory appeal. If the taxpayer wins his judicial review claim, HRMC will have to make its determination afresh, possibly with the guidance of the court as to how HMRC practice is to be applied. If such determinations are adverse to the taxpayer, he will again have to appeal. The statutory appeal had the potential finally to resolve the dispute concerning the taxpayer's residence. For these reasons, the Court of Appeal ruled that it is appropriate that the judicial review claim should be stayed whilst the statutory appeal proceeds to a determination.[82]

The same approach was adopted by the High Court in *R (on the application of Hankinson) v Revenue & Customs Commissioners*.[83] In contrast, the position will be different where judicial review requires no resolution of disputed facts and has the potential finally to dispose of the question. In *R (Davies) and Gaines-Cooper v Revenue & Customs Commissioners*,[84] Lord Wilson observed that, had Mr Gaines-Cooper's contention in his claim for judicial review prevailed, to the effect that he had only to show that he had kept his day count in the UK below 91 days, the 10-day hearing of his appeal before the Special Commissioners (now the First-tier Tribunal) would have been unnecessary.

10.15 Role of Upper Tribunal or Court of Appeal

Residence and domicile are essentially factual in nature. The right of appeal from a decision of the First-tier Tribunal to the Upper Tribunal is on points of law only.[85] Only one reported decision of the Special Commissioners on domicile[86] has been appealed. In *Agulian & Anor v Cyganik*[87] the Court of

80 At para 12.
81 At para 19.
82 At para 22.
83 *R (on the application of Hankinson) v Revenue & Customs Commissioners* [2009] EWHC 1774. See also **1.23**.
84 In *R (Davies) and Gaines-Cooper v Revenue & Customs Commissioners* [2011] UKSC 47, at para 6. See also **1.23**.
85 TCEA 2007 s 11(1).
86 See **9.01** above.
87 [2006] EWCA Civ 129.See also the non-tax case *Barlow Clowes International Ltd (In Liquidation) & Ors v Henwood* [2008] EWCA Civ 577.

Appeal was faced with the contention that the appeal was essentially against a finding or findings of fact by the court below and that it was not entitled to substitute its own assessment of the evidence for that of the deputy judge, who heard and saw the witnesses, preferred the evidence of his client and made a finding corroborated by independent evidence. Mummery LJ explained the normal role of the appellate court as follows:

> 'Further, this was not an appeal against the exercise of a discretion by the lower court nor was it a case in which the lower court was applying a fairly flexible and imprecise standard involving an evaluation of all the facts.... In those cases the appellate court is more reluctant to interfere with the trial judge's decision than in the case of a finding of primary fact or an inference from primary facts. This is an appeal contesting the correctness of an inference as to Andreas's relevant intentions between 1995 and 1999. The function of the appellate court is to decide whether the inference is wrong, making proper allowances for any advantages that the trial judge would have had and an appellate court would not have and not interfering with inferences which the judge could reasonably have made.'[88]

In appeals from the First-tier Tribunal, by contrast, the appellate tribunal or court has no such power. It must be satisfied not that the Tribunal's evaluation of the facts was wrong, but that they made an error of law.[89]

Such a re-evaluation of the facts on appeal is only possible where there is a question of mixed fact and law as in *Edwards v Bairstow*[90] in which Lord Radcliffe said:

> 'If the case contains anything ex facie which is bad law and which bears upon the determination, it is, obviously, erroneous in point of law. But, without any such misconception appearing ex facie, it may be that the facts found are such that no person acting judicially and properly instructed as to the relevant law could have come to the determination under appeal. In those circumstances, too, the court must intervene. It has no option but to assume that there has been some misconception of the law and that, this has been responsible for the determination. So there, too, there has been error in point of law. I do not think that it much matters whether this state of affairs is described as one in which there is no evidence to support the determination or as one in which the evidence is inconsistent with and contradictory of the determination, or as one in which the true and only reasonable conclusion contradicts the determination. Rightly understood, each phrase propounds the same test. For my part, I prefer the last of the three, since I think that it is rather misleading to speak of there being no evidence to support a conclusion when in cases such as these many of the facts are likely to be neutral in themselves, and only to take their colour from the combination of circumstances in which they are found to occur.'

In *Gaines-Cooper*, the fact that the Special Commissioners did not accept some of Mr Gaines-Cooper's evidence, or that 'in one short paragraph they

88 At para 12.
89 *Gaines-Cooper v Revenue & Customs Commissioners* [2007] EWHC 2617 (Ch) at para 27.
90 [1956] AC 14; 36 TC 207.

utterly fail to do justice' to the evidence of witnesses as well as a number of other factual criticisms, was held on appeal to reveal no error of law. A general assertion that the tribunal's conclusion was against the weight of the evidence and was therefore wrong was held impermissible in an appeal restricted to questions of law. In *Grace*, the Court of Appeal was careful to restrict its decision to questions of law. In remitting the case to be re-determined by the First-tier Tribunal on the basis of his legal rulings, Lloyd LJ noted:

> 'Respectfully, I part company from the judge on that. I agree that a finding of residence is a possible conclusion, and perhaps a likely one, but it does not seem to me that it would be right for the court to pre-empt the decision of the Special Commissioner on that issue. The responsibility of the Special Commissioner to make such decisions, having found the primary facts, is stated and repeated in many of the cases .... Of course there are cases in which, on a correct view of the law, only one conclusion is possible, but it seems to me that the courts ought to be particularly cautious in substituting their own view on this.'[91]

A distinction, he said, had to be drawn between whether Mr Grace's presence in the UK to perform his tasks as a BA long-haul pilot, with whatever regularity and length of stay that is involved, using the house which he retained, is not such as to qualify as presence 'for some temporary purpose only', so as to come within section 831, which could be decided by an appellate court. However, it was not for the appellate court to decide on the balance stands between factors connecting the taxpayer with the UK on the one hand, and his connections with South Africa on the other hand, in terms of satisfying the non-statutory tests for residence and ordinary residence.92

---

91 *Grace v HMRC* [2009] EWCA Civ 1082 at para 38.

92 At para 40.

INDEX

[*References are to paragraph number*]

www.ingramcontent.com/pod-product-compliance
Ingram Content Group UK Ltd.
Pitfield, Milton Keynes, MK11 3LW, UK
UKHW021037150926
475561UK00003B/144

9 781526 534590